BEYOND THE 'WILD TRIBES'

CERI OEPPEN AND
ANGELA SCHLENKHOFF (EDS)

BEYOND THE 'WILD TRIBES'

*Understanding Modern Afghanistan
and its Diaspora*

Columbia University Press
New York

Columbia University Press
Publishers Since 1893
New York   Chichester, West Sussex
Copyright © Ceri Oeppen and Angela Schlenkhoff, 2010
All rights reserved

Library of Congress Cataloging-in-Publication Data

Beyond the wild tribes : understanding modern Afghanistan and its
diaspora / Ceri Oeppen and Angela Schlenkhoff (eds).
    p. cm.
Based on a conference of the European Centre of Afghan Studies (ECAS)
held on Mar. 3, 2007, at the School of Oriental and African Studies (SOAS).
ISBN 978-0-231-70210-2 (alk. paper)
1. Afghanistan—Social conditions. 2. Afghanistan—Politics and
government—2001– 3. Afghanistan—Population. 4. Afghanistan—Emigration
and immigration. 5. Afghans—Foreign countries. 6. Refugees—Afghanistan.
I. Oeppen, Ceri, 1980– II. Schlenkhoff, Angela. III. Title.

DS371.4.B49 2010
958.1—dc22

                            2010011808

∞

Columbia University Press books are printed on permanent and durable acid-free paper.
This book is printed on paper with recycled content.
Printed In India by Imprint Digital

c 10 9 8 7 6 5 4 3 2 1

References to Internet Web sites (URLs) were accurate at the time of writing.
Neither the authors nor Columbia University Press is responsible for URLs
that may have expired or changed since the manuscript was prepared.

In loving memory of my father, Ulrich Schlenkhoff (1948–2007), who instilled in me a passion for knowledge and learning.

— Angela Schlenkhoff

Dedicated to the people of Afghanistan and the hope that one day they will find peace.

— Ceri Oeppen and Angela Schlenkhoff

ACKNOWLEDGEMENTS

This book has grown out of the launch conference of the European Centre for Afghan Studies (ECAS) held on 3 March 2007 at the School of Oriental and African Studies (SOAS), and would not have been possible without the essential contributions of a large number of people and institutions.

The conference was funded through a generous grant from Awards for All, as well as the in-kind support of the Centre of Contemporary Central Asia and the Caucasus (CCCAC), especially Bhavna Davé, who offered to host the event. Jane Savory from the CCCAC provided essential organisational support before the conference and on the day. Ahmad Farid Mall and the Afghan Association Paiwand supported the organisers throughout the planning phases, as well as on the day of the conference. The large team of volunteers, also recruited through Paiwand, was of immense help on the day of the conference, especially Milad Yousufi who looked after all the technical equipment. The Afghan Students Association also provided several volunteers. Our thanks also go to the Refugee Council, especially Gary Bell, for hosting the planning meetings before the conference. The British Library, the Royal Geographical Society as well as Shikyba Azizi from the University of Westminster enriched the event with their respective exhibitions. John Baily, Veronica Doubleday and Wasi Naleh rounded up the event with musical performances at the end of the day, and Zuzanna Olszewska read out Dari poetry. Finally our gratitude goes to all the presenters and workshop organisers, as well as the conference participants for making the event such a success.

CONTENTS

CONTENTS

SECTION II: SECURITY AND GOVERNANCE

SECTION III: A TRANSNATIONAL AFGHAN COMMUNITY?

ABOUT THE CONTRIBUTORS

Valey Arya is currently working towards a PhD at Brunel University in London. His research topic is the geopolitical identity of Afghanistan. His main interests lie in international relations, geopolitics, development studies and management. He has more than fifteen years of work experience in different managerial and programmatic positions in both Afghanistan and the UK.

Professor John Baily is director of the Afghan Music Unit and Professor of Ethnomusicology at Goldsmiths, University of London. He has studied the music of Afghanistan for over thirty years, and produced many articles, films and audio recordings on the subject. His other research interests include musical cognition, music and the human body, ethnomusicological filmmaking, and music in the South Asian communities of the UK.

Dr Kristian Berg Harpviken is the Director of the International Peace Research Institute, Oslo (PRIO). Harpviken is a sociologist, whose research interests include the dynamics of civil war (mobilization; conflict resolution; post-war reconstruction and peacebuilding), migration and transnational communities, and methodology in difficult contexts. His book *Social Networks and Migration in Wartime Afghanistan* was published by Palgrave Macmillan in 2009.

Dr Armando Geller is a Research Assistant Professor at the Center for Social Complexity at George Mason University and a Research Fellow at the Krasnow Institute for Advanced Study. He has a doctoral degree in conflict analysis and social simulation. His research focuses on evidence-based multi-agent social simulation of contemporary conflict, currently in particular Afghanistan.

Dr Antonio Giustozzi is a research fellow at the Crisis States Research Centre, based at the London School of Economics. He works on the security dimension of failed states and states in a critical situation. He is researching the political aspects of insurgency and warlordism, and the response of the state. He has published widely on Afghanistan, including the book *Koran, Kalashnikov and Laptop: the Neo-Taliban Insurgency in Afghanistan 2002–2007*.

Kathryn Lockett (MSc) is Programmes and Policy Manager for South Asia at WOMANKIND Worldwide, a UK-based international women's human rights development agency that has been working in Afghanistan since 2003. Kathryn has worked in international development for the last ten years in countries including Nepal, Russia, Kyrgyzstan, India, Sri Lanka and Romania, working with a variety of grassroots NGOs and international development agencies. She specialises in women's human rights, conflict and NGO development.

Dr Alessandro Monsutti is currently a Research Associate and Lecturer at the South Asian Studies Council, MacMillan Center for International and Area Studies, Yale University. He has carried out fieldwork in Afghanistan, Pakistan and Iran since 1993, and more recently amongst the wider Afghan diaspora, thanks to a grant from the MacArthur Foundation, Chicago. His work focuses on migration and transnationalism, local factions and ethnicity, and development and humanitarian assistance. He is the author of the book *War and Migration: Social Networks and Economic Strategies of the Hazaras of Afghanistan*.

Dr Ceri Oeppen is a Senior Teaching Fellow in Development Studies at the School of Oriental and African Studies (SOAS), University of London. Her doctoral thesis, completed at the University of Sussex, was about the interactions between transnationalism and integration for Afghan refugees in the wider diaspora, and their role in the reconstruction and development of Afghanistan. She has carried out fieldwork with Afghans living in California, London, New Delhi, Pakistan and Afghanistan. She is a founding member of the European Centre for Afghan Studies (ECAS).

Bijan Omrani was educated at Wellington College and Lincoln College, Oxford. Alongside *Afghanistan: a companion and guide*, co-authored with Matthew Leeming, he has written for *The Spectator*, and is also the co-author of the new Odyssey guide to Iran. He is a member of the editorial board of Asian Affairs Journal and currently teaches at Eton College.

Dr Angela Schlenkhoff received her PhD in Social Anthropology from the University of Kent at Canterbury. Her research focused on constructions and reconstructions of home and homeland in exile, using the case study of Afghan refugees in London. She has worked with several Afghan refugee community organisations and is currently Project Officer at Community Service Volunteers (CSV). She is a founding member of the European Centre for Afghan Studies (ECAS).

Dr Deborah J. Smith is the Senior Research Manager for Gender and Health at the Afghanistan Research and Evaluation Unit (AREU). Before moving to Afghanistan, Deborah worked at the London School of Hygiene and Tropical Medicine, where she conducted health policy research in Malawi and Zambia. She has a PhD from the London School of Economics and Political Science, for which she conducted fieldwork on gender issues in Rajasthan, India.

Major General Charles Vyvyan was formerly Chief of Staff at UK HQ Land Command, and then Defence Attaché at the British Embassy in Washington DC. He is now Chairman of Oxford Strategic.

GLOSSARY

Arbab	village leader
Bad	practice of compensating a murder by giving girls to the victim's family
Dabara	a practice in Pashtun customary law, loosely translated as a truce over a set period of time
Deya	compensation
Dutar	musical instrument
Eid	Islamic festival
Ghilzai	one of two major branches in the Pashtun tribal system (the other being Durrani)
Hawala	money transfer system
Hawaladar	money transfer agent
Hezb-e Islami	political party
Hijra	the Prophet's flight from Mecca to Medina
Jalasa	local meeting (name used in Bamiyan)
Jamiat-e Islami	political party
Jirga	local meeting
Kargar	worker
Khalq	the 'people' or the 'masses'; a wing of the People's Democratic Party
Kiliwali	popular music
Kuchi	traditionally nomadic *Pashtun* group
Madrassa	Islamic school
Mujahideen	a fighter in a holy war or Jihad
Mullah	religious teacher or leader
Parcham	banner or flag; a wing of the People's Democratic Party

Pashtunwali	Pashtun code of honour
Qawm	solidarity group, sometimes translated as tribe
Rubab	musical instrument
Sadozai	a Pashtun tribe
Shariat/Sharia	Islamic law; code of practice
Shinwar	large *qawm*, living in Nangarhar province
Shub-e-huquqi	department dealing with civil law
Shura	community council
Tabla	musical instrument
Teega	a practice in Pashtun customary law, loosely translated as a truce over a set period of time
Ummah	the Muslim community, transcending national borders
Ustad	honorific title for a teacher
Woliswal	district governor
Wazir	court official, often an advisor close to the ruler
Wolesi Jirga	lower chamber of the Afghan houses of parliament

ABBREVIATIONS

AAA	American Anthropological Association
ANDS	Afghanistan National Development Strategy
AREU	Afghanistan Research and Evaluation Unit
AWEC	Afghan Women's Education Centre
AWN	Afghan Women's Network
AWRC	Afghan Women's Resource Centre
BBC	British Broadcasting Corporation
CAREC	Central Asian Regional Economic Cooperation
CEDAW	Convention for the Elimination of all forms of Discrimination Against Women
CNN	Cable News Network
DDR	Disarmament, Demobilisation and Reintegration
DIAG	Disarmament of Illegal Armed Groups
DFID	Department for International Development (UK)
ECAS	European Centre for Afghan Studies
ECO	Economic Cooperation Organization
ENNA	European Network of NGOs in Afghanistan
ESRC	Economic and Social Research Council
FCO	Foreign and Commonwealth Office (UK)
IDP	Internally Displaced Person
IPI	Iran-Pakistan-India (proposed pipeline)
ISAF	International Security Assistance Force (in Afghanistan)
JCMB	Joint Coordination and Monitoring Board (Afghanistan)
KhAD	State Information Services (communist-era Afghanistan)
NATO	North Atlantic Treaty Organisation
NGO	Non-Governmental Organisation

OPEC	Organisation of Petroleum Exporting Countries
PDPA	People's Democratic Party of Afghanistan
PMC	Private Military Contractors
RCO	Refugee Community Organisation
SAARC	South Asian Association for Regional Cooperation
SCO	Shanghai Cooperation Organisation
TAPI	Turkmenistan-Afghanistan-Pakistan-India (proposed pipeline)
UK	United Kingdom (of Great Britain and Northern Ireland)
UN	United Nations
UNAMA	United Nations Assistance Mission in Afghanistan
UNHCR	United Nations High Commissioner for Refugees
US	United States (of America)
USAID	United States Agency for International Development
USSR	Union of Soviet Socialist Republics
WAD	Ministry for State Security (communist-era Afghanistan)

1

BEYOND THE 'WILD TRIBES'

WORKING TOWARDS AN UNDERSTANDING OF CONTEMPORARY AFGHANISTAN AND ITS DIASPORA

Ceri Oeppen and Angela Schlenkhoff

On 3 March 2007 the newly formed European Centre for Afghan Studies (ECAS) held its launch conference at the School of Oriental and African Studies (SOAS), University of London. The conference gave European academics and practitioners interested in Afghanistan a rare opportunity to come together, present their work and share ideas. This volume brings the research presented and discussed at that meeting to a wider audience.

ECAS was formed with the goal of bringing together researchers, humanitarian practitioners, and others interested in research about Afghanistan and the global Afghan diaspora. Integral to this goal is the aim of reaching across the boundary between researcher and researched; and a key success of the launch conference was that almost 50 per cent of the participants were Afghan. These Afghans were not just there in a position of 'research participants' or 'informants'; many Afghan intellectuals, academics and graduate students are currently based in London, and the conference benefited not only from their personal experience as Afghans in exile, but also from their intellectual input.

The majority of conference participants (Afghan and non-Afghan) were based in the United Kingdom but we also welcomed academics from institutions in Norway, Poland, Austria, Switzerland, Italy, France, Germany, the Netherlands, Denmark, and even Afghanistan itself. Participants came from spheres of study across the academic spectrum; although, as the chapters in this volume suggest, predominantly from those of the social sciences and humanities.[1] Among those who attended were practioneers from a variety of organisations[2] working in Afghanistan, or with Afghan refugee communities in Europe.

The conference was advertised via word of mouth and email. The enthusiastic response ECAS received suggested two things: the ongoing public fascination with Afghanistan, and the lack of opportunities for those working on Afghanistan to join together. As Afghan studies enthusiasts ourselves, we were not surprised by the former. However, the latter continues to be somewhat perplexing. Perhaps it is a result of the academic need to categorise people, places and regions: it has become a cliché to point out Afghanistan's position as being at a crossroads; but it is true that it does appear to be at the crossroads of standard academic regional categories, being variously described as Middle Eastern, Central Asian and South Asian.

Afghanistan is not an exemplar of any of these regions yet contains elements in common with its neighbouring countries. Those of us interested in the study of identity may ask where Afghans place themselves; but perhaps it is just as important to question where we, as academics and practitioners interested in Afghanistan, position ourselves within the institutions of academic disciplines and professional associations. Part of the impetus for ECAS, and arguably part of the enthusiastic response to the launch conference, stems from a feeling that symposia based on regional categories or single academic disciplines are not effective in furthering the process of 'understanding Afghanistan'.

The idea of 'understanding' the local, national and international processes at work in Afghanistan is of interest to a variety of actors, and it is worth considering who they are. The more obvious answers include governments, non-governmental organisations, inter-governmental organisations, and researchers and journalists working in Afghanistan: people who want information about the country in order to facilitate achieving their aims and objectives in being there. Less obvious, perhaps, is the desire amongst Afghans themselves to learn more about why and how their 'homeland' is in its current situation. There is also a whole generation of young Afghans who have grown up 'in exile', who are hungry for more information about the country they left behind, or never had the chance to experience—perhaps to help them understand their own identity, and what it means to be Afghan.[3] One of the many excitements and challenges we faced whilst doing our own research in the Afghan diaspora was managing the expectations of those research participants who hoped that we could help them uncover 'an answer' to understanding Afghanistan and the Afghans.

Of course, there is no single identifiable 'answer', despite the best efforts of scholars, travellers and politicians—from Elphinstone (1815) to the rash of books on Afghanistan hastily written or reissued after 11 September 2001. Further, whilst many of these texts on Afghanistan and the Afghans have been carefully and thoughtfully researched and written, some have not; and as Rubin (2002) suggests, many 'Western' efforts to understand Afghanistan may say more about our own society and politics than those of Afghanistan.

Rubin (2002: 3) suggests that the fascination of colonial-period writers with the Afghan people is illustrative of the Afghans' status as decidedly 'other', yet 'emblematic of a Western male romantic ideal' (*Ibid*: 3).[4] Shadl (2007) goes further, criticising colonial sources as 'not only permeated with pejorative undertones' but 'inclined to exaggerate the adventure that makes up the myth of "wild Afghanistan"'; and they 'virtually hanker after the exotic' (*Ibid*: 89). Whilst chauvinism in colonial texts is not limited to accounts of Afghanistan, there does seem to be a particular romantic vein in the descriptions of Afghanistan and Afghans, where violence and treachery are linked irredeemably with courage and loyalty, as Pennell (1909: 17) argues in his book, *Among the wild tribes of the Afghan frontier:*

...the Afghan character is a strange medley of contradictory qualities, in which courage blends with stealth, the basest treachery with the most touching fidelity, intense religious fanaticism with an avarice which will induce him to play false to his faith, and a lavish hospitality with an irresistible propensity for thieving.

Perhaps, as Shadl (2007) suggests, the inability of colonial aggressors to fully capture or control Afghanistan contributed to these qualities: and the symbol of the Afghan warrior, proudly holding on to their territory and resisting 'civilisation' became mythologised. Arguably, the myth-making did not stop with the Anglo-Afghan wars: representations of the *mujahideen* as proud but poorly-equipped warriors resisting the Communists were steeped in the same language and images. Even today, when many more people consider identity and character to be fluid concepts, some still try to somehow define the 'essence' of the Afghan character, as in this extract from a study on Afghanistan (published in 2002):

The main characteristic of the Pushtoons, particularly those of the hills, is a proud and aggressive individualism, practiced in the context of a familial and tribal society with predatory habits (Ewans, 2002: 7).

This kind of language inevitably seeps into media, politics and public perceptions, which in turn shapes foreign policy towards Afghanistan. As Shadl (2007: 102) argues, '[t]he modern perspective on the country, its people and its culture in general not only resembles the mystifications of the colonial period, but is actually rooted in them'.

Given the persistence of these problematic descriptions, rooted in the nineteenth and twentieth century, the need for continued contemporary research in Afghanistan and the Afghan diaspora is stronger than ever. There is research going on, as the contributions to this volume signify; however, much more has to be done in order to fill the gaps and create a substantial body of current information. Until that is achieved, scholars will have to continue to refer to older texts. It is telling that what is probably the key background text on Afghanistan, still used widely, was published in 1973 (Dupree, 1973).

Undoubtedly, the conflict in Afghanistan has been a major barrier to research. The difficulty of guaranteeing security for researcher and research participants severely limited research opportunities in Afghanistan between 1979 and 2001. Since 2001 there have been increased research possibilities, associated with the heightened interest in Afghanistan from donor governments and international organisations. However, the security situation still severely limits research opportunities, particularly in certain areas of Afghanistan such as the south and south-east. In general, the security situation, combined with the types of funding available, also severely limits the possibility for long-term and in-depth research—such as traditional ethnography—in any area.[5]

The majority of research that took place in the period 1979–2001 involved Afghans in exile, particularly refugees in Pakistan (see for example the edited volumes Anderson and Hatch Dupree, 1990; Farr and Merriam, 1987). However, the changes that have taken place as a result of the Communist period, the Jihad against the Soviets, the civil war, the Taliban era, and the current international control and associated insurgency, demand fresh research. For a start, a generation has grown up through conflict and displacement, which presumably will have an effect on social practice and norms. Even the enduring nature and strength of Islam is not immune to change, since various power brokers have (ab)used religion in various ways to achieve their goals.

During research in the diaspora, we spoke to Afghans who had gone back to visit Afghanistan after 11 September 2001. It was clear that they felt the country they returned to was not the one they left, and that the society and culture had changed in their absence. In a photo essay for the BBC, Esmet (2003) describes her feelings on returning to Kabul from the UK.

It was weird because all the people who I remember looking like city people were gone... In their place Kabul seemed to be a city of people who were from somewhere else. I don't know where, but they were not from the city I remember.

Similar sentiments were heard from others. In the United states, a research participant explained why he had decided not to return: 'It's not the same Afghanistan you left... I became discouraged... I don't have friends left there that I could, you know...that could help me out.'[6] And it is not only Afghanistan that has changed. The experience of living in a 'foreign' country and making it their 'home' is likely to also shape Afghans' perceptions, as will the human tendency to romanticise places and eras left behind.

The 'community' of those interested in Afghanistan has also changed over the last few decades. Prior to the 1980s it was possible to identify relatively clear disciplinary and national traditions amongst researchers interested in Afghanistan; for example, French academics were known for working on Afghan archaeology and anthropology. It was evident from the audience of participants at the ECAS conference that some of those established researchers rubbed shoulders with younger European researchers, and, importantly, different generations of Afghans.

Our perception, largely stemming from our research amongst the diaspora in the US and London, is that Afghans are willing to engage in, and demand to be included in, academic debates. For both Afghan and non-Afghan researchers, this means that they must become used to sharing their knowledge with their research subjects and participants. Admittedly this can be quite an intimidating experience, and some of the presenters at the ECAS conference expressed this on first seeing their audience. They consequently felt the need to temper certain expressions within their presentations in order to make them, in their opinion, more 'suitable' for the audience present. Schetter (2003) describes a similar experience when first presenting some of his research findings to Afghans in Germany, where he sparked off passionate and heated discussions about the meaning of 'ethnicity' amongst the diaspora. Nevertheless, these academic debates can contribute to dialogue amongst Afghans, whether in Afghanistan or the diaspora, and can be a catalyst for socio-cultural and political debate and change.

The issue of presenting research findings to the 'research subjects' is not new, and should arguably be a planned part of any research project involving human subjects.[7] It is a necessary process in which to engage, not only to ensure an inclusive approach and to initiate fruitful debates, but also to add depth and further reflexivity to research, as Horst (2002) illustrates when she describes her discussion of her research findings with some of her Somali participants.

With regard to European researchers, one can observe a generational change taking place: from the generation who engaged in pre-conflict research in Afghanistan to those who are now gathering, or seeking to gather, (post) conflict data in Afghanistan and the diaspora. Although some subjects of study are ongoing, such as issues of livelihoods and governance, others have come about as a direct outcome of the continuous conflict—for example, studies of militant groups and research on the diaspora. The latter subjects are relatively recent additions to the research agenda. Another tendency is that more recent research projects are using a more interdisciplinary approach—a tendency that can be observed across the academic sphere more generally.

Considered as a whole, these different groups of Afghan and non-Afghan researchers and professionals have much to contribute to the ongoing development of a thorough understanding of Afghanistan and its diaspora; and the conference sought to highlight and emphasise the importance of contact between these groups. Underlying the organisation of the conference was the strong belief that everyone involved should have a sense of ownership of and responsibility in this process; and that a common platform for all these types of knowledge to come together in discussion was vital. There are now many more opportunities for researchers and those interested in a particular subject to link up and exchange information—both virtually and in person—than ever before. ECAS seeks to become one of these tools of exchange. During the conference it became clear that a key need was for greater communication about the type of research and knowledge currently available.

The conference also demonstrated the wide range of research interests currently being pursued in Afghanistan and the diaspora. Neither the conference nor this resulting volume had a theme as such, except for presenting for discussion a multi-disciplinary cross-section of contemporary research efforts. Due to the conflict and related security challenges, it is not appropriate to highlight a particularly under-researched area, except to say that arguably, every aspect of Afghan life is under-researched.

With chapters on issues ranging from the features of protracted conflict to the future of Afghan music, this volume examines just some of the key issues facing Afghanistan and the global diaspora of Afghan people. It is subdivided into three thematic sections.

The first section, 'Afghan history, society and culture', explores several wide-ranging issues: lessons drawn from the country's historic wars (Bijan Omrani and Charles Vyvyan); the situation of women and girls in Afghanistan (Kathryn Lockett); the state of normlessness in protracted conflicts, using the example of Afghanistan (Armando Geller); and customary laws and informal dispute resolution (Deborah J. Smith). The second section, 'Security and reconstruction', draws together material covering several issures: the problems of governance in Afghanistan (Antonio Giustozzi); the geostrategic potential of Afghanistan as a landbridge (Valey Arya); and the image of the refugee warrior in relation to migration and armed resistance (Kristian Berg Harpviken). The final section, entitled 'A transnational Afghan community', brings together work on the global Afghan diaspora: the diaspora's involvement in Afghanistan's reconstruction process (Ceri Oeppen); Afghan music and its circulation between diaspora groups and Afghanistan (John Baily); and migration as a survival strategy and durable solutions to refugee crises (Alessandro Monsutti). Before these sections commence, however, the next chapter (Angela Schlenkhoff) explores some practical and ethical issues regarding fieldwork in Afghanistan and its diaspora—a cross-cutting issue that was repeatedly raised in discussions at the ECAS conference.

Afghanistan, its people and its future have aroused substantial interest at various points in history. Post-2001, international organisations, non-governmental organisations and journalists have added greatly to our knowledge of contemporary Afghanistan. However, as discussed above, in-depth academic work has been somewhat limited. Those academic studies that have taken place have often done so in isolation. The European Centre for Afghan Studies (ECAS) aims to bring together those working on Afghanistan, whatever their background. The conference of March 2007 was a good starting point, but much more needs to be done in order to improve understanding of Afghanistan and the Afghan diaspora. Whilst historical texts can provide a useful starting point in understanding contemporary Afghanistan (see for example Omrani and Vyvyan, this volume) there remains a pressing need for new research across the academic disciplines to bring our knowledge up to date. There is a need to move beyond the colonial understandings of 'wild tribes' and consider what it means to be Afghan in the twenty-first century. It is our hope that the passionate researchers, both Afghan and non-Afghan, who were so very active at the ECAS conference, will take up this challenge.

2

CHALLENGES TO RESEARCH IN AFGHANISTAN AND ITS DIASPORA[1]

Angela Schlenkhoff

This paper seeks to explore issues raised by researchers arising out of their fieldwork in Afghanistan and its diaspora. Since 2001, after almost two decades of virtual stand-still, research on Afghanistan and the Afghans has been on the rise again. There is a desire to close the gaps in information and understanding that were left open by decades of war and destruction, and in many ways the country almost has to be researched anew due to the lack of continuous information based on in-depth knowledge.[2]

As Afghanistan became a research location again, its wider diaspora has also moved into the spotlight of international interest. While almost completely ignored in the past, many research projects are now focusing on the situation of Afghan refugees in exile for various reasons: be it to understand what they could contribute to the reconstruction of their homeland (see Oeppen, this volume); or to analyse how they have formed an identity in exile (Schlenkhoff, 2006), and how this has the potential to alter in light of the changes in Afghanistan. A more cynical suggestion is that there may also be an interest in return migration from the diaspora and the role of return in solving the so-called refugee 'crisis' of Europe (Black, 2001). Further, research both amongst the diaspora and in a war-torn society such as Afghanistan poses specific ethical challenges. This chapter addresses some of these.

Why do we study war-torn societies?

Research in countries characterised by their involvement in national or international war is not a new interest. Disciplines such as anthropology have a long history of research involvement in war zones, and less favourable memories of the discipline's involvement still haunt anthropologists and researchers in general today. As Price states: 'Twentieth-century anthropologists applied their knowledge and ethnographic skills to warfare on many occasions, fighting with both books and guns' (Price, 2002: 14).

It is undeniable that some researchers have contributed in various degrees to questionable endeavours, or have seen their material being misused for such purposes. One example of the latter is Ibrahim al-Marashi's case. In 2002 he was a postgraduate student at the Monterey Institute of International Studies, and published an article entitled 'Iraq's Security and Intelligence Network: A Guide and Analysis' in the Middle East Review of International Affairs (al-Marashi, 2002). Large parts of this article were subsequently plagiarised (he had not been consulted on this) by the British Government for a briefing document in 2003, entitled 'Iraq: Its Infrastructure of Concealment, Deception and Intimidation'. It later also became known as the 'Iraq Dossier' or the 'Dodgy Dossier'. Together with other documents, this dossier was used by the government to justify its involvement in the war on Iraq, a purpose which al-Marashi never intended for his research.

However, there have also been numerous examples of a direct and conscious involvement of researchers in war efforts, which have informed many later discussions (for further discussion see Asad, 1973; Coon, 1980; Gough, 1968; Mabee, 1987; Nader, 1997; Price, 1998). While these debates are valid and should underlie the conducting of present and future research projects, they should not serve to paralyse current research projects and researchers. This does not mean that researchers should not conduct consultancy research for institutions, such as the military (see Ames, *et al.*, 2007)—especially when it is with regard to improving the living and working conditions of military personnel, and to contributing to a reduction in detrimental conditions, such as alcoholism or mental health issues. Furthermore, consultancy research can make these institutions more transparent in their structures and cultures. But while 'inside studies' can potentially have a beneficial effect, the researcher is faced by many ethical pitfalls in conducting research with subjects who find themselves in conflictive relationships with the military or respective government: 'The complication comes when [researchers] find themselves in a situation where the military is interested in their expertise because their informants have become enemies of the [researcher's] own government' (Gusterson, 2003: 25): in such cases any research activities for the benefit of informing the fight against these 'enemies' should indeed be seen as questionable.

The contributors to this volume conduct research in Afghanistan and the diaspora due to a genuine interest in the country and its people; and to make an informed contribution to improving the country's situation and to contribute to the understanding of forms of conflict and violence. What can studies of forms of conflict and violence teach us? According to Gilsenan (2002: 99) they:

...tell us much about the ways in which groups and persons organise and imagine themselves, constitute relations of power and hierarchy, and create social identities and meanings. Both are central to the world we live in and to our understanding of our place in that world.

The ethical, logistical and methodological challenges connected to research in war and the resulting view that it is impossible to gather reliable data in such situations have deterred many researchers as well as aid organisations from considering participation in in-depth research. However, it is also now widely recognised that any attempt to appease and (re)construct a war-torn country without up-to-date information about its historical and present situation has to remain futile. As Goodhand (2000: 12) rightly concludes:

If researchers and analysts are not prepared to engage until the guns fall silent, knowledge and understanding tend to be stuck at the pre-war level. Responses based solely on pre-war society which fail to account for the fact that society has moved on are likely to be inappropriate. Afghanistan is a classic example of a conflict zone that in the last 20 years has virtually dropped off the 'research map'. One could argue that, as a result, action has got ahead of understanding.

It is therefore very much a certainty that high-quality and in-depth research is desperately needed, not only to close the information gap that characterises our knowledge of long-term war countries such as Afghanistan, but, more importantly, to inform any kind of remedial action. However, this, of course, poses a whole array of questions and concerns for researchers, not least about how to ensure the establishment and maintenance of ethical research standards and quality data collection under what are often extreme research circumstances. As Hoffman (2003: 10) states, 'Frontline anthropology is still anthropology, and needs to maintain high disciplinary standards'; and this applies equally to representatives of other disciplines in the field. The next sections will discuss what these high disciplinary standards are deemed to be and how this transposes to a field site such as Afghanistan.

Ethical guidelines for empirical research

Adherence to ethical guidelines has been professional practice for a long while, and should be part of any research project. While it is undoubtedly of utmost significance that researchers analyse their research project on the basis of ethical considerations before embarking on it, external evaluation of ethics and of ensuing demands—e.g. by universities, funding bodies as well as local gatekeepers—are sometimes perceived to have a crippling effect, distorting the initial research project, or at times making it impossible to continue with the research project as initially envisaged (see for example Scheyvens *et al.*, 2003: 145). In most research settings, there is a debate between those who believe in absolutist ethical standards and practices (i.e. the principles of research must be adhered to at all times and under all circumstances), and a more relativist standpoint which states that the rational objectivity required in the first model [the absolutist view] is a false reality:

[R]esearchers are not apolitical, neutral observers but rather fully involved, self-aware, interacting people who are (or should be) ethically fully informed, therefore responsible for their actions (*Ibid.*: 140–1).

While the first model is criticised for being too rigid and offering one set of guidelines for a whole array of different situations, many of which cannot be foreseen at the onset of fieldwork, the second is contested for being seen as advocating an 'anything goes' mentality which might lead to unethical conduct during fieldwork. However, most ethical standards are now recognising that a certain level of flexibility is crucial to ethical as well as successful research. Thus, the ethical guidelines of the American Anthropological Association (AAA) state:

No code or set of guidelines can anticipate unique circumstances or direct actions in specific situations. The individual [researcher] must be willing to make carefully considered ethical choices and be prepared to make clear the assumptions, facts and issues on which those choices are based (Cassell and Jacobs, 2006).

The researcher will always be confronted by situations in which an ethical decision needs to be made; and which are distinctive and so require a unique approach. Ideally, the researchers, through the broader as well as the context-specific knowledge they possess, will have the ability to make judgements about the impacts of certain actions, and should be in a position to make an appropriate decision—bearing in mind that there is probably no one right course of action, but rather a choice between better and worse. An approach informed by specialist knowledge that answers to a unique situation will also aid the researcher in being transparent about decisions and being able to justify them.

Ethical guidelines are primarily written with the intention to safeguard vulnerable people and relationships that could be damaged during the course of research, and to whom researchers owe their responsibility and obligation. These are usually identified to be the following: those studied, the public, the sponsors, and the discipline itself. Researchers would also consider vulnerable the relationships with their own and host governments. To this list of obligations I would add that of one's own safety and security as the researcher, especially in a research location that is characterised by war or latent conflict. This will be subject to further discussion in the course of this chapter. Yet how do these obligations translate into good ethical practise?

The Economics and Social Science Research Council (ESRC) in the UK has stipulated several key principles of research in its Research Ethics Framework that researchers must adhere to in order to be eligible for ESRC funding. According to these:

- Research should be designed, reviewed and undertaken to ensure integrity and quality
- Research staff and subjects must be informed fully about the purpose, methods and intended possible uses of the research, what their participation in the research entails and what risks, if any, are involved[3]
- The confidentiality of information supplied by research subjects and the anonymity of respondents must be respected
- Research participants must participate in a voluntary way, free from coercion
- Harm to research participants must be avoided
- The independence of research must be clear, and any conflicts of interest or partiality must be explicit (ESRC, 2005)

Any breach of these principles could have serious repercussions for the researcher's aforementioned responsibilities and obligations. However, how can these principles be translated to and ensured in a research site such as Afghanistan?

Challenges to research in Afghanistan

An increasing number of research locations have either dropped off the 'research map' (Goodhand, 2000) or are only just being considered again as research locations due to ongoing war and conflict. Afghanistan is just one example. While all research locations and themes pose their own general and unique problems, data collection and analysis in a war-torn country like Afghanistan introduces a whole range of serious complications: the researcher is trying to meet academic standards of quality but at the same time is working towards ensuring personal security and the well-being of the research participants, and is also trying not to 'spoil the field' for other researchers. As a consequence, as Harpviken (2006: 88) argues:

the conditions of research are not conducive to the tallest ambitions of social research, such as to systematically test theoretical propositions or validate theories. The more modest aim is to engage in data and insights gathered during fieldwork, and to use them as a basis for developing new theoretical proposals and understandings.

This is exacerbated by the fact that there are only now available an increasing number of research projects and findings collected under similar conditions which researchers currently working in Afghanistan can use as a model for the design of their own project. However, this lack of existing models and of favourable conditions for research in countries such as Afghanistan also means that the researcher has some academic freedom to try new and creative approaches, methods and theoretical models. Thus, in a more positive light, research under such extreme conditions can force the researcher to re-think assumptions that were taken for granted, and to develop new models. The following sections will, in turn, highlight some of those issues that researchers have found particularly daunting: choice of and access to research location; various levels of trustworthiness on the part of researcher and researched; informed consent from the research participant; information reliability; various and often conflicting expectations placed on the researcher from multiple sources; and security risks and confidentiality.

Choice of research location and access

The first consequence of doing research in a war-torn country for the researcher is the limitations in the choice of the research location.[4] In a country like Afghanistan, it is often not the individual preference of the researcher and the suitability for the research project that determines the choice of the specific fieldwork site(s), but rather questions of security. Another significant criterion is the access to the field site: whether there are potential gatekeepers as well as supporters who can help solve logistical problems locally and facilitate communication at different levels. While gatekeepers more often than not pose specific problems for the researcher, they are almost unavoidable in every fieldwork project and can either provide much sought-after information and/or open up networks. This will be a discussion point throughout the remaining chapter sections.

In order to tackle logistical issues, many researchers link up with non-governmental organisations (NGOs) or international organisations; while others seek to distance themselves as much as possible in order to maintain their own neutrality and to avoid potential pitfalls when seen as cooperating with these actors. Opinions are divided when it comes to the issue of using contacts in local NGOs to access the field site. Hoffman states that 'making use of such institutions [...] may well allow a motivated researcher to conduct field research in spaces from which academics have previously been excluded' (Hoffman, 2003: 11). While Harpviken also affirms that in his case acquaintances within the NGO world were 'a major advantage—if not a prerequisite—for gaining access both to the authorities and to the local population' (Harpviken, 2006: 97), he was also aware that it impacted people's responses 'through their expectations that we might influence the level of assistance provided to them' (*Ibid.*).

Goodhand (2000), on the other hand, suggests working closely with a locally existing NGO, where possible and desirable. Thus data collected can be fed directly into an aid project and potentially improve the project's impact, while the research participants could see their words turned into actions. However, in line with aforementioned concerns, this partnership demands that strong communication and cooperation mechanisms are in place, as well as clarity on both sides about what the research, aid projects and work ethics entail.

Generally, it is advisable, if considering cooperation with an organisation, to collect as much information as possible about it and its local reputation, and to make a decision based on this, bearing in mind the reliability of information gathered. The same is also true if hiring local research assistants, since their personal background and behaviour will reflect onto the researcher. A researcher may hire local staff for a number of reasons but the decision of a particular research assistant over others may be seen as the researcher's preferred and conscious choice; for example, the choice of a Pashtun research assistant may be interpreted as the researcher favouring Pashtuns over other ethnic groups.

All in all, several researchers have found it useful to work with NGOs and a variety of local gate-keepers for the initial introduction to the field site, which primarily meant knowing to whom to introduce oneself, and making one's intentions known to various gatekeepers on all levels of the local and national hierarchies. At further stages during the fieldwork process, however, it has been seen as more beneficial to distance oneself, if possible, from the initial access contacts in order to be seen as separate from them and to protect them, as they are often the ones particularly at risk should anything go wrong.

Trustworthiness and informed consent

In order to gain access in a way that enables long-term fieldwork, and potentially even return visits, trustworthiness of the researcher is of critically importance, especially 'in situations where trust is a scarce commodity' (Harpviken, 2006: 97). As far as possible, therefore, informed consent should be sought, and interviewees as much as gatekeepers should be informed about the project, its intention, the use of data collected and any potential risks that it poses for the participant. Of course, in an environment such as Afghanistan, the issue of informed consent raises a whole array of questions about how 'informed' this consent can really be. Wilson (1992: 185) shares his own experience from the field:

To ensure that consent is really 'informed', regular meetings should be held with all concerned. [...] With the help of key informants, local leaders and research assistants, fieldworkers must struggle to understand how people perceive them and the research issues so that communication on these occasions can be effective. Furthermore, to maintain 'informed consent', researchers must be prepared to spend time continually explaining to people individually and collectively why they need certain kinds of data. Finally, researchers should realise that what is said about them by local officials and the people they are personally closest to will be critical, so that such people should be especially briefed.

This seems like a feasible strategy, especially in a country that has high illiteracy rates and/or where people may be hesitant to sign any declaration. It is also important that the same information is given to all who participate in the project in one way or another, because different versions, especially if seen as divergent, will cause suspicion.

Particular care needs to be exercised in working with gate-keepers. On the one hand, they 'provide access to their social networks, and in the process place at risk their own trustworthiness, which they may have spent considerable time and energy to build up' (Harpviken, 2006: 99). They take a considerable risk, especially when granting access to these networks to somebody they hardly know, and in a country which is being inundated by foreign aid organisations and researchers whose intentions are not always clear. Thus, the researcher should feel obliged to keep the risk for the gate-keeper to a minimum, particularly if they feel that the research project will depend on the involvement of the gate-keeper for some time to come. On the other hand, gatekeepers may also hamper certain research efforts, either to protect certain interests or to ensure the researcher's security, a distinction which, for the researcher, is not always easy to recognise. Several researchers (Harpviken, 2006; Valentine, 1997) have suggested not to rely on one gate-keeper but to collect information from several sources for a more balanced assessment.

Reliability of data gathered

Access to reliable information is generally seen as an issue by many researchers. Thus, Valey Arya, a contributor to this book, referring to his own experience stated that there are 'a lot of conspiracy theories flying around which can easily affect the findings of the research if one is not careful enough. [...] Sometimes respondents are [also] suspicious of researchers and think they are MI5 or CIA spies'.[5] Furthermore, 'racial, linguistic, religious and political leanings and prejudices influence the viewpoints of the interviewees to a great extent; again the interviewer should be extremely careful'.[6] When including Afghan politicians in the research project, he warns that 'personal vendettas make some politicians speak unrealistically and untruthfully about others'.[7]

How can the researcher work with this problem of information reliability? To a certain extent triangulation of information can limit the problems inherent in data collection. Several different sources should be probed about a certain piece of information; however, care should be taken not to favour one source of information over another, e.g. valuing the information an NGO provides more than that of locals, since its own information source could prove to be just as shaky as that of the researcher. Potentially, the researcher could end up with a range of different versions, each telling the same story from a different angle.

As I experienced during research amongst the Afghan diaspora in London (Schlenkhoff, 2006), sometimes giving up the search for scientific 'truth' can provide a whole range of other insights otherwise overlooked, e.g. why certain people feel they want to, or need to, provide a certain piece of information in one situation and not in another, depending on the audience and the purpose.

Research data like this can give valuable insights into current socio-cultural and political definitions of, for example, ethnicity and gender and situational identity markers (see Schlenkhoff, 2006) prevalent at a certain time and in a specific location. Thus, which of these is the 'true' version is not relevant, as the different versions serve various purposes depending on the narrating situation.

Managing expectations

An issue that came up in researchers' accounts about their experience of doing fieldwork in Afghanistan was the difficulty of managing the expectations of the research participants. How does the researcher avoid raising certain expectations about improved and increasing outcomes for the research participants, and avoid creating incentives to participate which will colour the data collected? Moreover, should the researcher recompense the time and risk research participants take in answering questions? Most researchers who contributed their ideas found it inadvisable to compensate research participants in terms of monetary means for their time (unless, of course, they were research assistants on a contractual basis). Harpviken (2006: 103–4) stated that his research team:

found that being generally helpful, for example in offering a lift to the city when possible, was enough. Despite such favours being extended to only a few of the informants, they are noticed as gestures of goodwill and positively affect people's motivation to contribute. It is essential, of course, that such favours be distributed at random, so they are not seen to benefit some people or groups at the cost of others.

Similarly, Wilson (1992: 188) stresses that:

during fieldwork researchers have to make decisions about the extent to which their research can usefully address different people's needs. In terms of benefits to local people, too much stress is generally put on the value of the 'products' of research, rather than its 'process'. Engaging creatively in community life is often the most effective way of having a positive impact on an area through fieldwork.

Generally, in order to manage expectations it is of utmost importance that the purpose of the research is communicated at all levels to people involved and potentially stressed at different points throughout the research stay. If research participants are left under the impression that the research project and their participation in it will improve their life (and the researcher may not be aware of this) and they find their expectations subsequently crushed because they do not see any tangible outcomes, they may become disillusioned with participating in research altogether. This will make future research more difficult.

Security risks and confidentiality

As Harpviken (2006: 87) has stated in his doctoral thesis:

risk aversion is a constraint among researchers of armed conflict. The response to this problem, however, is not that researchers must be willing to accept more risk, but that we need to upgrade our ability to assess and manage risk, both before and during fieldwork.

Furthermore, 'in a war situation, security criteria ought to be fixed. Other criteria—including those that have to do with the research topic—may be open to negotiation' (*Ibid.*: 90). The extent to which researchers may take personal risks is an individual decision; however, this should not apply to risks concerning others—interviewees, gatekeepers or anyone else involved. The ethical bottom line must be, without doubt, that if the personal security of the participants and assistants cannot be guaranteed, they should not be persuaded or coerced into participating.

However, as Haver (2007: 10) found, 'international staff [of aid agencies] often fail to realise that national colleagues may find it exceedingly difficult to decline potentially dangerous work for economic and/or altruistic reasons'. With an increasing number of aid organisations in Afghanistan, this has developed into a business that promises an income to locals. The same applies to researchers, and often the assumption is that national staff members will be less at risk because of their status as 'local', thus requiring less security measures. While in some cases local staff may be more secure in comparison to international staff (who may be vulnerable due to their 'foreign-ness', lack of specific local knowledge, language skills etc.), in others they may actually be at just as much risk:

[L]ocal staff may be 'too local', assumed, rightly or wrongly, to be aligned by ethnic or religious affiliation with a party to a conflict. In some contexts they risk being attacked due to their access to cash or agency assets, such as computer equipment or vehicles. They also face a potential loss of income for themselves and their families should a programme be terminated (*Ibid.*: 10).

Wilson (1992: 190) also attests that 'few researchers are sufficiently aware of the risks their assistants sometimes face. Field assistants are often blamed for the real and imagined crimes of researchers, and for the fact that researchers found things out that are not compatible with official views'. The question then arises as to what extent it is the responsibility of the researcher to ensure the security of research assistants even after their departure from the field. Wilson (*Ibid.*: 190–1) offers some potential solutions to ensure the safety of local staff:

Between the two extremes of the 'unavoidable' and the effects of 'inadequate fore-thought', there is much that a researcher can do to protect assistants. Strategies depend on context. In one situation, in a country with a highly developed sense of secrecy, I decided to keep the host country national (who worked with us as an equal) as an apparently insignificant subordinate, in case we inadvertently offended the government and he was blamed. In situations where research is likely to be highly critical I try to work with a large number of assistants to avoid victimisation...

Furthermore, the 'researcher should not put pressure on assistants to interpret events and spell out the implications. Assistants should be allowed to feel secure that all they did was to interpret word by word, and transmit the facts according to their contracts, and did not operate as 'informers'" (*Ibid.*: 191).

As a consequence, the security of local staff, if employed to provide support with certain parts of the research project, should be considered just as much as the researcher's security, as well as anybody else involved in the project. If their safety cannot be guaranteed to a reasonable standard, the researcher should consider other alternatives.

Particular care should also be taken to store any data collected securely, so that no unauthorised person finds access and misuses the often sensitive data. Most researchers will have their own preference for data storage in order to ensure a systematic process that will facilitate data analysis during the field-work period as well as afterwards. In the case of researchers who are sufficiently proficient in a language not commonly known in the research location, writing down the data in this language may already provide some security. However, research participants need to feel sure that the confidentiality of data and their anonymity are guaranteed at all times: 'It is clear that the ethical bottom line [...] must be that if information systems cannot be used safely and responsibly, they should not be used at all (Editors Forced Migration Review, 2007: 28).

While minimising risk and protecting research participants is of paramount importance, researchers also have some means of controlling their own security, e.g. by choosing the time of entering the field, the fieldwork location, and the methods used:

'Armed with an understanding of the patterns and dynamics of conflict, researchers can make informed decisions about when, where and how to do research. Conflicts are often characterised by dynamic and mutating patterns of violence. These may be spatially, temporally or seasonally determined. For example, fighting in Afghanistan tends to follow a seasonal pattern, with the spring and summer being the periods of greatest intensity' (Goodhand, 2000: 8).

The following section will now focus on some of the challenges encountered while conducting fieldwork amongst different Afghan diaspora groups. Much of this is based on my own fieldwork experience amongst the Afghan diaspora population in London between 2003 and 2004 as well as the result of discussions with colleagues embarking on similar research projects, such as Ceri Oeppen's research with Afghans in California and London.

Challenges to research amongst the Afghan diaspora

While the research projects I am referring to here have not been conducted in war-torn countries, they still reflect some of the difficulties encountered while doing fieldwork in Afghanistan. One major similarity is the fact that large parts of the population have experienced traumatising events and can be suspicious of people with an unknown background to them. Furthermore, London is home to a refugee population that mainly arrived at three different intervals,[8] thus uniting people of different political groupings in one place, which creates potential tension lines. At each of these points in time, the society and its predominant norms and values were very different; and it can be argued that the intensity of ethnic affiliations and religious piety has increased continuously (Schetter, 2003).

Thus, refugees fleeing at different stages have distinct memories of their homeland and its norms and values, which influence their life in exile, and are coloured according to the level of antagonism within Afghanistan at the time that they fled. This, of course, also has repercussions for the way they identify and view other Afghans around them, especially the refugee community organisations (RCOs) (see Schlenkhoff, 2006). The following will now address some of the issues encountered by myself and other researchers working with Afghan diaspora populations.

Gaining access

Gaining access to a population that is not only scattered all over a metropolis like London, but that can also be suspicious of attention, proved quite difficult for my fieldwork. It took me the first three months of my fieldwork in London to build up contacts and establish a rapport with a small number of people until they felt comfortable enough to be interviewed by me, and to refer others to me through 'snowballing'. In the same way, Omidian (1996: 33) describes her experiences of fieldwork with an Afghan community in California:

[W]ithout the help of Afghan friends, a study of the Afghan community would have been very difficult. Afghans do not trust strangers or outsiders, making the anthropologist's task all the more difficult. This distrust stems in part from living under a communist regime in which informants were afraid to talk about mundane aspects of everyday life for fear of being overheard by spies who would report to the police. [...] Also, in Afghan culture outsiders are viewed as being potentially dangerous, and only close in-group connections are trusted. The only way to talk to an Afghan is to be introduced by a mutual friend.

However, once these relationships were actually established, they were cordial, and many have lasted until now, several years after the initial fieldwork. Of course, relying heavily on snowballing involves certain risks, since the problem could arise that the researcher only scratches at the surface of a population and gets to know some of only the most prominent members. The researcher also needs to be aware of the Afghans' perceptions of research and interview; for example, I was told by a potential Afghan interviewee that I should interview his brother rather than himself as 'he is the one doing interviews for Sky and BBC'. In some cases it took some explaining as to how my intentions were different from those of a journalist: Ceri Oeppen and I found in research in both London and California that media coverage after 11 September 2001 has certainly had a major impact on the way many Afghans perceive interviews generally. But overall I received very positive responses to my research project.

I attempted to 'snowball' from different angles of the Afghan population— e.g. by contacting people living in different areas of London and being affiliated to various networks. This way I not only got into contact with people from different sections but I was also often able to collect data on how the different networks interlinked. However, despite my efforts, my research project inevitably failed in reaching those particularly isolated, either through their own choice or due to various barriers such as language differences and poverty.

Opening old wounds

When working with a refugee population, there is always the danger of touching on sensitive subjects that might open emotional wounds from the experience of war and escape. While some interviewees may be quite keen to share their experiences and express their traumas in words, others may choose silence as one way of coping. Goodhand (2000: 14) raised a similar issue concerning traumatised populations in general, whether in the country of war or outside:

> For traumatised individuals and groups, silence may be a coping, not just a survival, strategy. Researchers may inadvertently re-open wounds by probing into areas respondents may not wish to talk about. Dialogues must always be based on mutual consent. Researchers need to show restraint and know when to stop.

Refugee community politics

Part of my methodology was to maintain contact with as many RCOs as possible in order to gain a full picture of the framework and network of institutional actors. Many of these RCOs had problematic relationships with each other, linking with some when necessary but ignoring or criticising others. Although I was told that the situation between the different RCOs had already markedly improved, there were still several who had not mended rifts with each other, and I became, in part, a resource to fight over. Occasionally I was told not to associate with specific others because they were of the 'wrong type', as they consisted of the former Communists, *mujahideen*, Taliban-sympathisers or a variety of other ethno-political groups. It became a rich source of information, but I did not feel comfortable and at times became frustrated. It demanded a lot of sensitivity and I was very aware of and careful about my conversation with people whose background I was not familiar with.[9] To some extent, it can be argued, these dilemmas are probably inevitable when studying a population which has experienced so much internal conflict, heightened by outside forces, and which now lives in a situation where various conflict actors live in close proximity. Yet I found that the more I became familiarised with the arguments and conflict lines, as well as their historical background, the better I could steer my own boat through these sometimes rough waters.

Outside perceptions

Another issue with which I struggled was outsiders' perception of refugees and asylum-seekers in general, and of Afghans in particular, as presented in the media, in the offices of policy-makers, and among the general public. I do not aim to go into detail here about the reputation of refugees and asylum-seekers, and I do not wish to take side vehemently.

However, I would argue that researchers generally find themselves in a difficult position if they come across instances which at first sight seem to confirm certain internal and external accusations. This is almost inevitable due to the nature of their work and the relationships established through the necessary long-term close contact. Thus, 'every anthropologist finds himself in possession of facts that he cannot publish, since to do so would injure the reputation or betray the confidence of friends and informants with whom he has been working' (Stirling, 1968, accessed April 2006). This is an ethical dilemma which follows the researcher right through fieldwork into the writing-up phase (and arguably even beyond that). In most cases, ethnography is the result of a long process of considering which information to use and how to describe certain events without exposing oneself 'at one and the same time to the danger of charges of condoning immorality, and of charges of publishing malevolent calumny' (*Ibid.*).

Conclusion

As the above discussion of challenges to research in war-torn countries such as Afghanistan and its diaspora shows, researchers are faced with a huge array of demands on their role: the academic quality of their work as judged by peers and employers, and the nature of the relationships they form in the field—with gatekeepers, research participants and authorities. Often the latter pose conflicting demands, and researchers might find that the realities they face in the field are difficult to view from a professional distance. For now, ethical guidelines, such as those compiled by the AAA or the ESRC, can only be seen as guidelines that researchers should adhere to as much as possible. However, much within these guidelines will depend on the individual researcher's ability to judge the field that they are working in and to make informed decisions in terms of ethical challenges on the basis of the specialist knowledge and experience they possess. In a country such as Afghanistan, this might often mean using less orthodox and more creative approaches, and research in both Afghanistan and the diaspora will demand a certain amount of flexibility and confidence from the researcher.

However, rather than striving to avoid harm from happening during the course of and as a result of fieldwork, there is also some scope to do good, as Goodhand (2000) identified. One benefit researchers can bring concerns the value of gathering data:

research can play an important role in countering myths and stereotypes, identifying information blockages and giving voice to the suppressed. If research can help us better understand the complex information economy in war zones, this will be a major contribution to more informed and appropriate responses (Goodhand, 2000: 8).

This, of course, raises the issue of representation. However, considering that in war-torn countries (as well as their diasporas) researchers are often the only ones in a position to gather data and spread information, do they not have an obligation to their research participants as well as the wider research community to do the best possible under the present circumstances? As the following chapters will show, quality research is feasible even under the most extreme circumstances, and serves to enhance our knowledge and understanding of Afghanistan and its people.

SECTION I

AFGHAN HISTORY, SOCIETY AND CULTURE

3

BRITAIN IN THE FIRST TWO AFGHAN WARS

WHAT CAN WE LEARN?

Bijan Omrani with Maj Gen. Charles Vyvyan

It has become a commonplace to draw comparisons between the current conflicts, both in Afghanistan and in Iraq, and the First and Second Afghan Wars (1839–1842 and 1878–1880) (see for example Beeston, 2006; Loyd, 2007). However, for all the British military and political experience in Afghanistan over two campaigns with objectives not dissimilar to that of the current operation, more effort has been put into research regarding the Soviet occupation of the 1980s and its lessons—primarily in the tactical field—for the current situation (see for example Cordesman, 2002; Kulakov, 2006). By contrast, little attention has been paid to the more detailed aspects of the first two British campaigns in Afghanistan, and what they might have to teach us. This chapter is an attempt to rectify this deficiency. It lists a number of the similarities over many fields—political, governmental and strategic—between British involvement in the first two Afghan Wars and the current conflict in Afghanistan, also referring to parallels with Iraq where relevant. It then attempts to determine what of value NATO and the coalition governments can learn from these comparisons.

Points of similarity

Causes of war

The ultimate cause of the First Anglo-Afghan War (1838–1842) was the British fear of Russian encroachment into Central Asia and Persia, and the threat that this would bear against British possessions in India.[1] In 1837, Persia undertook a siege of the city of Herat, then a *de facto* independent principality under a renegade Afghan prince, Kamran of the Popalzai clan. Russia held considerable influence at the court of the Shah of Persia, and the siege of Herat was conducted with Russian logistical help, subsidies and encouragement. It was believed by the British government in India that should the city fall, the governors of nearby Kandahar would also pledge allegiance to the Shah of Persia, and thus themselves fall similarly under Russian influence; Russian power, therefore, could be projected to within a short distance of the frontiers of British India (Durand, 1879; Kaye, 1851). In order to avert such an eventuality, the Indian Government held that it was vital to have a friendly power controlling the remainder of Afghanistan (then including the cities/regions of Kandahar, Ghazni, Jalalabad, Kabul, Charikar, Bamiyan). The ruler who then held Kabul, Dost Mohammed Khan, was well-disposed to the British, and could easily have been drawn into a strong alliance with little financial and diplomatic outlay; however, the Indian Government were not prepared to make this, demanding his obedience, but promising nothing in return. Although Dost Mohammed refused to assent to these demands, he nevertheless preserved his independence, not conducting any intrigues with Russia, despite many rumours to the contrary (see Kaye, 1851).

The first parallel may be drawn here with the campaign against Iraq. The British Government failed to support a stable power for diplomatic and military advantage, trusting instead in the idea of regime change, and installing an exiled placeman of unknown and doubtful ability.

Manipulation of intelligence

The Governments in India and London, fearing Russia, were not able, for the sake of diplomatic relations with Russia, to cite this fear as a reason for their invasion of Afghanistan. Instead, they set out to blacken the reputation of Dost Mohammed Khan, and set him up as a straw man for their armies to attack. In two documents—the Simla Declaration of 1838, published in India, and an edited selection of official correspondence published in London—Dost Mohammed Khan was incorrectly portrayed as intriguing with the Persians and Russians; as a serious threat to the stability of northern India and the Sikh principality of the Punjab; and as an unjust, unpopular and tyrannical ruler, unable to maintain unity amongst his chiefs. They held that their own candidate for the Afghan throne, Shah Shuja (who had been deposed from that position in 1809, and had since then lived as a British pensioner in Ludhiana) had been illegitimately deprived of the kingship; that he was popular amongst the Afghan people; and would make a strong and capable ruler, friendly to British interests.

However, this depiction of the situation ran quite contrary to much of the intelligence which was actually received by the Governments. A number of British agents, news-writers and travellers with experience on the ground in Afghanistan, all testified to the abilities of the Afghan ruler, Dost Mohammed Khan (Burnes, 1834; Masson, 1842; Vigne, 1840). Masson and Burnes in particular also gave it as their opinion that Shah Shuja was not at all Dost Mohammed Khan's equal, and that he did not possess the capabilities to rule adequately over Afghanistan (Burnes, 1834). Moreover, the anthology of documents published in London in 1838 made many omissions from official correspondence, with the result that it portrayed Sir Alexander Burnes as giving his wholehearted support to the enterprise, when this in fact was far from being the case.

We may adduce several parallels here with Iraq: the failure to take into account critical evidence from intelligence agents; the misunderstanding (wilful or otherwise) of the long-term intentions of the regime in question; the manipulation of the media, and even the production of spurious intelligence to achieve this (the so-called 'dodgy dossier'); and the masking of a wide and poorly thought-out geopolitical objective by petty and incorrect complaints about small-scale infringements.

Committing troops

The invasion of Afghanistan in the First Afghan War (1838–42) was made according to an agreement between the British, the Sikhs under Maharajah Runjit Singh, and Shah Shuja (Kaye, 1851). It was originally envisaged that the great bulk of forces that would carry out the operation would be Sikhs sent from the Punjab, and Durrani Afghans loyal to Shah Shuja; the British contribution would be light, with a small number of troops, officers to help lead the Sikh and Durrani men, and logistical support. The reality, however, was very different. The Durrani contribution was slight and irregular; the Sikh contribution, after the death of Runjit Singh was also severely curtailed, so that although they would draw many political and financial benefits from the invasion, they would in military terms contribute little.

This is similar to the fashion in which today countries contribute forces to Afghanistan through the NATO-led International Security Assistance Force, but those forces are slight, and hampered by restrictive rules of engagement, leaving the larger contributors to do even more of the work than would otherwise be the case.

Assumptions of quick victory

The advance of Keane's column to Ghazni, and the capture of the city on 23 July 1839, was in itself a brilliant military exploit, and it had the result of cowing the Afghan opposition into an initial submission.[2] However, the reaction to it betrayed a terrible hubris on the part of the war's supporters, who assumed that this military triumph was both a vindication of the overall policy, and a guarantee of its future military and political success. The clamour over the victory shut down further debate about both the validity of the policy, and whether the policy was, in the long run, militarily viable. A flavour of the mood in the wake of the capture of Ghazni is given by the speeches made in the House of Commons, for example:

Sir John Hobhouse: That the very stations on which the British flag is now flying, were the resting places of the great Alexander, and that, since his days, the standard of no civilised nation has been seen on the banks of the Indus. We may be allowed to dwell on this bold and brilliant achievement—and most pleasing is it, instead of the conflicts of party and struggles for political power, to be enabled to direct our attention to subjects of national interest, and to unite in doing justice to those who have upheld the honour and renown of the British empire and the British army.[3]

It is notable that the motion on which these speeches were made, on a message of thanks to be sent to the Army of the Indus, seems to have been the only time that the matter of Afghanistan was debated in Parliament between 1839 and receipt of the news of the disastrous 1842 retreat. Even during this debate, it was stressed that the essence of the discussion would be limited to a review of the achievements of the army, and not to consider the policy, or any of the wider questions.

This finds parallels in both modern-day Afghanistan and Iraq: a lack of proper debate, planning and consideration of the military and political requirements in the medium- to long-term, and the tendency of an immediate victory (e.g. the toppling of Saddam's statue in Baghdad, the immediate evaporation of the Taliban in 2001) to shut down the mind of government to the more extensive long-term problems that the military campaigns both brought about. As the Duke of Wellington commented on the First Afghan War, the problems would begin for the British when the military success was completed (Kaye, 1851, vol. I: 363). Similarly, Cordesman says of the present conflict in Afghanistan:

There is a curious irony in the fact that the US Government and Department of Defense seem to have been only marginally more concerned with planning for conflict termination and grand strategic outcomes in Afghanistan than they were during the Gulf War and Kosovo (Cordesman, 2002: 55).

War expenditure

Not long after the troops had left on the Afghan expedition in 1839, it soon became obvious to the Governor-general of India, Lord Auckland, that their absence could well imperil the security of India itself, and that he could little afford to spare them. As soon as Kabul was occupied, Auckland wrote:

I am anxiously desirous that the forces which compose the Army of the Indus should be once more stationed within our own provinces. The political effect of their return could not but be advantageous. It would put an end to the injurious speculations which have been founded on their absence (Kaye, 1851, vol. I: 465).

It is also worthwhile to note in this connection the general calculation, quoted in Parliamentary debates on 23 June 1842 and 1 March 1843, that the First Afghan War cost the Government in India on average around £1.5 million sterling every year.

This echoes the modern-day problem of imperial overstretch, and crippling expenditure to maintain this, for an exiguous result.[4]

Mission creep

As soon as the British reached Kabul in August 1839, and reinstalled Shah Shuja as ruler of Afghanistan, it became clear that he was not capable of government, and the British forces, who had hoped to leave, would be required to stay in order to maintain him on his throne:

The Shah had no hold on the affections of his people. He might sit in the Bala Hissar, but he could not govern the Afghans... The palace of his fathers had received him again; but it was necessary to hedge in the throne with a quickset of British bayonets (Kaye, 1851, vol. I: 463–4).

As with Iraq and Afghanistan, there was a serious tendency for the circumstances of the place to lead to 'mission creep', and for the British forces to become engaged in the toils of an exceedingly complex situation from which there seemed to be no possible means of escape. With respect to Afghanistan, the original over-optimistic forecast of the then United Kingdom Defence Secretary, John Reid, was that the period of British Military deployment could be for up to three years (see BBC, 2006b). The latest suggestions by the current Defence Secretary, Des Browne, are that the deployment could now last indefinitely beyond 2009 (see BBC, 2007a).

Military strategy

The ruler deposed by the British, Dost Mohammed Khan, fled with a number of his supporters to the regions north of the Hindu Kush. In order to guard against attacks from him, and the unsubdued country to the north and west of Kabul, a number of small detachments were placed in isolated fortresses towards and in these regions (e.g. Bamiyan). Sir John Kaye calls this strategy of 'planting small detachments in isolated positions... one of the great errors which marked our military occupation of Afghanistan' (Kaye, 1851, vol. I: 473). These detachments were often pinned down, at the mercy of tribesmen and tribal politics; and they were difficult to communicate with and supply, so were not able to achieve very much. An example of one of these detachments is given in the account of the occupation of Bajgah (about 50km north of Bamiyan), and the attack on its garrison (*Ibid.*). Similar situations arose in the Second Afghan war. Of the siege of the British in the Sherpur Cantonments, an embedded correspondent Howard Hensman wrote: 'To defend it, simply, is now comparatively easy... but beyond defence, we can do nothing' (Hensman, 1881: 224).

This is very close indeed to the current situation in the south of Afghanistan, and echoes exactly the strategy used in the early occupation of Helmand in 2006—putting small numbers of troops in isolated outposts, where they are difficult to supply, vulnerable to attack, and can achieve next to nothing in terms of pacification, reconstruction, projection of central government power, and law and order. Leo Docherty, a former British officer who participated in the battle for Sangin in May 2006, recently wrote:

The decision to scatter small groups of soldiers across the north of Helmand, in isolation, in an intelligence vacuum and with complete disregard for the most basic tenets of counter-insurgency, was, quite simply, a gross military blunder... These teams were deployed despite the fact that DFID [Department for International Development] and the FCO [Foreign and Commonwealth Office] had absolutely no effective practical measures in place in northern Helmand... The troops, deployed in isolation, had no real means of winning hearts and minds; they could offer no practical developmental improvements and were unable even to state the British policy on opium production (Docherty, 2007: 188).

Resentment toward occupying forces

It was found that the positioning of British military outposts, particularly in Pashtun tribal territory, often had an effect contrary to that intended. Instead of pacifying the tribesmen and local population, their mere presence often roused them to arms. Actions which were also calculated to stop low-level disturbances almost always brought about a significant revenge attack from the tribesmen, which led to a vicious circle of fighting between the British and the Afghans. A specific example is the occupation and fortification of Kelat-i Ghilzai on the road north-east of Kandahar, which led to heavy fighting with Ghilzai Pashtun tribesmen in May 1841 (Kaye, 1851).

A similar problem has been found in Afghanistan's Helmand province today—the mere presence of foreign troops stirs up insurgent attacks, giving them a specific target against which to fight. Any deaths amongst the Afghans caused by British action cause the tribesmen to seek, for the sake of their family's honour under the *Pushtunwali* code, revenge against the British—thus leading to a spiral of violence.[5] This allows the troops little liberty to achieve anything else. As Docherty goes on to say:

[The presence of the troops] soon became antagonistic; like honey-pot targets, they attracted anyone fancying a crack at the invading infidel, seemingly no better than the Russians before them. Once attacked, these teams were quickly sucked into lethal high-intensity war fighting... Over-exposed and often outgunned on the ground, British troops have had to rely on close air support... This escalation of violence is their primary means of survival. But these weapons are not the surgical tools best used by the counter-insurgent: they are blunt-edged, indiscriminate and have killed numerous civilians (Docherty, 2007: 188).

Similarly, in the First Afghan War, Sir Alexander Burnes remarked in a letter to the political officer who instigated the earlier action at Kelat-i Ghilzai, 'I consider we shall never settle Afghanistan at the point of the bayonet' (Kaye, 1851, vol. I: 592). Burnes considered that a policy of bribery and other political measures would be more satisfactory in maintaining the peace. Similarly today, political and economic measures are more likely than overt employment of military force to bring about a climate of security. Again, Docherty writes:

It would be absurd to suggest that war-fighting on a broad front, supposedly 'drawing out' the Taliban, is a necessary prelude to the reconstructive phases of the comprehensive approach. Violence begets violence, as thousands of new local recruits, previously uninterested in radical Islam, are drawn to the Taliban cause, hungry for revenge after civilian deaths in their communities (Docherty, 2007: 189).

Parallels also may be drawn between the offences caused to public morals by the sexual licence of British troops in the First Afghan War, a major contributory factor in the 1841–2 uprising, and the recent treatment of the people of Kabul by international—particularly US—forces. A significant example is the rioting which took place in response to the high-handed behaviour of the US army after a traffic accident in Kabul in May 2006 (see Leithead, 2006); but impositions on everyday life—such as hold-ups of traffic as security measures, and crash barriers erected to protect international buildings—also cause great resentment, though are little reported.

Reasons for failure

When the British announced their policy of a regime change in Afghanistan in 1838, they gave their attention solely to the form of the new government, but not its substance. After the Brisish incorrectly assumed that Shah Shuja would be able to hold Afghanistan without their help, besides the installation of a British Envoy in Kabul,[6] the British gave no prior thought to the sort of government that would be set up under Shah Shuja—neither to the people that would run the administration, their competence, nor other policies. Not thinking that theirs would be a long occupation, they did not contemplate beforehand that there would be a difficult co-existence in Afghanistan between British and Afghan authority. This lack of planning allowed a number of serious problems to flourish in the everyday administration of government, which would eventually contribute to the British defeat in 1842:

First, there was the problem of a lack of clarity in the administration of the Afghan government:

The more we found the people quiet, the more steps we took in shaking off their confidence. We neither took the reins of government in our own hands, nor did we give them in full powers into the hands of the Shah Shuja-ul-Mulk. Inwardly or secretly we interfered in all transactions, contrary to the terms of our own engagement with the

Shah; and outwardly we wore the mask of neutrality. In this manner we gave annoyance to the king upon the one hand, and disappointment to the people on the other (Lal, 1846, vol. II: 313).

The lack of clarity also seriously damaged the authority of the Shah (*Ibid.*: 365–6).

Second, attempts to impose reforms on the country against its natural inclinations caused difficulty:

Notwithstanding all these points of grave concern, we sent a large portion of the army back with Lord Keane to India, and yet we interfered in the administration of the country, and introduced such reforms amongst the obstinate Afghans just on our arrival, as even in India, the quietest part of the world, Lords Clive and Wellesley had hesitated to do but slowly, and to extend them over many years (*Ibid.*: 311–2).

Third, the disorder and lack of clarity in government led to ample scope for corruption amongst government officials. For example, Burnes promulgated a reduction in commercial tariffs; and so the traders, who accumulated wealth on account of this reduction, were mulcted by the corrupt *Wazir*, Mulla Abd-al Shakur Ishaqzai:

…every day complaints were made to us, and we permitted ourselves to interfere by giving notes to the complainants, requesting the Mulla to settle their cases; but this did no good, for instead of having redress to their grievances they were beaten, and sometimes confined, for coming and complaining to us against the Shah's authority (*Ibid.* and see also Noelle, 1997).

It should be noted that Mulla Shakur was a notoriously dishonest official, who had been in Shah Shuja's previous regime, and had managed to enter into the new government without the British initially trying to prevent him from doing so, despite his corruption. Under the same heading, the confusion of authority made it very difficult for Afghans to make their grievances known and find redress, especially against corrupt officials (Lal, 1846).

Fourth, the foreign occupation led to serious price hikes and inflation, especially in Kabul, with the result that there was starvation and hunger amongst the poorer inhabitants of the city (*Ibid.* and see also Noelle, 1997).

Fifth, the use of native Afghans to work for the occupying army in various capacities drove up the price of labour in and around Kabul, and also led to serious labour shortages for other civilian work—even when that work was for the Shah's own government (Lal, 1846).

Sixth, there was the difficult task of effectively re-establishing the Afghan army, and of securing of a force sufficiently loyal for the preservation of Shah Shuja (*Ibid.*).

All of these points find parallels in present-day Afghanistan: the authority of the Afghan government undermined by a foreign presence (Gall and Sanger, 2007), corruption and difficulties of finding redress through official government channels,[7] inflation,[8] and shortages of food, services and skilled labour.[9] However, the main fault behind all of these problems is that the coalition thought too much about the form of the government it would impose—a democracy—without thinking carefully enough about the daily practicalities it would have to face. The military intervention and the imposition of a particular form of government were seen as a panacea, and not enough was done to ensure the practical success of the government. In the words of Cordesman '[the] failure to give conflict termination the same priority as military operations... is particularly striking...' (Cordesman, 2002: 55).

Lack of local knowledge

Although there was a certain amount of fraternisation between British soldiers and the population of Kabul during the 1839–42 occupation, the British officials found it difficult to gauge the public mood, and were often unable to discern the warning-signs of the government's unpopularity. This was partly because of the wilful self-deception of British officials—for example, the Envoy Sir William Macnaghten's oft-quoted and complacent comment about the security situation, just before the 1841 uprising, that 'the country is quiet from Dan to Beersheba' (Kaye, 1851, vol. I: 609).

Further, the channels of communication and intelligence were often disrupted or manipulated. One curious example is that the Shah's government bribing the British news-writers to report that the Kabul government was more popular than it actually was, and to conceal or discredit reports of discontent (Lal, 1846). Also, the British officials often refused to see or take into account the problems on the ground, because the Supreme Government in Delhi did not wish to do so, and wished to spin the policy as a success. It is useful to bear in mind the comment of one of the British civilian residents in Kabul over the First Afghan War, Lady Florentia Sale:

[Our] state of supineness and fancied security... is the result of deference to the opinions of Lord Auckland, whose sovereign will and pleasure it is that tranquillity do reign in Affghanistan [sic]; in fact, it is reported at Government House, Calcutta, that the lawless Affghans [sic] are as peaceable as London citizens; and this being decided by the powers that be, why should we be on the alert? (Sale, 2002: 16).

There are many echoes of this in present-day Afghanistan: from accusations that the various development agencies are isolated from the people and little able to understand their needs (Nixon, 2007), to the pronouncements of the British Government in 2006, at the start of the Helmand deployment, about the situation into which they were placing sixteen Air Assault Brigades— perhaps best summed up by the former Defence Secretary John Reid's optimism that they might be able to do the job 'without a single bullet being fired' (see BBC, 2006b). Further, Docherty describes similar break-downs specifically on the ground—in the communications with local people and in the flow of intelligence (Docherty, 2007).

Changing priorities

Vacillation and lack of clarity about policy have been prominent, especially in the earlier stages of the Second Afghan War. An 'Army of Retribution' was dispatched after the murder of the British Envoy Sir Louis Cavagnari, but the form the retribution was to take remained unclear until long after the force reached Kabul; a number of people thought to be involved in the murder were summarily hanged, but the policy after a short while was reversed. The Bala Hissar was partially dismantled, only to be reconstructed a short while later. The King, Yakub Khan, whom the British were instrumental in installing, abdicated, leaving the British in unexpected executive charge of Afghanistan—to the deep resentment of the people, and with no obvious way forward; some hoped to solve the problem by annexing Afghanistan up to the Hindu Kush; others hoped to dismember it, keeping Kandahar as an Indian possession, leaving Herat as an independent principality; others advocated scouting around for another successor to place on the throne as a puppet ruler. The official policy wavered for many months between all of these alternatives, leaving the British 'Army of Retribution' to get caught up in running battles against insurgents, with no concrete function or mission.[10]

This echoes the earlier points on mission-creep, and lack of clarity of policy or mission in Afghanistan. In a similar fashion, we see the evolution of the current British mission from one of 'support for reconstruction' to daily warfighting and active pursuit of insurgents.

The 'Kabul bubble'

During the Second Afghan War, the presence of British forces could not maintain the unity of the country, nor guarantee that the provinces would answer to the centre. This was a problem which the British Army between

1878–80 were not adequately able to solve. One example of this is the expulsion of the Governor of Ghazni in November 1879 by 'local *moollahs*, who [had] been preaching a *jehad* on their own account, and [had] gathered together several thousand tribesmen from the villages in the district' (Hensman, 1881: 156). Also:

An authority, to be respected, must be tangible. The British authority at Cabul is in the tangible shape of a conquering army: it is respected—at Cabul. But Cabul is not Turkistan [north of the Hindu Kush], and it is idle to expect a Proclamation, or even a thousand, to cause provincial governors, now free from all control, voluntarily to submit to an authority which makes, apparently, no effort to reach them (*Ibid.*: 181).

Exactly the same problems are suffered today in Afghanistan with respect to the centralisation of authority. At present, within Helmand province itself, ISAF forces are struggling to maintain the unity of the province and to project the authority of the provincial centre into the outlying and isolated regions; yet throughout all of Afghanistan, many regions answer neither to regional centres, nor to the capital (BBC, 2006a). A case in point was Kabul's long and often violent struggle to dislodge the former *Mujahideen* commander Ismail Khan, who ruled Herat as a virtually independent fiefdom, much in the fashion of the former *Sadozai* Prince Shah Muhammed at the beginning of the nineteenth century (BBC, 2004).

Lack of resources

The unwillingness of the British government to spend sufficient money on the campaign during the first and second Afghan wars has caused many problems—political, military and logistical (despite the fact that huge amounts of money were spent—see point 5). A political example from the First Afghan War might be the cut in subventions to the Ghilzai tribes to keep the roads to India open, which resulted in the various garrisons throughout the region becoming cut off (Noelle, 1997). A logistical example from the Second Afghan War might be an incident in which two Sappers were killed on 23 December 1879: they lacked a proper supply of fuses for mines on account of cutbacks, and as a result were killed by faulty improvised fuses (Hensman, 1881).

Much has been said about the parsimony of the government with respect to military supplies and levels of troops in Afghanistan and Iraq, and one need not go into it in detail here (see BBC, 2007b). One may call to mind Hensman's further comment:

The memorandum of a military secretary in India, who can seek to reassure the country by the absurd statement that 2,500 men can garrison a cantonment with over four miles of walls and trenches to man, must not be allowed to weigh against the ugly facts we have had to face (Hensman, 1881: 285).

The statement of the Indian military secretary echoes the many early pronouncements by the British government on the subject in 2006.

An uncertain future

The British Army, during the Second Afghan War, were not able to solve the problem of insurgents intimidating or attacking Afghan villagers who had helped the British (*Ibid.*). Hensman further comments that a sense of impermanence about the British presence, and lack of certainty about the settlement of government made it difficult for people to show greater support for the British; the sense that they would shortly be gone, and that the insurgents might soon be in power, prevented them from approaching the British too closely.

Similar problems are prevalent in Afghanistan today. A recent report by Human Rights Watch has found that in 2006 'there were at least 350 cases in which insurgent attacks caused civilian deaths or injury. These attacks—including bombings, shootings, kidnapping and executions, and other violence—killed at least 669 Afghan civilians' (Human Rights Watch, 2007b: 70). Many of these people were involved in, or were relatives of those involved in, the government, development, security, healthcare and education: the objective was the intimidation of the general population, to deter them from associating with the agencies of government.

Conclusions and policy recommendations

It would be too easy to say that because foreign involvement in the affairs of Afghanistan has never been effective—from Alexander the Great in the distant past to British, Soviet or NATO interventions—it should not be countenanced again; That is not the argument of this chapter. As we have seen, there are parallels aplenty in the failed experiences of the past and the failing practices of the present—on the strategic, operational, and tactical levels of both military and political activity. But we can learn from the past: it can be repeated as the basis of success, not failure—if the appropriate lessons are learned. It does not appear that they have been. One should not believe that this current mission will fail because of either the nature of the country, of its people, or of its society; albeit historically it is perhaps not the most fertile soil in which to embark on a nation-building project. Rather, it is likely to fail because it has not been established on the secure foundations, nor developed on the well-founded principles which the lessons of past campaigns suggest are necessary.

Such lessons demand that, first, there must be a clear and identifiable aim with a clear purpose and a clear and definable end state; there is not. Are all the governments involved in the mission at one over its purpose, its tasks, and the practical results which will define success? As with the Tripartite Treaty in the First Afghan War, and the confusion over purpose in the Second, they are not.

Second, there must be a coherent, coordinated, and robust strategy designed by all the stakeholders and accepted by them; there is not. Even if the policy is agreed by all those involved, has an associated strategy been agreed to deliver that policy? Clearly not. The integration of the civilian sector, both Government and non-governmental, has not occurred—a situation which is comfounded by the national caveats placed upon the activities of both the military and civilian agencies in this international mission.

Third, there must be sufficient resources devoted to the achievement of the mission; there are not. A UN official has said that this is the most poorly resourced peacekeeping programme since World War II. The lack of sufficient military resources—both manpower and machines—has been well documented; and there has been a similar failure to deliver the civilian and financial resources promised—whether at Tokyo in 2002, or more recently in Paris or London. Let us remember that Iraq is half the size of Afghanistan and holds a smaller population of 22 million compared to Afghanistan's 33 million (CIA, 2008); but it has attracted three times as much military commitment, at least five times more financial funding, and a far larger civilian engagement.

Fourth, there must be a clearly defined and resilient chain of command and responsibility; but as with the confusion between British and Afghan authority in the First Afghan War, there is not. This is perhaps the most egregious area of concern. To be effective, such a mission must be tightly coordinated and directed, preferably by the host government. The current situation within the mission is verging on the anarchic, with a lack of overarching coordination and with too many agencies answering to the requirements of their own capitals rather than to those of Kabul. As a result, instead of bolstering the positions of the President and his Administration, the actions of the international community are undermining them.

Fifth, there must be overwhelming political commitment to the mission and to its conduct; there is not. Coalition projects, whether military or civilian, will only succeed where there is determined and sustained political engagement from the national governments. This must include the commitment of resources, and, most significantly, the acceptance of risk. The heavy lifting in NATO is being done by at most half a dozen of the twenty-seven members; and in the wider international community the commitment is one more of presentation than substance.

Afghanistan is a place where history is scarcely ever distant from the minds of the people. 'Remember Maiwand' is a refrain that is often heard in the south of the country near Kandahar in praise of Afghan martial prowess; and intrepid visitors to the region might often be proudly shown the pit into which the bodies of the dead British soldiers were flung after that terrible military disaster of 1880. Given that the geopolitical stresses on Afghanistan have changed little since the nineteenth century, it is hard to ignore these historical echoes of British engagement: the situation then is all too similar to the situation now. Twice in the nineteenth century, in closely comparable circumstances, the British attempted to solve problems similar to those which Afghanistan now faces, and too little has been learnt by policy-makers from that wealth of historical experience. This chapter scratches the surface of that historical experience by elucidating the mistakes. But deeper research into the abundance of available material could do much better than this; and more than pointing to mistakes, could uncover more viable solutions to Afghanistan's problems, already tested by experience and the passage of time.

4

THE SITUATION OF WOMEN
AND GIRLS IN AFGHANISTAN

Kathryn Lockett

This chapter came about as a result of a workshop facilitated by the women's human rights and development organisation, WOMANKIND Worldwide at the European Centre for Afghan Studies (ECAS) conference held at the School of Oriental and African Studies, University of London, in March 2007. It draws heavily on WOMANKIND Worldwide's research reports into the situation of women and girls in Afghanistan, including our most recent report, 'Taking stock update: Afghan women and girls seven years on' (WOMANKIND, 2008),[1] as well as our ongoing work with local development actors in the country.

The chapter outlines evidence of a clear and urgent need to do more to promote women's human rights in Afghanistan, to protect women from violence, to meet their basic needs and to promote their full participation in decision making at every level and within civil society as a whole. It forms part of an urgent call to the international community and to the Government of Afghanistan to provide women with greater opportunities, resources and support.

About WOMANKIND worldwide

WOMANKIND Worldwide is a United Kingdom (UK)-based, international women's human rights and development agency. WOMANKIND works in the UK, Latin America, East Africa, Southern Africa, Europe and South Asia to end violence against women; to promote women's civil and political participation; and to inform and influence policy and practice on women's human rights at local, national and international levels. In most cases we do not implement projects directly. In Afghanistan we work in partnership with local Non-Governmental Organisations (NGOs) to ensure our international development work is sustainable, owned by communities, and is informed and directed by the grassroots needs of the beneficiaries whom we and our partners support. We support our partner programmes through funding, information sharing, training, policy and advocacy initiatives, and capacity building.

Whilst the aims of our Afghan partners are often similar to WOMANKIND's, their approaches to tackling violence and discrimination and empowering women are tailored to the Afghan context and Afghan needs. As such, work to tackle violence against women includes providing support services to survivors, helping survivors get justice, eradicating harmful practices (such as early and forced marriage) and challenging and shaping the underlying attitudes that perpetuate violence. Work to increase women's and girls' participation in civil and political life includes promoting and supporting local networks, such as youth groups, and encouraging women and giving them the skills, knowledge and confidence to take part in elections or to sit on their local council or decision-making body. In influencing policy, our support includes helping partners draft new legislation or gather data, providing training and support in how to engage with policymakers, and research on key issues. We also work in the UK and internationally to bring the grassroots perspectives of our partners and beneficiaries in Afghanistan to the attention of national and international policymakers, and to document and promote best practice.

Women's human rights in Afghanistan

WOMANKIND has been working on women's issues in Afghanistan since 2003—following the events of 11 September 2001 and the subsequent war in Afghanistan, and from a sense of the urgent need to address women's human rights at the first stage of the reconstruction process. As well as supporting programmes with three NGOs in the country, including the Afghan

Women's Resource Centre (AWRC), the Afghan Women's Education Centre (AWEC) and the Afghan Women's Network (AWN), we also produce regular research reports on the situation of women and girls in Afghanistan—to monitor ongoing developments and ensure that women's human rights issues are kept at the forefront of the international development agenda.

WOMANKINDS's latest research report, 'Taking stock update: Afghan women and girls seven years on' (WOMANKIND, 2008), was launched in the UK Parliament in February 2008 by WOMANKIND and Partawmina Hashemee, Director of the AWRC. Whilst data on women's human rights in Afghanistan remains limited, this report was able to build on three earlier WOMANKIND research reports—'Taking Stock: Afghan women and girls six months on' (WOMANKIND, 2002), 'Sixteen months on' (WOMAN-KIND, 2003) and 'Five years on' (WOMANKIND, 2006)[2]—to pull together a wide range of secondary evidence and case studies from national and international sources.

These reports make it clear that many years on from the international community's entry into Afghanistan there remain a great number of serious challenges and ongoing risks to women and girls. Despite the rhetoric of gender equality and women's rights that surrounded NATO and the International Security Assistance Force (ISAF's)[3] entry into, and long-term involvement in, Afghanistan, it is questionable how much has really changed for most women since 2001. As such, the 2008 report formed part of an urgent call to the international community not to forget the women of Afghanistan. There remains an urgent need to make the promotion of gender equality and women's rights an explicit goal of all programmes in Afghanistan, whether military or development-oriented; and to set clear targets and indicators for measuring progress on gender equality and women's rights in *all* areas.

2001: A window of opportunity

A window of opportunity opened up for women and girls in Afghanistan in 2001. Following the harsh regime of the Taliban and decades of war came a promise of peace and stability from the international community. With the signing of the Bonn Agreement in 2001 and democratic elections in 2005, women's organisations in Afghanistan successfully lobbied for participation, inclusion and representation. A number of positive legislative changes were made, which, at least in theory, should improve the situation of women and girls. Women participated in voting (over 40 per cent of registered voters) and exceeded the 25 per cent quota reserved for them as Members of Parliament in the lower house (*Wolesi Jirga*) in the 2005 elections,[4] giving them unprecedented political representation. The new Afghan constitution of 2003 granted Afghan women equal rights with men (Islamic Republic of Afghanistan, 2003: 22); and a Ministry of Women's Affairs was established, along with the Independent Human Rights Commission to monitor and promote women's human rights in the country.

In the years following 2001, many women's NGOs, who had been operating from neighbouring countries such as Pakistan and providing support to refugee communities, returned to Kabul and grew in strength and number. In addition, Afghanistan became a signatory to the Convention for the Elimination of all forms of Discrimination against Women (CEDAW) and party to the United Nations (UN) Security Council Resolution 1325 (UN, 2000), which guarantees women protection, participation, promotion of their human rights and access to justice. Yet despite these theoretical gains, the situation remains extremely difficult for many women and girls in the country, who are affected by violence against women, a lack of civil and political rights, limited judicial protection, poor social and economic status, and major health issues. These difficulties will now be explored in greater detail.

Violence against women and girls in Afghanistan

As outlined in WOMANKIND (2008), violence against women—including sexual, physical and psychological violence—remains pervasive at household, community and state levels in Afghanistan; and is both a serious human rights abuse and a barrier to the long-term development of the country. An estimated 87 per cent of women are affected by domestic violence, at least 60 per cent of all marriages are forced in Afghanistan, and 57 per cent of girls are married before the age of sixteen (some are as young as six).

Women and girls are still regularly exchanged in marriage as compensation for debts, disputes or crimes between tribes, communities or households (see also Smith, this volume). In addition, Afghan law does not require court permission for a second, third or fourth marriage, fuelling polygamy and the related difficulties for women in negotiating sufficient resources for themselves and their children.

Cases of self-immolation have risen dramatically over the last few years, particularly in the west of the country; and this horrific phenomenon has been linked to forced marriage[5] and the devastating effect this has on women and girls who have little social mobility, access to disposable income, or recourse to protection and justice outside of their husband's family, and who are often married to men significantly older than themselves. Child marriage in particular has led to higher rates of sexual abuse of girls by older males. So-called 'honour' crimes are also on the rise, and trafficking of women both internally and to other nearby countries remains a serious and unaddressed concern. Discussion of sexual violence remains taboo in Afghanistan, despite studies that have found that sexual violence constituted 46 per cent of the type of violence perpetrated by family members, and that abduction and rape were the type of community violence most often reported to be committed against women in Afghanistan (UNIFEM, 2006).

Such violence denies women their most basic rights and undermines the social and economic development of communities and whole countries. It undermines good governance by preventing women's participation in decision-making at all levels; and deprives women and girls of their education, healthcare, self-determination and social mobility (see WOMANKIND, 2007). Yet, shelters for women escaping violence in the country are a low priority for most donors, despite the rate of violence against women in Afghanistan being one of the highest in the world: shelters are rare and found only in major cities.[6] A new Violence Against Women Law has recently been developed by the Ministry of Women's Affairs and NGOs working in Afghanistan, but this remains to be signed, ratified and implemented by the Afghan government. In early 2007, the Supreme Court of Afghanistan approved a new marriage contract or *Nikah Nama* (Women Living Under Muslim Laws, 2007), which has the potential to end child marriages and empower women's legal status. The contract calls for the registration of marriages and fixes the legal age of marriage for girls at sixteen. However, there is currently little awareness about, or implementation of, this new legal instrument.

Civil and political rights for women in Afghanistan

Civil society can be understood as the realm where citizens act 'collectively in a public sphere to express their interests, passions and ideas, exchange information, achieve mutual goals, make demands on the state and hold state officials accountable' (Diamond, 1994 cf. Brand, 2001: 963). The nature and intensity of civil society has been directly correlated with good governance, well-established democratic processes and a healthy economy (Harriss and De Renzio, 1997). As such, the development of civil society remains especially relevant to the Afghan context following the many years prior of conflict that tore apart the country's social, political and civil structure.

In particular, there is a real need to promote women's and girls' involvement in civil society, following the gender apartheid suffered under the Taliban and the many years prior of conflict which effectively removed women and girls from public life. Developing women's and girls' opportunities and capacity to take part in Afghan civil society through providing meeting spaces and resources, forming networks, sharing information and knowledge, providing support for each other, and pushing for their needs to be met at a local and national level, is particularly important at this time. Working together, women and communities can hold the state accountable to the equality granted under the constitution and the various international instruments outlined above.

Women's organisations on the ground in Afghanistan, and NGOs in particular, have proved their ability to address women's needs and rights effectively; and their contribution, voice and experience have been valuable to the country's ongoing processes of governance and accountability. Women's participation, often facilitated through their involvement in NGOs, in drawing up the constitution, in the 2005 elections, and in advocating for and contributing towards necessary legislative reforms, as well as through their role in preventing human rights abuses,[7] have all contributed towards long-term development in Afghanistan. Yet during the last ten years, women's organisations across the globe have seen their funding reduced, which has created obstacles for both the delivery of long-term programmes and their organisational sustainability.[8] Afghanistan is no exception: resources for women's NGOs remain scarce, which is highly problematic since women's organisations continue to be largely reliant on international donor funds for their advocacy work, community-development activities and service delivery.

Even today, most women in Afghanistan do not have access to the public spaces necessary for participation in social, civil and political life. Whilst the patriarchal social system and notions of 'honour' promote women's seclusion in general, this is exacerbated by a lack of recreational, educational and cultural activities for women and girls. The lack of identification documents for women also contributes towards the denial of their social mobility and right to vote. In addition, with female illiteracy estimated at 88 per cent, most women simply cannot access everyday services such as public transport, chemists and shops, by means of which they could engage with political processes, or develop an understanding of Islam based on reading the Qur'an. Female representation in the political sphere, as members of parliament, is far from significant: currently, only one out of twenty-five Cabinet ministers is female; and she runs the Ministry of Women's Affairs, which is severely sidelined within the government. In addition, women who take a prominent role in public life are often at risk of threats, intimidation and killings.[9]

Limited judicial protection

Women's and girls' access to justice and legal representation in Afghanistan remains extremely limited (WOMANKIND, 2008). Judges frequently resort to tribal or customary law instead of codified law when resolving local cases or disputes that affect women and girls—particularly in areas of the country where the state has limited reach (see also Smith, this volume). Authorities rarely investigate women's complaints of violent attacks or rape; and murders or suicides of women and 'honour' crimes are rarely reported. Even if these crimes are brought to court, offenders are rarely prosecuted.

Impunity for perpetrators of violence against women, therefore, remains a serious concern in Afghanistan. Women who report rape risk being imprisoned themselves, through being tried customarily for crimes of *zina*—sexual intercourse outside of marriage. As outlined recently by the ENNA[10] NGO Working Group on Afghan Women's Human Rights,[11] the majority of women and girls held in detention[12] in Afghanistan have been detained or convicted for crimes against social mores, including elopement and adultery (Medica Mondiale, 2007). Once incarcerated, there are significant difficulties for women and girls in reintegrating back into Afghan society, particularly if they are shunned by their families and have no other structures of support.

Poor social and economic status

Whilst clear improvements have been made since 2001 to ensure the schooling of Afghanistan's five million children—more children are now in school than at any other period in the country's history—the majority of primary-school-aged girls are still not enrolled in school. Human Rights Watch suggest that only 35 per cent of school-age girls were in school in 2006 (Human Rights Watch, 2007a). Insecurity appears to be the primary reason for families banning their girls from school, leading to concerns that girls are some of the first to suffer as security deteriorates in Afghanistan.[13] In light of the recent attacks on Afghanistan's education system (see Human Rights Watch, 2006) and the resulting closure of hundreds of schools throughout the country, the lack of girl attendence has also had a real impact on girls' schools, not least because there were fewer girls' schools to begin with (only 19 per cent of schools were designated as girls' schools throughout the country, and many districts have no schools for girls at all) (WOMANKIND, 2006). Poverty also has an impact on the education of girls, as families struggle to pay for school supplies, shoes and books. In addition, early marriage can be a factor, as it often abruptly ends a girl's education.

Another factor in Afghan women's poor social and economic status is that they are largely dependent on men for their economic and social survival: gender discrimination combines with the lack of social mobility and education to limit the employment opportunities for women. In addition, it is estimated that even when they do find work, women earn only a third of male earnings. Such economic dependency can limit women's ability to provide for themselves and their families and to have negotiating power at a household level; and can prevent women from leaving abusive marriages.

In situations of conflict, often the women's role as carer or guardian of family members left at home means that they are required to take on increased economic responsibilities within the household (El Bushra, 2004)—particularly if they have lost the household breadwinner or their homes have been destroyed, which impacts heavily both financially and emotionally (Amnesty International, 2004). Female family headship tends to be particularly high in the aftermath of conflict (Chant, 1997), especially in countries where gender discrimination already exists. As Cockburn (2001: 26) suggests, 'in the absence of the kind of jobs they can do, of training they can get access to, and of capital, credit, and land, many women fall more deeply into the poverty they knew before the war began'. Such is the case in Afghanistan: there are approximately one million widows in the country, who are often dependent on begging and are denied basic services such as clean water and healthcare. Such women are particularly vulnerable to exploitation and abuse. Denial of inheritance rights and traditional protection for women[14] also contributes to the grinding poverty many women continue to suffer in one of the world's poorest countries.[15]

Major health issues

Women and girls still lack access to healthcare in Afghanistan—a reason why the female life expectancy is lower than that of men, at only forty-four. (UNDP, 2004). Maternal mortality is among the leading causes of death, with one of the worst rates of maternal mortality in the world—1,600 deaths per 100,000 births (Human Rights Watch, 2007a). Tragically, it is estimated that 40 per cent of deaths due to pregnancy complications are preventable with access to the right healthcare. In addition, some women are prevented from seeking healthcare due to a lack of women doctors or, in extreme cases, because their husbands will not give them permission.

Research suggests that, like experiences of conflict, post-conflict trauma is also related to gender (see Cockburn, 2001). Rape can be a deliberate policy of war that is used to terrorise women, wrest personal assets from them, promote the futility of resistance and to harm the interests of enemy men (Turshen, 2001). As such, 'the impact and trauma of rape extend far beyond the attack itself', and, due to sexual violence, women suffer from 'emotional torment, psychological damage, physical injuries, disease, social ostracism and many other consequences that can devastate their lives' (Amnesty International, 2004: 23), including the birth of children conceived in rape (Pankhurst, 2004). Further, a culture of impunity often persists during times of conflict, since both perpetrators and victims remain faceless (Enloe, 2000) and many more vulnerable women risk losing the respect and support of their communities if they speak up about their experiences (Yuval-Davis, 1997). Despite the fact that post-traumatic stress disorder, major depression and severe anxiety are common amongst Afghan women, provision of psychological support has not been a priority amongst the aid community. In addition, there is an urgent need to re-invigorate Afghanistan's Action Plan for Transitional Justice (see AIHRC, 2005), to ensure that war crimes, including those relating to sexual violence against women and girls, are excluded from amnesty provisions.[16]

An urgent call to the International Community

As WOMANKIND (2008: 7) stated:

In Afghanistan, seven years after the fall of the misogynist Taliban regime, Afghanistan is still one of the most dangerous places in the world to be a woman... Several years into this large-scale international intervention, we urgently need to ensure the necessary reforms, capacity and institutions are in place to guarantee women the rights promised to them in Afghanistan's new constitution.

Based on these findings, there is a clear and urgent need to do more to promote women's human rights, protect women from violence, meet their basic needs including employment and health, and promote their participation in decision-making at all levels of society. Recommendations from WOMAN-KIND's 'Taking Stock' report (2008) include urgent judicial reform and the implementation of laws that protect women's human rights; ensuring the registration of marriages, divorces, births and deaths; and more support to survivors of violence against women, including increasing the number of shelters and rehabilitation programmes. Fundamentally, more work needs to be done to raise awareness of women's existing human rights within the country and to provide women with the skills, knowledge and support to defend their rights at a household, community and national level.

Women's involvement in civil society can be facilitated through long-term financial and technical support to women's NGOs, and through a greater provision of spaces, education and activities for women and girls. Security for women and girls can be further enhanced if the realisation of basic human rights and standards of living, such as access to education and healthcare, are made the benchmark of success in the NATO-led mission in Afghanistan. In addition, in line with the UN Security Council Resolution 1325 (UN, 2000), women should be involved at every level of ongoing peace negotiations, as well as supported in their grassroots peace-building work at a community and intra-household level. Whilst women and girls have proven their ability to make significant changes to the country's development, more must be done to provide them with greater opportunities, resources and support to continue and build on their ongoing work.

A way forward: working with local NGOs in afghanistan

WOMANKIND currently provides technical and financial support to three partner organisations in Afghanistan: the Afghan Women's Resource Centre (AWRC),[17] the Afghan Women's Network (AWN)[18] and the Afghan Women's Educational Centre (AWEC).[19] Our Women's Empowerment Project in Afghanistan is funded by the UK Department for International Development (DFID) and the UK Foreign and Commonwealth Office. It aims to educate individual Afghan women on their human rights, support them to engage in, and with, local and national social, civil and political bodies; and to build the skills and knowledge of Afghan women's organisations and women's human rights activists to further assist Afghan women in actively participating in political and civil life within Afghanistan.

Our partners run a variety of programmes to meet these aims—in Mazar-i-Sharif, Jalalabad and Kabul in Afghanistan, and Peshawar in Pakistan (home to many Afghan refugees). These include working with youth and women's groups to train them on their political and civil rights, and to build their leadership skills and confidence to advocate for women and girls' rights within their communities; offering basic, vocational and health education to vulnerable women and girls; undertaking peace-building workshops with communities to explore the causes of and tackle violence at a household level; holding workshops to train women and girls on their rights under Islam; and providing psycho-social support and counselling to survivors of violence.

These programmes are having a huge impact on the thousands of women and girls who have no other access to such support within their communities.[20] In addition, we support our partners through providing access to materials, resources, training, networks and additional funding. We also liaise closely with partners to ensure the voices of the women and girls they support are heard at a UK and international level by the relevant policymakers. However, more urgent is the need to promote and protect women's human rights in Afghanistan itself, and to encourage women's full participation in its development.

ECAS workshop discussion: what more can be done?

The ECAS conference workshop in March 2007 focused on what more can be done to support women and girls in Afghanistan. It was well attended by both Afghans and non-Afghans and a variety of age groups and yielded some interesting discussions. The need for more resources to be allocated to grassroots women's organisations working to meet the needs of their communities was identified, as was the need for a political will at a state and international level to push through much-needed reforms that would create an environment which enables women and girls to claim their human rights. Economic programmes that create more employment for women and, therefore, more access to disposable income, would provide more women with decision-making power at a household level, and enable them to meet their basic needs. Such programmes would also give a vital lifeline to widows and female-headed households. Education and support programmes for young women and girls were also seen as key to Afghanistan's future development.

In line with the current thinking on development, the need to engage men in the struggle for gender equality was highlighted by the group. This included educating men in Afghanistan about women's human rights as guaranteed under the constitution, and as compatible with Islam.[21] The need for positive male role models to act as champions for women's human rights within the country was also seen as a crucial step to address underlying attitudes of gender discrimination and to promote future change.

Conclusion

There has been significant progress since 2001 towards entrenching women's and girls' rights in Afghanistan, and the local women's movement has played a key role in ensuring these gains. Progress made includes women's increased representation within national and provincial political structures; a national constitution enacted in 2004 that recognises their equality with men; the signing of key international agreements; a growing number of shelters and police family response units; a new Marriage Contract; increased attention to girls' education; and a growing international recognition of the need for judicial reform and the effective implementation of laws.

Yet, significant challenges remain for women and girls in the country; and progress towards ensuring women's and girl's participation and inclusion in society, and the implementation of their human rights, has been unacceptably slow. Realising women's human rights in Afghanistan still requires a long-term financial and political commitment from both the international community and the Government of Afghanistan.

There remains an urgent need to tackle violence against women, improve women's access to health and education, advance family law, increase women's access to public space and to enforce women's human rights. Women and girls in Afghanistan have demonstrated their ability and determination to take part in the development of their country. It is crucially important that an environment is created which enables and encourages them to do so.

5

THE POLITICAL ECONOMY OF NORMLESSNESS IN AFGHANISTAN[1]

Armando Geller

The problem of normlessness in contemporary conflict

'I don't recognise my own people anymore!' This is an exclamation often heard nowadays in Afghanistan made by exiles returning home. It is also expressed by Afghans who have never left their country. '*Tempora mutantur, nos et mutamur in illis*'—the times change as we change with them. Things have obviously changed in Afghanistan since 1979, the time of the Soviet invasion, and so have the inhabitants of this country, the subjects of this conflict-torn society. This chapter focuses on norms and social conventions that have changed during the conflict and that have altered people's behaviour. The opening statement refers exactly to this change in individual behaviour which, in the case of Afghanistan, is often connected to a deprivation in 'traditional' values, social conventions and norms.[2] Thirty years of conflict have also had an effect on the norms, social conventions and values steering the actions of the Afghan elites' pursuit of goals. They are of special interest to this analysis.

So-called emergentist social science suggests that the evolution of social structure depends on individual behaviour, and is caused by individuals interacting with each other; and, vice versa, that individual behaviour and interactions respectively are influenced by and depend on social structure (Sawyer,

2005). The emergentist paradigm, however, is not only interested in agency and structure, but also underlines the importance of analysing processes: it is not only of interest to know who is (inter)acting, how and with whom, and what structural outcomes these interactions generate; but also what social dynamics, i.e. social processes, result from this interplay between agency and structure.

Societies of conflict are societies '*sui generis*' (Sofsky, 2002: 115–6). They exhibit distinctive, i.e. conflict-related, social processes and structures. In such societies virtually anything goes. The notion of normlessness illustrates this. Normlessness is the situation in which the upper and lower normative boundaries—for example the maximum and minimum salary that one should earn—for the aspirations of individual members of a society are discarded (Marks, 1974). Normlessness is thus a state of deranged order in which one no longer knows what is feasible and what is not; what appears appropriate and what does not; nor which claims are adequate and which ones are not. Individual aspirations become boundless, the result of which is also an increasing appetite for personal satisfaction and gain. A normless situation emerges when the means to satisfy this appetite run out of (social) control (Merton, 1938).

Societies of conflict are not only situated in spaces characterised by normlessness, but also exhibit institutional weakness. They lack legal stability, property right protection, and the state's monopoly of organised violence. Consequentially, societies occupying spaces characterised by normlessness can be easily instrumentalised and misused. Special consideration must therefore be given to the anthropogenic nature of power structures (cf. Popitz, 1992: 12): stakeholders in normless spaces can shape social (power)structures according to their will and need. An emerging prevailing organisational principle in such circumstances is neo-patrimonialism (Geller, 2006; Médard, 1990). Neo-patrimonial behaviour can take many forms: instrumentalisation and manipulation of groups; creation of ethnic, religious or political affiliations; and organised violence, intrigue, corruption, alliances, clientelism, patronage, nepotism and so forth (Médard, 1990: 30). In general, it can be described as an unregulated accumulation and redistribution of material and social resources, the purpose of which is to establish, maintain or increase a ruler's social power, as well as his grace and mercy (Kaldor, 1997; Weber, 1978).

The notion of normlessness (or *anomie*, the proper socio-scientific term) links the micro and macro-level (i.e. agency and structure; see above for the introduction of the notion of emergence) of society and provides a framework to explore and explain the relations between normlessness and protracted conflict in Afghanistan from a processual and structural perspective. Actor behaviour and interaction deviating from the norm gives rise to normless social processes, allowing normless social structures to evolve, which in turn influence actor behaviour from a point of social normlessness.[3] The evolving social setting is a state of normlessness, of which Afghanistan is only a historical variant amongst others. The following sections analyse this state of normlessness in Afghanistan from an emergentist perspective, and corroborate the above assertive demonstrations with evidence.

Exploring normlessness in Afghan society

The roots, expansion and consolidation of the state of normlessness in Afghanistan cannot be examined separately from one other. There is a historical, but not teleological, connection between pre-conflict Afghan society, the Soviet occupation (1979–1989), the time after the Soviet retreat (1989–1992), the civil war period (1992–1994), the Taliban era (1994–2001) and the period of President Hamid Karzai's administration (2001– the time of writing).

The roots of Afghan normlessness: resistance against the Soviets (1979–1989)

What accounts for being the norm depends on one's historical and social perspective. The state of normlessness therefore needs to be pitted against the background of what is perceived as being a norm.[4] A number of context-dependent concepts in Afghan society provide strong normative directions for what is to be perceived as socially acceptable or even ideal behaviour, and for what needs to be dismissed as socially unacceptable behaviour in particular circumstances. A well known example is the ideal-type of the warrior-poet, i.e. a man who is brave and articulate at the same time (cf. Dupree, 1979: 52). The Pashtun code of conduct, *Pashtunwali*, makes equally strong declarations of what has to be perceived as normatively desirable. An ideal Pashtun is a man of honour, who is heroic and proud, and whose honourableness interferes with his conduct towards neither a senior nor weaker person (Janata and Hassas, 1975: 84). Finally, many practises exist which appear to be normless from a modern state's point of view but for which there exist different and endorsed notions in Afghan society (Schäfer, 1974). Examples for such practises are reported by various scholars (e.g. Dupree 1973, 1984; Sigrist, 1994) and include: corruption; poppy cultivation; contrabandism; regular feuding amongst families, tribes and villages; and raiding of government institutions.

The Jihad (1979–1989) against the Soviet occupation forces had a catalytic function in increasing extremism in various spheres of society, since it radicalised ethnic and religious identities (Roy, 1995; Schetter, 2003). Afghanistan's dependence on foreign aid basically dates back to the time of the Second Anglo-Afghan War (1878–1890), but the Jihad politicised humanitarian and military aid—as it did society in general—and aggravated the struggle for these resources (Baitenman, 1990; Barakat, 2004; Dupree, 1973; Goodhand, 2004a; Jalali, 2007; Roy, 1994; Rubin, 1992, 2002). It intensified the relatively old conflict over traditional and modern values, dating back to the reformist government of King Amanullah (1919–1929) (cf. Dupree, 2004: 184; Roy, 1998: 199). It further factionalised Afghan society, not only along the faultline between the Soviet backed government and the opposition, i.e. the *mujahideen*, but also within these two groups (Rubin, 2002; Sigrist, 1994). The Jihad also started to weaken qualities that formerly served a cohesive purpose, such as loyalty and tolerance, and instead increased mistrust, nepotism and cronyism (Dupree, 2004; Sigrist, 1994). Finally, materialism became more important. In general, the pristine war aim of fighting the Soviets gave way to an intensification of individual struggle for power and self-enrichment amongst newly evolving elites.

A state of normlessness is not established when norm-deviating incidences occur sporadically and in isolation. Rather, it materialises when the scale of this deviation regularly attains a level which fundamentally differs from what used to be the norm. The changed system of norms inevitably becomes a part of social memory and cultural heritage, and the result is social change. During the Jihad norm-deviation reached an extent that left Afghan society deeply mutated, and which caused increasingly norm-deviating behaviour of its members. The boundaries of the aspirations by members of Afghan society, especially amongst elites, gradually started to shift. To this end, the Soviet-backed state system provided an alternative in the form of a potentially functioning state and government, which was, however, dissatisfying; and was questioned by many Afghans.[5]

Fostering the system of normlessness: 1989–2001

The withdrawal of the Soviet forces in 1989 meant that this normative alternative faded away, until it completely vanished with the fall of the government of Mohammad Najibullah in April 1992 and the subsequent beginning of the civil war. The state of normlessness was consequentially fostered.

Many of the different *mujahideen* group leaders ended up being more powerful by the end of the Jihad than at the beginning. They formed part of a new Afghan elite, which had originally been supported by Iran, Pakistan, Saudi Arabia and the United States, but which had lost most of its sources of income after the war (Rubin, 2000). A result of this was the intensification of an interfactional struggle over resources and power, and the emergence of regional and local fiefdoms (Rubin, 2000; Tarzi, 1993). Such a political environment did not allow the *mujahideen*—nor later the Taliban—to govern sovereignly; instead they were the object of clientelistic networks' interests (Schetter, 2004: 10). The fiefdoms allowed the various strongmen—frequently named 'warlords'—to consolidate their informal economic systems, which they had built up during the time of the Jihad (Giustozzi, 2007b). Afghanistan's borders were further eroded, indirectly facilitating the strongmen's economic interests (Goodhand, 2004a).

The consolidation of the state of normlessness between 1989 and 2001 had two major effects: first, the ascent of a number of *parvenues* disseminated an 'anything goes' mentality; and the boundaries which restricted the elite's aspirations finally dissolved. Secondly, people were massacred in the name of ethnicity and religion, and unbridled material desire culminated in predatory-like behaviour (Rubin, 2000).

The epicentre of Afghan normlessness was Kabul, where Ahmad Shah Massud, the factual leader of *Jamiat-e Islami*, Gulbuddin Hekmatyar, the leader of *Hezb-e Islami*, and Rashid Dostum, the leader of *Junbesh-e Melli*, as well as many other strongmen, were fighting over power and resources. Those Kabulis who survived the carnage caused by indiscriminate shelling with rocket launchers and urban guerrilla warfare—at the time several million civilians lived in the Afghan capital—became increasingly disillusioned with leaders they saw as corrupt and power-hungry (Tarzi, 1993). Inter-ethnic massacres irrevocably shattered inter-ethnic relations.[6]

The Taliban did not bring an end to the state of normlessness, despite improvements in the security situation and the introduction of political rule, *qua sharia* law and edicts. Neither did they provide an institutional alternative to it since the formation of a modern Islamic state was not their aim. Their imposed system was riddled with arbitrariness, favouritism and barbarism.[7] Paradoxically, for example, the banishment of women from public life also had to do with the Taliban leadership's fear that some of their younger ranks could sexually harass women (Dupree, 1998). Thus, even amongst the Taliban, who wanted to shape society according to strict religious norms, individual 'aspirations' of some members had to be controlled for. Despite the theological justification of their regime, the Taliban's *terreur* and aspiration for power—and to a lesser extent their aspirations for self-enrichment[8]—were boundless. The state of normlessness continued to exist.

Normlessness as an institutionalised form of government: the Karzai era

After the fall of the Taliban, it would have been Hamid Karzai's mission to re-install state structures and institutions. Instead, an institutionalised form of the state of normlessness arose; and Hamid Karzai's government was, and is, part of the problem, since it consists of former strongmen and corrupt bureaucrats. This makes the government hive of power games; and one which lacks integrity, characterised by intrigue and self-enrichment (Jalali, 2007: 45; Rubin, 2007). Because it does not exert power beyond Kabul, Afghanistan remains a non-state territory, cobbled together from a number of fiefdoms (Burke, 2007). Many governors do not even intend to govern their province, but pay up to $100,000 to get assigned to a post that helps them to enrich themselves (Burke, 2007: 69). Hamid Karzai's brother, the government official Ahmed Wali Karzai, is allegedly involved in the drug business, as are other government officials, who use drug money to sustain their solidarity groups (Goodhand, 2005: 212). Government officials enrich themselves by extracting bribes from international contractors in return for lucrative government contracts.[9] Further, the Afghan security forces are corrupted—sometimes even by Private Military Contractors (PMCs)—to the extent that they are even affiliated with organised crime (Rubin, 2007).

As at the onset of the Jihad, when *mujahideen* had been trained by Pakistani and British officers in guerrilla warfare, a mode of warfare that has been so far unknown in Afghanistan, some of this norm-deviating behaviour has been 'imported' to Afghanistan.[10] Western contractors bribed Afghan government officials in the early stages of Afghanistan's reconstruction.[11] PMCs, for example MPRI and DynCorp, sometimes leave a bad impression on Afghan security forces, for their behaviour has deteriorated since 2001.[12] Likewise, suicide bombings, previously unknown in Afghanistan, have been imported—presumably from Iraq—though they are rejected by many Afghans on ethical grounds.

The population, again, is disgusted with this apparent lack of norms (Barakat, 2004: 6). Nevertheless, people tend to be optimistic, as two polls reveal; but optimism decreased from 2005 to 2006, and the situation worsened in 2007 (ABC News, 2005; ABC News/BBC World Service, 2006).[13] The fact that people attest to the Taliban parallel 'state' emerging in the South as being more just and having more efficient courts, compared to the official ones, is a sign that there is a desire to replace the state of normlessness with a system that is governed by more unambiguous norms (Rubin, 2007). To equate this with a desire to return to the harsh and arbitrary rule of the former Taliban is, in all probability, wrong, since the south is ruled by a new generation of Taliban (see below).

Implications of the perpetual lack of norms

During a decade of conflict, the social behaviour rooted in Afghanistan's culture has been perverted into a form of normless behaviour. Decreasing optimism amongst the majority of the population suggests that a return to a social state lacks a viable future. This decreasing optimism is closely linked to a general absence of property rights, legal stability, bureaucratic predictability and security. For the elite, this lack of social structure helps them to maintain a system that keeps them in power and ensures access to material and social resources. This state of normlessness has led to the emergence of an endemic conflict, the implications of which have a considerable impact at various levels of society.

On the micro-level, mistrust amongst members of the Afghan society moulds specific forms of individual behaviour. Government officials, for example, often have to compensate for a lack of trustworthiness by close cooperation with non-Afghan third parties, such as Non Governmental Organisations (NGOs) or International Organisations. Such cooperation also compensates for their lack of legitimacy—a result of the general lack of trust in the government. An 'anything goes' *weltanschauung* among many members of the Afghan elite creates the sort of behaviour that identifies them as being above the law and outside the norm. This is why the current struggle for resources and power (political, religious, economic, military, etc.) is accompanied variously by boundless personal enrichment, personality cults and unaccountability.

Afghan society is structured along many often overlapping social networks, *qawm*, an Arabic term used in Dari and Pashto. The notion of *qawm* varies not only in the literature, but also amongst Afghans themselves. It can mean (extended) family, tribe, descent group, ethnicity, 'people like us' (Tapper, 2008), 'an occupational group' (Roy, 1992: 75); or it can be a discourse of solidarity which is applied in fluid ways to different groupings: it can connote a complex interpersonal 'network' (Roy, 1995: 22) of political, social, economic, military, and cultural relations (Mousavi, 1997; Rasuly-Paleczek, 1998; Roy, 1995; Shahrani, 1998; Tapper, forthcoming). These meanings are not exclusive: *qawm* do not have clear boundaries nor do they divide Afghan society into mutually exclusive groups. *Qawm* need to be sustained, and it is not so much an Afghan leader's ability to accumulate social and material resources, but his ability to redistribute them that makes him powerful and eventually successful (Roy, 1994: 74). They can be created to attain a particular goal, which is also perceived as a demonstration of power (Azoy, 2003: 36). *Qawm* still 'have a powerful and pervasive effect on contemporary political discourse and the behaviour of Afghans' (Shahrani, 1998: 220) and have during the years of conflict been instrumentalised and misused by new elites in the pursuit of aggressive and criminal aims (Roy, 1994; Rubin, 1992; Shahrani, 2002; Tapper, forthcoming).

Hence, as with many other Afghan social concepts, *qawm* were subject to change during conflict (cf. Canfield, 1988). The state of normlessness gave rise to neo-*qawm*. Neo-*qawm* are not unprecedented socialities with regard to their inherent mode of operation (functionality), but with regard to the criminal energy they unfold.[14] Depending on the reasons for their establishment and function, neo-*qawm* materialise in various forms (cf. Rasuly-Paleczek, 1998). In the security sector, for example, an amalgamation of the police, private security firms and organised crime has taken place (Rubin, 2007). Jalali (2007) reports on an even wider nexus existing amongst politicians, businessmen and militaries (see also Gellner, 2006). In general, strongmen of different social (ethnicity, tribe, family), political and functional (commander, religious leader, politician, etc.) backgrounds affiliate with each other, as well as with government officials, the military and police officials, NGOs, International organisations, neighbouring countries, international businessmen and organised criminals, to establish neo-*qawm* committed to a particular cause.[15] This neo-patrimonial pattern also dominates the neo-Taliban, who are more heterogeneous than the Taliban were before 2001.[16]

Besides leading to a flourishing illicit economy, as a result of establishing criminal networks, neo-*qawm* have two important consequences for Afghan society. Firstly, the build-up, dissolution and shifting of alliances has become more erratic, as the whole politico-economic situation can no longer be clearly divided along 'traditional' lines, such as political affiliations, religious background, ethnicity, tribe or family. Neo-*qawm* are more pragmatic and opportunistic than their 'traditional' forerunners. Secondly, neo-*qawm* not only foster the system of role pluralism incorporated by many strongmen since the Jihad—a commander can be a religious authority and a businessman at the same time, as, for example, Ismail Khan has been until September 2004 in the city of Herat, but can legitimise it by providing *qawm* members with sovereignty.

While the state of normlessness has caused individual behaviour and social group configurations to change, it has also had an impact at the macro-level of Afghan society. Organised violence and crime have changed entire systems of incentive (Goodhand, 2004b): although 'traditional' systems of values such as *hisiyat* (character) and *e'tibar* (credit) are still of importance (Azoy, 2003), more mundane values such as fancy cars and pretentious houses play an increasingly important role, and appear to be for many an incentive to engage in the illicit economy. These status symbols of the *nouveau-riche* also function as regalia of power, giving expression to the fallacious notion of power preponderant amongst the new elite. Thus, power has been systemically perverted from an office of responsibility and reputation to a crude means of extraction and accumulation of materialistic values. This is tantamount to the dissolution of the 'traditional' system and the evolution of a new social order (Burke, 2007; Giustozzi, 2007b).

Throughout history the Afghan state has never been able to exert power over its entire territory.[17] However, there have been times when a government coexisted with pockets of land that resisted the idea of statehood. Recently, this was the case during the Jihad and the reign of the Taliban (1996–2001); but as a result of a prolonged state of normlessness, this coexistence broke up and a once failed state has become a 'failed' failed state. Not only is the Afghan state unable to exert its monopoly of power, but the government itself has become an institutionalised version of the state of normlessness.

Decade-long organised violence, political intrigue and mistrust, involving ethno-politics and religious radicalisation, and foreign actors' influence, destroyed the political communication among communities and estranged them from each other (Sigrist, 1994). More than ever, Afghanistan has become a deeply factionalised society.

How a lack of norms leads to protracted conflict

Goodhand's argument that conflict gives rise to innovation certainly applies to the case of Afghanistan (Goodhand, 2004b). *Qawm* are not only effective social entities for the management of power: they are also highly adaptive systems of reinvention (Gellner and Moss, 2008; Rasuly-Paleczek, 1998). Whenever a new situation emerges, such as a third-party intervention, Afghans quickly adapt to this new situation—for example by making newly available resources accessible (Monsutti, 2004; Rasuly-Paleczek, 2004). This, in turn, leads to changes in the social structure, as new incentives are created and as systems of accumulation and redistribution need to be redefined. As a consequence, power structures are reconfigured. The transformations that occur on this higher social order inevitably influence and alter social behaviour. This leads to a further change of social structure—the system continually recreates itself.

One reason this process escalates into a state of normlessness is the lack of socially confining boundaries. Little guided by norms, individuals react time and again in creative ways to system changes. Because the system is in itself only little guided in its development by binding norms, the variety of its mutations is virtually limitless. The perverse results are hypercapitalism, organised crime, extreme organised violence and even acts of genocide, as well as acts of ineffable cultural and human barbarism. Justification of such behaviour is not sought by the perpetrators, and retribution is difficult to demand or to enforce by the victims.

There are two other reasons why the state of normlessness protracts conflict. The first is the availability of renewable resources, i.e. poppies and (open or covert) foreign aid. Both consistently nurture the various systems of incentive, and either validate or falsify them, leading in the latter case to the evolution of an adapted version. The second reason is Afghanistan's pivotal geostrategic location. Being located on the 'Silk Road' assures a constant flow of goods. Due to poorly guarded borders and a weak central state, smuggling networks flourish. In both cases there are no boundaries that limit the appetite for maximising revenues—which, again, reinforces the state of normlessness.

The perpetuation of the state of normlessness itself is reinforced by competing perceptions and implementations of norms. Fiefdoms are not only sovereign territories, but are also spatial antitheses to the state of normlessness: they contest the state of normlessness. Although condemned by various NGOs for humanitarian abuses and by the Afghan government for insubordination,

Ismail Khan, for example, recreated in Herat what many perceived as a vibrant economic and cultural city: trade and commerce were booming, security was guaranteed, the streets were tarred and clean, buildings and cultural sites were reconstructed, and authority was predictable, albeit dictatorial.[18] Mazar-i-Sharif is a similar example (Shahrani, 2002). The Taliban's successive return in the south of Afghanistan after 2005 might have been supported by similar mechanisms: Afghanistan's disillusionment with the state of normlessness is a fertile breeding ground for such projects. Unless there are no viable and sustainable alternatives to the state of normlessness, the emergence of fiefdoms, and their dissolution as a result of newly arising political circumstances, will propell a cyclical process.

A critical appraisal of the thesis of normlessness

To apply the thesis of normlessness to the case Afghanistan could imply that Afghan society in general has become detached from normatively routed behaviour. This is of course not the case, and neither is it argued here. A variety of examples epitomise that norms have played, and still play, an important role throughout the Afghan conflict.[19]

One reason the Taliban are able to successfully recruit new fighters is that a number of norms are being violated by their opponents. This drives people towards the side of the Taliban. The US-led coalition and the International Security Assistance Force (ISAF), for example, crack down on Afghan villages and private homes during counterinsurgency operations. Aerial bombardment causes casualties among the civilian population. PMCs and military personnel behave recklessly on the streets. A US military convoy, for example, caused a major accident in Kabul in 2006, which left fourteen people dead and sparked off anti-American riots.

Norms still play an important role in interpersonal relations in Afghanistan. The socio-economic conditions during the years of conflict in Afghanistan have put enormous pressure upon individuals; and livelihood strategies within and among families and neighbours have, to a certain extent, brought relief. These strategies rely on trust among family members and their neighbours (Monsutti, 2004). The drug trade is another example where trust plays an important role—between poppy farmers and dealers.

Further evidence for the importance of norms is their constant appropriation by radical movements, such as the Taliban or, outside Afghanistan, Hamas in Israel. Both groups are able to mobilise deeply rooted normative sentiments in their areas of operation. Because the international community tries at the same time to win the hearts and minds of the population, the result is a battle about norms and, finally, legitimacy. Hence, the state of normlessness is neither a space emptied of norms, nor is it a static entity. It is rather a condition that may lead to the emergence of a new body of norms as a result of concurring perceptions of normlessness and normality.

At present this is apparently happening amongst those Afghans who have been born and raised in the various refugee camps in Iran and Pakistan.[20] Some members of this generation have been educated in *madrassas* and occasionally joined Jihadist organisations. Others have had the chance to visit higher education institutions in Iran and Pakistan; and others have lived in Western exile for many years before they returned to Afghanistan. In each case they have been confronted with different circumstances and different sets of norms. This generation has a different perspective of traditions and norms in contrast to those who have been living in Afghanistan for all their lives. Accordingly, a state of normlessness must not be seen as a definitive condition. As has been laid out above, the state of normlessness is part of a conflict's dynamics, and therefore is also a sphere where innovation can emerge.[21]

These examples also suggest that a coherent notion of norms cannot exist in a society as diverse as Afghanistan—where different spheres of norms, linked to different conceptions of identity, exist on the individual and social level (Tapper, forthcoming). Hence, different reifications of norms exist on different levels of society and within different groups. As with many macro-sociological concepts, when applied to Afghanistan as a whole the 'state of normlessness' thesis is likely to be too coarsely grained to identify these idiographies. However, there is no reason not to apply the idea of normlessness to selected cases located at the micro-level, and to take specific notions of norms explicitly into account.

One particular problem with the idea of normlessness is that of coherently determining the scope of its boundaries. Societies are not free from arbitrariness applied without sanctions against its members by other members. For example, research shows that power holders of Uzbek tribes indeed have the right to break norms without being sanctioned; whereas ordinary members of the same tribe are not allowed to do the same without being sanctioned.[22] Hence, the borders of a state of normlessness need to be defined contextually—i.e. with regard to the construct of identity—against the background of what is the norm. In conflict-torn societies such as Afghanistan, this point of reference could be: situated before the onset of war; emerging as a result of evolving new and vanishing old norms; defined from scratch.

Last but not least, the state of normlessness thesis is not a reprisal of the new-war-thesis conceptual arguments (Kaldor, 1997). Greed and barbarity are not offered as the main driving forces of conflict in Afghanistan (Roy, 1994: 74). Rather, they are emergent properties of a year-long state of normlessness; they are instruments in the struggle for power; and they are antipodes to the state of norms in the dialectics of contemporary organised violence.

Conclusions

The state of normlessness is a social setting prone to boundless material exploitation and to the exploitation of identity politics. A number of actors stemming from the elite—but also from abroad—do well out of Afghanistan's state of normlessness, as norm-deviant behaviour ensures access to the centres of power. Moreover, they often become respected members of society. The consequence is a state of comfortable impasse among stakeholders, which contributes to prolonged conflict.[23] At the same time, 'ordinary' people lapse into an agony of mistrust, which renders conflict resolution even more difficult.

The state of normlessness is a fluid and evolving situation in which a set of established norms consistently interacts with newly emerging and exogenously introduced norms. The dynamics of the state of normlessness result from interactions among people, whose intrinsic normative systems have been distorted; and from the interactions between these people and the social structures of normlessness, which are an emerging consequence of these people's interactions. The question of how the state of normlessness influences the transformation of 'traditional' norms and the emergence of new norms, as well as the ensuing social effects, is therefore of particular interest.

Other points of interest in this context are related to breaking the vicious circle of the state of normlessness. Obviously, boosting the economy cannot be the only answer, as it has the effect of creating hypercapitalism, and so of further widening the gap between the rich and poor. By contrast, it should be possible to make use of the innovations inherent in a state of normlessness, of which perhaps the emerging fiefdoms are the most auspicious—but also the most dangerous (Geller, 2006; Giustozzi, 2007b). Does a good dictator know where his boundaries are and when to leave the stage? What is the capacity of these fiefdoms to transform a state of normlessness into a state of norms, to maintain the latter and to integrate themselves, if necessary, into a larger political entity, i.e. a state?

Finding empirical answers to the questions raised in this chapter and to corroborate the argument made is difficult and requires an appropriate methodology. Otherwise, research on the state of normlessness and its social transformation risks disregarding developments of new forms of power and methods to control territory, people and parties, by crystallising an academic idea of norms. Hence, a good starting point would be to collect micro-data and analyse norms on various levels of Afghan society, in several regions and in diverse contexts.[24] Particularly interesting could be the study of institutional change in the context of normlessness through the notion of folklore. Folkloristic notions, such as 'traditional' beliefs, myths, tales and practices, could be contrasted with currently persisting variations of the same notion and lend insight into similarities and differences.

Man is a *zoon politikon;* and therefore the question of 'what should we do in accordance to live a better life together?' is an important one. Besides taking into account questions of social transformation in general, and in particular the transformation of norms and values, the concept of normlessness may help to articulate answers to this most important question in political theory. Any society not exhibiting normatively institutionalised processes and structures which effectively control behaviour related to organised violence and crime, is, in the long term, not viable. This also holds true for Afghanistan. How these processes and structures should be embellished, is a question that can only be answered by Afghans themselves, and only by lending respect to a cultural heritage of centuries-old political life.

6

KEEPING THE PEACE; GENDER, JUSTICE AND AUTHORITY

MECHANISMS FOR COMMUNITY BASED DISPUTE RESOLUTION IN AFGHANISTAN

Deborah J. Smith[1]

'If a village doesn't have white-beards it is like a pot which doesn't have a lid.'
(Police officer from Nangarhar province)

This chapter presents findings from an ongoing research project being conducted by the Afghanistan Research and Evaluation Unit (AREU) on community based dispute resolution mechanisms. The research focuses on four central themes: the processes used for dispute resolution; the links between these processes at the community level and state institutions at district level; the principles underlying the outcomes of dispute resolution processes; and equity within these processes, with a particular focus on gender equity. Each of these themes is addressed in this chapter. It is argued that community based dispute resolution processes, rather than remaining static in an imagined version of tradition and custom, have varied and continue to vary across both time and space, proving themselves adaptable to changing social and political structures in Afghanistan. The underlying principles, used to rationalise the outcomes of dispute resolution processes, are complex, drawing on Islamic and customary ideals, negotiation and pragmaticism. Although perhaps not 'formally' recognised or legislated for, community based dispute resolution processes do not operate in isolation from state institutions. Gender equity has been analysed across four dynamics: first, women's ability to access dispute resolution mechanisms which are dominated by men; second, women's ability to contribute to these processes, in comparison to men's contribution; third, women's role as decision makers in resolving disputes; and fourth, the outcomes for women as compared to those of men of the decisions made within these processes. This paper argues that although women's access to and participation in these processes is constrained, spaces can be found in which women do access and influence dispute resolution processes. Further, women's restricted access to these processes and of participation in them, and the vulnerable position women may find themselves in as an outcome of these processes, are not a symptom of community based dispute resolution or customary law per se, but are instead a consequence of the gender roles and relations prevailing more widely in Afghanistan.

Research methodology

Until now, qualitative data has been collected in Bamiyan and Nangarhar provinces. These two provinces were selected in order to research a commonly discussed customary code used for dispute resolution, *Pashtunwali*, practiced in Nangarhar, and the less often referred to customary practices for dispute resolution of Hazarajat, of which Bamiyan forms a part.[2] In Bamiyan province the research has been conducted in one district, incorporating data collection from district level actors as well as working in two villages of the district. Of the two villages selected one is relatively close to the district's central town—an hour's drive in good weather—and the other is far more remote—taking approximately four hours by car during good weather and up to ten hours during the winter when there is a lot of snow. In Nangarhar the research was conducted in two districts. Work in these two districts allowed the research team to capture the dispute resolution processes of two different *qawms*[3] living in the area, *Shinwar and Momand*. However, due to security concerns all the districts available for the research team to work in were too small to capture the affects of differing levels of remoteness from the district's central town.

The primary methods used for data collection have been semi-structured interviews, informal conversations and focus group discussions. District level actors, including the judge, *woliswal* (district governor), police commanders, and prosecutors were spoken to. In the villages, those involved in dispute resolution and those who have had or who currently have an ongoing dispute, as well as members of all these different actors' families, were interviewed. Roughly an equal number of men and women were interviewed in the villages. In order to avoid responses based on expected behaviour or normalised practices, the research team gathered stories from both decision makers and disputants about particular disputes, as well as more general information and opinions. These different methods were used in both a flexible and open-ended manner in order to give respondents the opportunity to define the most important issues for them.

The data collection was divided into two phases, with a first round of interviews and informal conversations being conducted in all research sites of Bamiyan and Nangarhar. This was followed by preliminary analysis of the data, before returning to all research sites to conduct further interviews with different respondents and follow up interviews with previously spoken to respondents, where it was deemed necessary. Conducting the data collection in this two-phased manner allowed the research team to reflect on the data collected from both provinces and to consider what might be missing from the data and what themes could be further looked into before returning to all research sites for a second time. It was during this second round of fieldwork that focus group discussion was conducted—in order to have different groups of community members discuss some of our preliminary findings and make suggestions for how disputes could in future be resolved more effectively in their own communities.

Community based dispute resolution: actors, institutions and processes at the community level

Community based dispute resolution refers to the processes whereby disputes are regulated or resolved within the community in which the dispute has taken place. The parameters of the 'community' in this context, therefore, depend on the nature of a dispute.[4] In most cases community refers to the residents of the village in which the dispute takes place. However, some disputes may be contained within a particular *qawm* community or extended family within a village. Other disputes may incorporate more actors from different geographical locations, such as disputes between villages or *qawms*.

Processes of dispute resolution are also referred to as 'informal justice' or 'customary law'. However, it became apparent through the course of the research that neither of these terms accurately describes the processes under discussion. Referring to these processes as 'informal justice' fails to recognise that the outcomes of disputes are often documented, and that government officials may hold copies of these documents. Further, using the term 'informal justice' sets community based dispute resolution in an artificially dichotomous relationship to the formal justice sector, when in reality both systems of justice may work in collaboration. 'Customary law'⁵ is perhaps a more accurate description; however, a study which focused solely on customary law could be limited and fail to recognise other principles, viewed by those implementing them as distinct from customary law—primarily *sharia*. Indeed, decision makers in community based dispute resolution processes, spoken to by the research team, often made a clear distinction between *sharia* and *qanoon-e-urfi* (customary law), describing how they choose between using one or the other principle for the resolution of a particular dispute.

A wide variety of disputes are resolved at the community level; most common among these are disputes about access to and use of resources—in particular land, but also water and sources of fuel. Other disputes which may be resolved at the community level are, among other things, deliberate and accidental killings, disputes about marriage arrangements, theft, and payment for services. Thus, disputes of both a criminal and civil nature are resolved at the community level. Indeed, often criminal actions have their root causes in civil disputes, such as physical fighting as a result of a land dispute; violence in the family because of disagreements over marriage arrangements; and so on. As such, it is not possible to make a definite distinction between the resolution of civil and criminal cases: this is both contrived and unhelpful. However, arguing that community based dispute resolution mechanisms have a role to play in criminal cases does not deny the duty or right of the state to prosecute criminal cases. Instead, this recognition takes account of the role community based dispute resolution bodies have in resolving the causes of criminal actions and reconciling the families of those involved.⁶

The *right* to be a decision maker in community based dispute resolution processes is based on being in a position of authority. Authority in this context is seen as a form of power, which is distinct from power achieved through coercion. Power based on authority is contained and achieved by an individual due to the level of respect they receive from others, whereas power through coercion involves an individual or group to enforcing obedience.⁷ The idea of the *right* to be a decision maker in dispute resolution—a right which is based on authority—does not negate the reality that others using more coercive forms of power also influence these processes. They, however, should they use coercive power, are not seen by the general community as having a *right* to this influence. It should be noted that coercive power and authority are not mutually exclusive; rather, an individual may be in a position of power because he is respected, but also because he is able to wield coercive power. Decision making which is based on authority rather than coercion is important for the long-term acceptance of decisions made. For example, it was reported that many decisions regarding access to and use of land made by commanders during times of conflict, particularly in Bamiyan province, have returned to village dispute resolution bodies since the power dynamics in the area have changed. In the communities where the research was conducted, the opinion expressed was that most, if not all, disputes are currently resolved by those with authority—rather than by those with influence through coercion of one form or another.

This form of authority is vested mainly in particular elder men, commonly referred to as *reesh-safedan* or *spen-zharie* (white-beards).[8] Often it was difficult for respondents to the research to express exactly how a man becomes recognised as a community white-beard . It seems that it can be a heredity status; or can be based on a perception of someone as just and knowledgeable, particularly in regard to the relationships between community members and the social, political and economic history of the area. A formal education can also contribute to acquiring this status.[9] At times younger men may also be found among the pool of decision makers in community based dispute resolution. For example, in one of the villages where the research was conducted the local school teacher participates in resolving disputes, being perceived to have a form of knowledge and skills of use to dispute resolution, as well as being in a respected position in the village. These men form a pool from which individuals are selected to resolve a particular dispute.

The most overt processes of dispute resolution take place in a meeting or series of meetings, called a *jalasa* in Bamiyan, and a *jirga* in Nangahar.[10,11] These meetings are attended by white-beards, disputants and any witnesses to the case, if they are men. If the disputants and witnesses are women, whether they attend or not and how they participate is far more complicated and is discussed below.

Particular elder women, referred to as *sar-safedan* or *spen-sari*, white-hairs, in the communities are also in positions of authority . It is extremely unusual for these women to be included as decision makers in an inter-family or inter-*qawm jirga* or *jalasa*. Nevertheless, their role as decision makers is recognised within domestic disputes, specifically those involving women. Their authority is similarly based on knowledge, but a specialised knowledge of family relationships and 'women's problems'. The recognition of women's knowledge in a different arena was most clearly expressed when both female and male respondents from both provinces expressed the opinion that women should play some role in the resolution of marital disputes or other disputes related to the domestic realm. Likewise, the idea of women-only *jirgas*[12] and *jalasas* for the resolution of 'women's problems' was seen as a positive suggestion by some respondents. Women in Bamiyan province were both reported to and seen to have a slightly greater influence over male-dominated dispute resolution processes. However, the reasons for this are related to a stricter sex segregation of space among the Pashtun communities in Nangarhar than among the Hazara communities in Bamiyan, rather than Pashtun communities having less respect for the elder women's knowledge.

The institutions of *jalasa* or *jirga* are flexible bodies, the structure and location of which not only changes from dispute to dispute but also over the course of the resolution or regulation of an individual dispute. For instance, a *jirga* or *jalasa* may be held to resolve a dispute over a small amount of land on the land that is being disputed or it may be held at the home of one of the white-beards. For larger inter-*qawm* or inter-village disputes a *jirga* or *jalasa* may be held at a white-beard's home, in a public space or even be at the *woliswal's* office. On occasion the *woliswal*, or for very large disputes provincial governor, may attend a *jirga* or *jalasa*. Indeed the size of a *jalasa* or *jirga*, where it is held, who attends, and the nature of the outcomes, are flexible and depend on the needs of the community members regarding its resolution.

One example of this is a large dispute between two *qawms* (one of settled villagers and one of *Kuchi*,[13] who had migrated to the area for generations, and who during the Soviet-*mujahideen* war had settled in the village more permanently) in one village in Nangarhar. This dispute about use of land in the village eventually erupted in the villagers burning the houses of the *Kuchi*. This original dispute over the land had been back and forth through the different justice systems of different regimes in Afghanistan since the departure of the Soviets, but no outcome had been reached. It was finally resolved in a large *jirga* presided over by the then governor of Nangarhar province. Despite representatives of the state being present, and the police having been involved during various stages of the dispute, no one was prosecuted. Instead customary practices were used to resolve the dispute and maintain peace in the village. Those who had burnt the houses had to give *Urz* (roughly translated as apology) in the form of providing a feast for the villagers and walking, without showing pride, to the side of the village where the *Kuchi* live to give their apologies. In exchange the *Kuchi* had to promise allegiance to the village and to defend the village and the other residents against incursions from outsiders.

In another example from Nangarhar, two different groups of *Shinwar*[14] people have had a similar dispute over land which was allocated to one group under the Communist regime. There is a great deal of animosity between these two groups. *Jirgas* are regularly held at the *woliswal's* office in an attempt to resolve the dispute. Although no resolution satisfactory to both sides has been reached, this process of *jirgas* appears to be what is preventing the dispute from erupting into large-scale violence between the two groups. This example demonstrates how community based dispute resolution processes, while not always able to resolve disputes, play an important role in controlling or regulating them—in keeping a lid on the pot.[15]

Choices, motivations and authority: Links and relationships between community and state actors

The two examples above also highlight how state actors work with community based dispute resolution processes to resolve and regulate disputes. In these examples state actors have a very direct role in resolution of the disputes. This interaction between the community and state actors is also found to be the case in smaller disputes between individuals. The primary actor from district level state institutions in community based dispute resolution is the *woliswal*, who is part of the executive branch of government. The *woliswal* plays three primary roles in dispute resolution. First, as has been illustrated, he can be a participant and decision maker in a particular *jirga* or *jalasa;* second, he acts as a gatekeeper to other district level actors, such as the police, *shub-e-huquqi* (department dealing with civil law) prosecutor and courts;[16] third, the *woliswal* acts as a point for registering and further legitimising the process for and outcomes of dispute resolution mechanisms, in the eyes of the community. It was commonly reported for many different types of disputes how in the first instance or at some point in the process of the dispute, the *woliswal* would be made aware of the dispute by either disputants or white-beards. The dispute would then be referred back to the village, by the *woliswal*, for resolution, with either the *woliswal* choosing or more likely the disputants deciding which white-beards would represent them. In some, but not all cases, once a dispute was resolved the documentation showing the outcome of the resolution would be given to the *woliswal*.

Many disputes do not ever reach the *woliswal;* and relationships between the communities, the white-beards of the communities and the *woliswals* vary from district to district and village to village. However, it is important to recognise that a strong relationship often exists between the state and the community for dispute resolution; and that the *woliswal* is the primary liaison in this relationship, acting as both gate-keeper to other state institutions and as a form of legitimisation for dispute resolution. It should be noted here that this relationship is similar for criminal and civil disputes: in the districts where the research was conducted, *woliswals* referred both civil and criminal cases back to the village *jalasas* and *jirgas* for resolution.

Most other district level respondents (including judges, prosecutors, officials of the *shub-e-huquqi* department and police department heads) expressed support for the *woliswal* in their district, referring cases back to villages for resolution. These same respondents also said that on occasions when disputants do come directly to them, they encourage disputants to resolve cases using their white-beards, except perhaps for cases of a very serious criminal nature. Pragmatism was the rationale expressed by district level respondents for referring as many disputes as possible to the village white-beards for resolution. They explained how if the case goes to the state justice system, it would go on for a long time and be expensive for the disputants. Contrary to this most common perspective, in one district in Bamiyan province two district level respondents felt that the *woliswal* should not be referring cases back to the village white-beards: they felt that it was not his responsibility, it was illegal, and that the *woliswal* would only be doing this to lessen his own workload.

The question of why disputants and white-beards continue to bring their disputes to the *woliswals* in the first place, knowing that they will most likely be encouraged to resolve their dispute within the village, is an important one in understanding state community relations at district level; as is the question of why the disputants virtually without exception go to the *woliswal* and not to other officials at district level . The answer to both these questions lies in the authority of the position of *woliswal*, which can in part be seen to come from the historical stability of the position of *woliswal*.[17] At least in the districts where this research was conducted, throughout the different regimes and times of conflict in Afghanistan there has virtually always existed the post of *woliswal*. The *woliswal* is viewed not only as the government's representative in the district, but also as the government in the district. Other reasons for why disputants go to the *woliswal* instead of other offices are related to their fears of these other officials—some believe that if they go to the courts or the police with a problem they will be imprisoned or punished in some way.

It was felt by virtually all those spoken with that having a letter authorising the white-beards to resolve the dispute gives their decisions further authority and could help in the maintenance and implementation of the decision. Indeed, state recognition of the decisions they make was an area that many white-beards said they wanted to be strengthened. This was expressed in terms of the state giving them further authority in implementing their decisions; and in preventing disputes from being taken to the state justice system—in case a disputant is not satisfied with the outcome of a *jalasa* or *jirga*, and then the dispute is referred back to the community for a second decision to be made.

The relationship between the *woliswal* and community actors is not always as collaborative as this analysis might suggest. For, example many respondents perceived either the current or previous *woliswal* of their district to take bribes or be ineffectual. Indeed, in one village in Nangarhar province the white-beards, during group discussions, laid much of the blame for increasing inequities and corruption within their *jirgas* with the *woliswal's* involvement in these processes. In this case the state is seen as directly corrupting the outcomes of the *jirgas* through 'paying agents in the *jirgas*' to ensure that the outcomes of disputes are favourable towards the *woliswal* or his clients.

Interestingly, while many respondents in Nangarhar province believed the *jirga* system to be becoming more corrupt, in Bamiyan province respondents pointed to improvements in community based dispute resolution. It was reported that since the time of the Soviet-*mujahideen* war and as a consequence of conflict and migration—both internal and external—the traditional hierarchical power relations in the villages had broken down. It was reported that previously *arbabs*[18] had made all the decisions regarding the outcome of disputes. People reported *arbabs* as having been corrupt, with the decisions they made being influenced by patronage and bribery. Most people said that things were now better, with many people able to choose which white-beards will resolve their dispute. Interestingly, during group discussions women expressed this opinion most strongly—particularly in one village, where it is suspected that the last *arbab* had been particularly corrupt. However, a couple of elderly men, when spoken to, did talk about missing the ultimate power of the *arbabs*, as it had meant that disputes were resolved very quickly and decisions never challenged.

Collaborating pragmatism: divergent principles

As the discussion above makes clear, significant links already exist between representatives of the state and community based dispute resolution, and are relationships which have changed over time, and which vary from one place to another. However, the principles underlying dispute resolution in the state justice sector as compared to those underlying the community based dispute resolution differ considerably. An analysis of how people choose or are motivated to use community based dispute resolution as opposed to state justice reveals how the nature of the principles underlying state justice and those underlying community based justice differ from each other. It is recognised that people's choices, and particularly women's, are highly restricted.

Perhaps the most important difference in the principles underlying the two mechanisms of dispute resolution relates to peace-making function of the community based dispute resolutions: keeping the peace is paramount, whereas individual rights take precedent in state based justice. This was expressed by the community in terms of there being winners and losers if disputes are resolved in the courts, whereas if their disputes are resolved in the community it will be through negotiation and ensuring all parties are satisfied with the outcome. For example, in disputes over land between two parties, even if one party was 'proven' to own all the land in a community forum it might be agreed that a small portion of the land be given to the other disputant. However, practices intent on resolving disputes and maintaining peace within the community can overlook individual rights, which can lead to abuse of the individual's human rights. For instance, one of the most often cited practices in critiques of community based dispute resolution is the use of *bad* to resolve a dispute. *Bad*[19] is the practice of compensating a murder (or even an accidental killing) by means of the family of the murderer giving usually either one or two virgin girls in marriage to the victim's family. From the research data it is clear that *bad* is recognised, even by those who practice it, to be harmful to the girls and against Islamic principles. Nevertheless, it is also viewed as an effective way to end disputes and maintain harmony in the village.

Since without exception respondents with whom this practice was discussed recognised it as both un-Islamic and highly detrimental to the well-being of the girls concerned, it is likely that its continuation comes from a lack of alternative means of reconciliation. However, it was generally agreed that occurrences of *bad* have decreased considerably in recent years. It is important to recognise that the practice of *bad* is a consequence of the value placed on women in society, which allows them to be seen as objects to be transferred between their natal and marital families.

A further key difference between community and state based dispute resolution is the differing values placed on subjectivity and objectivity, with subjectivity being a highly prized attribute among decision makers in community based dispute resolution. Respondents described how it is better that disputes are resolved in the village because the white-beards know the people and know about the dispute; they know who is 'really telling the truth'. In state justice systems, on the other hand, an objective standpoint for those passing judgement tends to be seen as ideal.

Concerns of a more practical nature were also a reason for most respondents expressing a preference for resolving disputes within the village context. These were most closely related to the expenses involved in rural residents taking a dispute to institutions for state justice, which are located in the district centre. This included both legitimate expenses in terms of travel, accommodation and food at the district centre, and illegitimate expenses: there was a common perception that a dispute would not be resolved using state institutions such as courts, police and so forth, without bribes having to be paid. Time was also a considerable factor: both the time that an individual would have to spend away from home, and the time the state system would take to resolve the disputes.

Another reason why village residents spoken with think it more desirable to resolve disputes within the community than within state justice systems is that they view it as shameful to share details of a dispute beyond the confines of the village or *qawm*. This is particularly the case for disputes involving women—specifically younger women; however, taking any type of dispute beyond the confines of the village community has elements of shame attached to it.

Challenging gender norms: women's access to and participation in community based dispute resolution processes

Similarly, notions of shame and honour are inhibiting factors for women taking disputes to white-beards in their villages. Despite this, it is considered far more appropriate for a woman to approach the elders of her own village than go to the *woliswal*. It was generally agreed across all the research sites that women had a right to access community based dispute resolution processes. However, social norms of sex segregation and association mean the women's ability to access institutions outside the family for dispute resolution are highly circumscribed. For instance, it is considered far more acceptable for a woman to approach a white-beard or a man in her own family to act as a representative for her. Regardless of these social restrictions, in all the research sites examples were provided when women had taken their disputes and difficulties to the white-beards in their villages. In the main these women were older, several being widows; and as such male elders who institute *jirgas* and *jalasas* are more accessible to them due to their greater freedom of movement, and to their ability to breech norms of sex segregation. Despite this, younger women, whose movement and association are severely restricted, do, at times, find ways to access dispute resolution mechanisms. For example, a wife of one of the elders in the village reported to the research team that she had found out about a problem a young woman was having in her family, and then reported the problem to her husband, who involved other white-beards to resolve the dispute.

The acceptability of women taking disputes to community based dispute resolution bodies varies considerably from village to village.[20] It was made clear to the research team that women are seen to have a right to access community based dispute resolution mechanisms; but that ideas of sex segregation and behaviour appropriate for women, affected by age and status in the family, restricts this access.

The data regarding women's actual participation in *jalasas* and *jirgas* more generally is both complex and contradictory. Many of the generalised responses given by both men and women, which were often expressed in focus group discussions, clearly stated that women do not sit in *jirgas* or *jalasas*. However, a conflicting story is found in the data looking at specific disputes. A significant number of examples were found of women not only taking their disputes to community based dispute resolution bodies but also sitting in the *jirgas* and *jalasas* to resolve these disputes. In other examples older women explained how they were called on to be witnesses in disputes: either to report on injuries a woman had incurred in a violent attack, or because they had actually witnessed a woman being beaten. Some examples were also provided of younger women acting as witnesses, but in Nangarhar province, where sex segregation is more strictly enforced, these women sit in a separate room to the main *jirga*, with one white-beard going to collect their evidence. It is beyond the scope of this paper to discuss the many disputes which women have participated in. However, one case from a village in Nangarhar illustrates how women do bring their disputes to *jirgas*, that *jirgas* can be found in their favour, and that in specific examples the community generally agrees that women's presence is essential for a just outcome.

Janwara[21] was betrothed in an exchange marriage at the age of five. Janwara's brother, being older than her, was married to the sister of Janwara's future husband. Janwara's mother did not want her young daughter to be married at this time; consequently her future in-laws demanded money from Janwara's parents as a form of compensation for having to wait until they could marry their son to Janwara. Janwara's parents were not in a position to pay this money. Despite the protests of Janwara's mother, Janwara's mother-in-law took her to Pakistan without the marriage actually taking place. In Pakistan, Janwara was severely abused and beaten by her in-laws, including being burnt to the extent that she had visible scarring. Eventually Janwara's parents managed to bring her back to Afghanistan and their village; but Janwara's mother-in-law came and took her back to Pakistan. By this point, Janwara's mother-in-law decided that she no longer wanted to marry her son to Janwara and instead wanted to find a reason to sell her.[22] She made up a story that Janwara had been having sexual relations with the son of a poor widow woman. Janwara's mother-in-law tortured Janwara until she confessed to the affair and recorded her confession on an audio cassette. Janwara's mother-in-law then went to the village white-beards and asked for a *jirga* to be held so she could accuse Janwara, release her son from the engagement, damage Janwara's reputation, and take her back to Pakistan to sell her on. Both Janwara's mother and mother-in-law participated in four or five *jirgas*, both arguing their cases. The *jirga* eventually decided that the dispute was too big for them alone to handle and that they had to go to the *woliswal*. Janwara and both her mother and mother-in-law accompanied them to the *walwiswal's* office. When the *woliswal* asked Janwara whether what was on the tape was true, she managed to tell her story of abuse and showed the *woliswal* the scars on her arms and ears from the burns she had received. The *woliswal* believed Janwara, as did the white-beards. The case was referred back to a village *jirga* where it was decided that Janwara was innocent and should be allowed to leave her in-laws and return to her parents. It was also decided that *deya* (compensation) should be paid to Janwara's family; however, by this point the mother-in-law had returned to Pakistan, and *deya* has never been received.

Women whom the research team spoke with about this case invariably said that women should participate in *jirgas*, since otherwise no one would have seen Janwara's scars and believed her. Unfortunately, it was not possible to speak about this case to any of the men involved in the resolution of it, as it was only the women in the village who talked to the women on the research team about it.

Throughout the research it was found that women's participation as either disputants, witnesses, or particularly as decision makers is highly constrained. Nevertheless, in the context of dispute resolution, in both provinces where the research was conducted, spaces do exist for women's participation, as this case illustrates. Similarly, while certain customary practices and gender dynamics in Afghan communities can on occasion lead to disastrous outcomes for women in community based dispute resolution processes, these processes can protect and have the potential to protect women's rights, again as this case exemplifies.

Conclusion

While not wanting to romanticise the role that white-beards, *jalasas* and *jirgas* play in communities in Afghanistan, this chapter has demonstrated that community based dispute resolution processes play an important role in maintaining peace and social cohesion in their communities. Further, it has been argued that these processes for regulating and resolving disputes have demonstrated themselves to be highly flexible to both external and internal social and political factors, and to the nature of the disputes being resolved. This ability to be flexible illustrates that community based dispute resolution processes can adapt in accordance with changing social circumstances—namely, those which demand the abolition of the more negative aspects of customary law.

From the research conducted so far, it is clear that community dispute resolution mechanisms, rather than existing in opposition to state processes, often work in co-operation with agents of the state. Indeed, most community level actors spoken with would like further recognition for the work they do, and would like to some degree a further involvement of the state in these processes. However, extreme caution is recommended in any process aimed at strengthening the links between state and community based dispute resolution, in order that the advantages of the principles applied in dispute resolution at the community level, such as negotiation, resolution and maintaining peace, are not lost.

State intervention and regulation of community based dispute resolution processes are often necessary in order to protect individual human rights, and more specifically women's rights. However, it should be recognised that further intervention from the state will not necessarily protect women's rights. Legislation is only one part of a strategy for improving the outcomes for women of community based dispute resolution: more significant changes will come about through wider social change and a change in attitudes and opinions towards the relative positions of men and women in society. This chapter has argued that the negative outcomes and limitations women face in accessing, participating and making decisions in community based dispute resolution processes are a consequence of gender roles and relations in Afghan society more widely, rather than of dispute resolution processes *per se*. Further, the spaces that women have found to access and in which to participate in existing community based dispute resolution processes should not be underestimated, but instead highlighted and recognised.

SECTION II

SECURITY AND GOVERNANCE

7

DILEMMAS OF GOVERNANCE IN AFGHANISTAN

BETWEEN PATRIMONIALISM AND BUREAUCRATISATION

Antonio Giustozzi

The origins of the Afghan state are those of an imperial polity: a patrimonial state based primarily on coercion and conquest. The empire was initially created by Ahmad Shah Durrani in the eighteenth century, but it was King Abdur Rahman at the end of the nineteenth century who perfected the internal structure of the remainder of the original empire after the loss of much territory. He indulged, more than any other ruler before him, in the manipulation of local conflicts and in the mobilisation of sections of the population against others (Rubin, 1995). Furthermore, he introduced a new dimension to the practice of tribal/community manipulation, investing a lot of energy in splitting local polities into smaller units and in trying to link them directly to the state (*Ibid.*). By appointing his own trusted representatives in the place of local rulers, Abdur Rahman laid the basis of what would become Afghanistan's subnational administration. Abdur Rahman was also the first ruler to start the policy of deporting whole communities to distant regions. In particular, he targeted rebellious Pashtun tribes and transferred them to northern Afghanistan, ensuring that once surrounded by hostile Uzbek and Tajik communities they would turn into loyal supporters of the central government. He eliminated the endemic banditry which affected the country by ordering that:

[I]f a traveller is killed, or his property is stolen in the vicinity of a town or a village, the people of that town or village are either to find the wrongdoer or answer for the injury themselves (Al-Rahman Khan, 1900: 69).

The system created by Abdur Rahman was in its own way very resilient, as it made internal mobilisation against the ruler very difficult to achieve on a large scale, as long as the web of alliances with local leaders was maintained and managed effectively. However, if the system produced strong support for the ruler, it also produced strong potential opposition among local rulers and communities who had been excluded from alliances with Kabul or were being antagonised by local rivals aligned with the 'state'. This strong minority, fragmented as it was and opposed by local rulers aligned with Kabul, was in normal conditions unable to challenge the ruler. However, in the presence of external support, such disgruntled local leaders could relatively easily be mobilised against the central government. Abdur Rahman was aware of this and this is partly why he took care in establishing good relations with Afghanistan's neighbours. Since the Russians, and most of all the British, started seeing Afghanistan as a useful buffer state between the two empires, the rulers of Afghanistan became able to play them against each other and extract resources from them (initially from the British).

In an apparent paradox, Abdur Rahman was also the first Afghan ruler to invest heavily in efforts to build a bureaucratic, centralised state (the standard texts on Abdur Rahman are Kakar, 1979; Kakar, 2006). The focus of his efforts was the army, on which he invested large resources and subsidies provided by the British. Another aspect of this 'modernisation' of the state under Abdur Rahman relevant to governance issues was the establishment of a powerful intelligence network inside the country (Saikal, 2004). This was, however, only the beginning of such efforts: the attempted transition from an imperial, patrimonial polity based on arbitrary power to a more institutionalised,[1] bureaucratised[2] and inclusive one dominated Afghan politics from the late nineteenth century to the early twenty-first century.

Abdur Rahman's paradox had in reality illustrious historical precedents. Several scholars, starting from Weber and Eisenstadt, have pointed out how patrimonial rulers have often used political and administrative tools which were non-patrimonial and transcended the basis of their legitimacy, in order to increase the rulers' ability to mobilise resources and exercise control. In this regard it is necessary to distinguish between patrimonialism as the legitimising principle of the state (i.e. the state is owned by the ruler(s) by right of conquest etc.) and patrimonialism as a tool of government. All states may use patrimonial tools, but only patrimonial states are defined by that use. In this sense patrimonialism and institutionalisation are not antinomies, but just different tools of state-making and ruling. While institutionalisation serves to provide a degree of stabilisation and predictability, charismatic patrimonialism provides the element of decisiveness and innovation required for fast, effective political decision making. The two, therefore, can be complementary. Strong institutions, widespread entitlements, etc., historically played a key role in stabilising states; but in certain circumstances can come to be seen as obstacles by specific actors, even at the centre of the state. Reforms, for example, are rarely carried out through institutional processes, which is why revolutions tend to be led by charismatic leaders and often result in at least temporary (re-)patrimonialisation. In Afghanistan, this phase was the Saur 'revolution' (1978–9).

It is a rare occurrence that long-term development will be the conscious choice of rulers, unless they came to form a group with a strong *esprit du corps* and/or high ideologisation. The creation of a bureaucratic, 'modern', 'Weberian' state in Afghanistan was the agenda of radical leftists and Islamist groups, but not of the ruling dynasty. If state-led developmental processes require a degree of ideological abstraction, they can only occur in non-ideological environments as unwanted consequences. Rulers might start 'modernisation' processes with limited aims (have a stronger army, etc.) and unwittingly set off much larger processes (for example, formation of an intelligentsia), eventually leading to their own demise.

It is also important to add that once its original aims are achieved or lose importance, patrimonialism can be severed from charismatic leadership. It can then acquire a life and justification of its own, as strong interests may coalesce around it, which are not directly related to the existence of the state and the viability of leadership. In this case we have elites not necessarily bent on developing their states, but rather focused on securing short-term survival and/or gain. This seems to have been the case of Afghanistan throughout most of the monarchy and after 1992.

How did this dialectic between patrimonialism and bureaucratisation impact on governance issues? Throughout 1880–1978, the quick responsiveness guaranteed by charismatic patrimonialism was privileged at the expense of institution-building, even if there was a slow trend away from the former.

The instability of the Khalq[3] period (1978–9) was followed by a new phase of institution-building under Soviet sponsorship. This stabilised the centre of the state, but the democratic republic under Karmal (1980–6) confirmed once again that heavily institutionalised polities tend to be slow at decision making. This was a phase of paralysis in terms of decision making, even though improving governance was a priority of this period. During this period, there was, initially at least, a coincidence of views between the government and its international patron (the Soviet Union), concerning the desirability of an increasingly strong institutional framework at the core of the state. This was not the case after 2001, when two alternative visions confronted each other, often paralysing action. The definition of governance held by international actors, focused on procedures, institution building, transparency and account-ability, was at odds with the understanding of governance which predomi-nated among the Afghan ruling elite—which remained essentially patrimonial in character. In this sense, on the Afghan side the post-2001 period was in line with the period of *mujahideen* rule (1992–6). The period of Taliban domina-tion, by contrast, was characterised by a comparatively high degree of institu-tionalisation, although one of a different kind.

Maintaining order and territorial control

Throughout its modern history, the Afghan state relied on the legacy of Abdur Rahman's regime of terror to maintain internal stability. The creation of a police force as separate from the army can be read as an attempt to 'civi-lise' the regime and rely less on purely military means to maintain order. Although some urban police force existed already in the nineteenth century, the development of a 'modern' police force in Afghanistan can be traced back to the 1930s. Between the 1930s and the 1970s Afghanistan's police force grew from a mere façade of the army into a more substantial entity—even if by the late 1970s it was still relying on army backup to effectively guarantee territorial control. Its presence at the sub-district level (covering several tens of villages) was limited to half a dozen policemen, and at the district level to a few tens; but there was a somewhat stronger force based in the provincial centres. However, in the case of serious trouble, the army was expected to provide support. The still partial characterisation of the forces of the Ministry of Interior as a 'police' is demonstrated by the fact that its top officers were as a rule coming from the army. The army was as rule given priority in terms of recruitment (second-rate recruits were sent to the police) and of equipment.

Police also remained reliant on cooperation with local communities and notables for law enforcement, particularly among Pashtuns.[4]

Nonetheless, the system allowed the central government to maintain constant control over its territory despite little equipment and extremely limited technology. The typical provincial police force had only one or two vehicles at its disposal, which were usually at the disposal of the chief of police and other officers. Some horse-mounted units existed, but largely policing was done by walking. Policemen, either individually or in small groups, would periodically visit the villages to make sure that nothing suspect was going on. Strict supervision of police activities existed, particularly from 1973—after Daoud Khan took power. Although by the 1970s all low and middle-rank officers were professionals, the system was relying more on a tight routine and strict supervision than on the quality of its human resources.[5]

Under Karmal, the strengthening of the police was prioritised, while at the same time the intelligence service (commonly known as KhAD and from 1986 as WAD) started playing an ever greater role. Thanks to Soviet support, the forces of the Ministry of Interior expanded considerably, and a gendarmerie ('operational units') was created to fight the *mujahideen* insurgency under a deputy minister. The new force was equipped with motor, armour and light artillery; and was organised in battalions and brigades. Under the strong discipline imparted by Minister Sayyed Mohammad Gulabzoi, the police had a reputation for honesty and mostly stayed out of direct political repression. By the late 1980s, KhAD/WAD had developed into a very capable force, which had a fairly accurate picture of what was going on in the country.

Corruption was restrained, and the administration of this period was most likely the most honest Afghanistan ever had. In this context, it is very significant that during the second half of the 1980s President Najibullah moved towards a re-patrimonialisation of governance—by increasingly relying on militias to maintain or re-establish territorial control, despite the opposition of the Minister of Interior and others within the power structure. A two-tier structure gradually emerged, with police controlling urban areas, towns and most highways; and militias the rural settlements. KhAD/WAD acted as the link between the two worlds: a difficult task given that the high level of discipline of the police was at odds with the indiscipline and riotous behaviour of the militias.[6]

After 1992, centralised policing disappeared, and regionally-managed police forces appeared in the west and north. Tribal policing appeared in the east and the south-east, while anarchy dominated in the south. Between 1992 and 1996 the legacy of Abdur Rahman's system seemed to be about to be wiped out; but it was in part re-established under the Taliban (1996–2001), though within a context of stronger institutionalisation. Theirs was not a developmental regime in any obvious sense; but, rather successfully used religious law and ruthless but targeted repression to deliver strong if basic governance. The clerical-judicial core of the regime provided an institutional framework which contained abuses and de-personalised issues. The Taliban did not really have a real intelligence service, but they used sympathising clerical networks for information-gathering—a system which proved to be quite effective. Thanks to them, the Taliban were comparatively well informed about what was going on in the villages, and were able to single out opposition elements (real or presumed) and target them accurately. Although the leadership of the Taliban was overwhelmingly Pashtun, these clerical networks were the closest thing to a nationwide base than any Afghan government has ever had previously and since. The Taliban maintained some uniformed police force in the urban centres, but relied on small detachments of their own 'army' to control the provinces. Their system was sufficiently effective and their reputation sufficiently ruthless to discourage widespread opposition. Only in some remote mountain areas of northern and central Afghanistan did pockets of resistance form, but they never represented a serious threat to the regime. Rural security was as good as ever, and banditry effectively rooted out.[7]

After 2001 the system created by Abdur Rahman once again entered a crisis. The monopoly of force was lost due to the proliferation of militias, and was not re-established due to the façade character of internationally-sponsored disarmament programs[8] (Giustozzi, forthcoming). Such political compromise made the creation of an effective police force very difficult. Any sign of a bureaucratic process disappeared, to the extent that by 2007 most policemen did not even know the regulations, and there was little effort to teach them. The situation was only compounded by the spreading Neo-Taliban insurgency (see Giustozzi, 2007a), which made it very difficult to enforce the rule of law and to get professional police to operate in dangerous areas. The result was that although from 2004 attempts to reform the Ministry of Interior were multiplying, they had little appreciable effect on the ground. The logical consequence of compromising on the establishment of a monopoly of military force should in principle have been to accept a modern 'facade only' police, abandoning the dream of building a centralised state; but the growth of the insurgency added a new sense of urgency to plans to reform the Ministry of Interior. In part this urgency was due to the growing awareness that abuses by undisciplined, untrained and uncommitted police forces were an important factor in driving popular support for the insurgency (Amnesty International, 2003; ICG, 2007; Wilder, 2007).

At the same time, Kabul and some of its international partners continued to favour local militias as a way to maintain influence in parts of the country. This reproduced the dualism of Najibullah's time; though while formerly the expansion of the militias was balanced by the existence of a strong and disciplined police, now the professional police was very weak. Militias were usually paid higher salaries than the police and were often handed large discretionary sums (Nixon, n.d.), which indirectly undermined the status of the police and harmed its ability to recruit locally. Further, not only were provincial governors authorised to create their own militias, but several technically illegal ones were allowed to exist and operate openly, particularly in the south.

The judiciary is another important aspect of governance and, more specifically, the maintenance of order; but in Afghanistan's history has mostly played a limited role. Executive power was always paramount in implementing governance, with police until 1992 responding to the Ministry of Interior and being authorised to carry out investigation and arrests without any intervention of the judiciary. Only during the time of the Taliban did that change, and the judiciary played a greater role. It appears that in 1996–2001, even in the provinces *Shariat* judges were called in to supervise the actions of police and administration, and were independent of the executive (Dorronsoro, 2005). After 2001, in principle the police force was subject to the judiciary and lost most of the discretionary powers which it had had until 1992, but the impact of this development was largely affected by the state of disarray of the judicial corps. Staffing problems and extreme corruption prevented the reform from improving the status of rule of law in Afghanistan, while at the same time constraining the ability of the police to quickly pursue wrongdoers (Papa, 2006; UNAMA, 2007; Watson, 2006a, 2006b).

Sub-national administration

As mentioned in the introduction, Afghanistan's provincial administration first saw the light of the day during Abdur Rahman's time, as he started the practice of appointing governors from outside their region of competence. The system, initially very basic, gradually developed into something more sophisticated, if still primitive compared to those in force in the surrounding polities. Throughout the twentieth century, the central government intensified its administrative coverage of the country. From a mere six provinces, in some cases so large that they could encompass huge territories such as all of southern Afghanistan, the number of major administrative divisions reached fourteen in 1960 and thirty-four in 2005. Similarly, the number of districts climbed from 164 in 1930 to 398 in 2005. The main rationale for such growth was, at least until the conflict started, the desire to bring some administrative control, conflict resolution and services to areas remote from the main roads and urban centres.

Reflecting their limited tasks and the even more limited allocation of resources, during the 1930s the boundaries of sub-provincial units were ill defined and could even vary seasonally. The administrative services provided were very modest—in practice being limited to the mediation of local conflicts—and people were expected to refer to the most easily accessible location. Otherwise the main tasks of the administration were tax collection and conscription into the army. The personality of the governor was integral to the ability of the central government to establish and maintain relations with local leaders. Throughout Afghanistan's history, to maintain contacts with rural settlements at the local level, sub-national administration was dependent on local notables, whose importance mostly derived from the fact that they had been selected for such a role. In other words, local notables were themselves dependent on government support for maintaining their influence, a fact which clearly compounded state vulnerability in time of crisis. However, the limited capabilities of the system were compatible with the limited tasks of the administration.

Only after the Second World War, and thanks to external aid, did Afghanistan's sub-national administration have access to more substantial funds, which were used to develop some additional governance-related tasks, such as issuing identity cards (Schiewek, 2000). The provision of new services such as health and education also helped the administration to expand its influence in the villages. However, the administration remained dependent on coercion in order to implement its decisions, particularly in non-Pashtun areas, since the population perceived it as working in the interest of Pashtuns and tended to be passively hostile. Indeed, Pashtuns largely dominated the administration, even in the north; and Turkic speakers in particular were almost never found within its ranks. One aspect of the effort to institutionalise the administration was that officials were rotated—often to prevent them from developing strong links with the locals or from building their own fiefdom. The drawback was that officials were as a result primarily concerned with maintaining good communications with Kabul, rather than with developing good relations within their area of responsibility. The effectiveness of the administration also suffered from a deepening urban-rural split (Barfield, 1984).[9]

When the leftist Khalq took power in Kabul in 1978 through a military coup, the new rulers tried to enforce ambitious reform programs, largely using the existing administrative structure with all its weaknesses. They tried to reinforce it through the despatch of teams of activists to the districts in order to implement specific programs, such as land reform; but this was no real surrogate for a capable administration. The result in 1979–1981 was the rapid erosion of the state's territorial control due to a spreading insurgency, initially driven mostly by local actors. Recovering territorial control turned out to be a major challenge for the pro-Soviet governments of Karmal and Najibullah, and by the early 1990s they had still made only limited gains, mainly by using irregular forces. However, this does not mean that the governments of the 1980s did not try innovative approaches in an effort to improve governance: under Karmal sub-national administration was separated from the Ministry of Interior, with the creation of a department under the Presidency—a measure which Karzai took again in 2007; and one key initiative taken by Karmal's successor Najibullah was to start appointing governors from within the province they were going to rule—an indication that, in his opinion, in times of crisis personal relationships matter more than strong institutions.[10]

In 1992–1996 the old administrative structure mostly survived after some purging, but its importance was reduced by the emergence of alternative arrangements—such as provincial councils of military commanders, or by the personal power of individual strongmen, who relied on personal authority and usually bypassed established chains of command. Governance therefore returned to the fragmented and fully patrimonial condition of the pre-Abdur Rahman time. The effectiveness of local administrations depended on the wealth of the factions or strongmen controlling different chunks of it: in isolated, poor and remote provinces, it almost completely decayed, while in wealthier areas such as Herat and the north it maintained a degree of functionality. However, even where the administration continued to work, governance was largely the prerogative of military-political groups which operated outside any institutional framework (see Christensen, 1995; Dorronsoro, 2005; Giustozzi, forthcoming).

Under the Taliban, the state administration was cut to a minimum both in Kabul and in the provinces. District administrations in particular were reduced to the bare essentials again—namely maintaining peace through mediation and negotiation—and staff levels fell correspondingly. Provincial governors were appointed from the centre once again, usually from outside the province, and rotated periodically. While the ambitions and tasks of the administration had gone back to Abdur Rahman's time, the Taliban were at least able to deliver on their promises. Helped by the Taliban's 'police', the administration was able to play an important role in maintaining stability, and in many areas effectively succeeded in collecting weapons from the population.[11]

After 2001, the sub-national administration was gradually re-activated. Initially captured by local players (militias), provincial structures were slowly brought under the influence of the central government, which once again started appointing governors from other regions. The rule was not enforced consistently: President Karzai eventually replaced allied local strongmen as governors in southern provinces like Helmand or Uruzgan only at the beginning of 2006, under pressure from foreign embassies; and as of 2007, some provinces were still run by local strongmen, depending on political contingencies—the most notable example was that of Balkh in the north. Another aspect of Kabul's arbitrary dealings with governors is the use of discretionary funds to strengthen or weaken governors. While this patrimonial aspect of government could be argued as necessary in a situation of instability, in order to quickly deliver funding to administrators operating in critical areas of the country, it was in fact often misused to channel money to governors linked to Karzai and other key players in Kabul, at the expense of the more needy ones. This period was also characterised by chaotic management even of relatively simple issues such as the creation of new districts. About fifty new districts, mainly created in the 1990s but without their borders defined or any administration effectively set up, were hanging in the balance with Karzai unable to decide over their establishment.[12]

The quality of sub-national administrators, which was never great, had seriously depleted by 2002, as a consequence of repeated purges in 1978–1980, 1992, 1996 and 2001. Moreover, even many of those who were not purged had left their jobs because of ageing, migration or other reasons. However, the functioning of provincial and district administrations had always been relatively basic and advanced skills were rarely required, so that in many cases even recently recruited clients of local patrons were able to do their job once Kabul's ministries re-activated their local branches. Indeed, the worse problems in re-activating the state bureaucracy seemed to be occurring at the centre rather than in the periphery. Although many seemed keen on occupying positions in the local administrations (see Manning, *et al.*, 2003), that might have been for the wrong reasons. After 2001 it was difficult to detect much commitment to duty or to the offering of services to the local population: the rationale for hanging on despite low salaries is likely to have been linked to opportunities for influence or bribery rather than anything else. Often, lack of supervision from the centre resulted in the embezzlement of funds, distribution of state assets to local clients and arbitrary actions by the administrators. Various reform attempts were launched throughout 2002–2007, initially aiming at improving financial management, and then increasingly with a focus on establishing alternative forms of transparency and accountability—for example to elected bodies (Lister, 2005, 2006; Lister and Wilder, 2005). While financial management did improve (Evans and Osmani, 2005), after 2007 attempts to secure greater accountability had had little appreciable impact, but bore witness of growing despair about the ability of the ministries to get their act together and exercise effective supervision.

Conclusion

The two most effective systems of governance ever set up in Afghanistan—those of Abdur Rahman and of the Taliban—were essentially 'governance on the cheap', based on retaliation. These systems, however, in order to work and not to cause a general insurrection, had to be based on detailed local knowledge. Abdur Rahman initially relied on his own extensive experience of the country and then set up a vast intelligence network; while the Taliban relied on the support of extensive clerical networks, extending right down to the village level. Both systems were able to exercise strict supervision on the administration, having subjugated the population; but the way in which such supervision was exercised varied: Abdur Rahman's was based on a strongly patrimonial system centred around the king, while the Taliban's was centred on the clergy—to both supervise and staff the higher levels of the administration.

The principle that a demonstration of overwhelming strength and relentless retaliation is conducive to the monopoly of violence, and is hence an essential ingredient of governance, was also well understood by both the Soviets and the Americans. Both tried to deliver the message that hostility to the central government would be met with overwhelming retaliation: the Soviets applied it on a very large scale during the first half of the 1980s, the Americans more cautiously so from 2001. However, neither had detailed local knowledge, and as a result both were unable to carefully target their repression. As the Soviets and their client government began to gather such knowledge, they adopted a more cautious and targeted policy; but the extent of the damage done up to that point was such that by 1991, when the Soviet Union collapsed, the process of repairing it was still in its early stages (see Giustozzi, 2000; Giustozzi, 2007a). The Taliban too adopted a similar system of ruthless retaliation when they were in power, but despite their immensely more limited technical and financial resources, they were much more successful because they had detailed knowledge.

The development of a sophisticated and effective intelligence service is only one aspect of achieving detailed local knowledge. A key challenge is the development of a local but disciplined military force (gendarmerie), as opposed to being a patrimonial para-military force under the control of a local strongman. Such a force would be based in a specific locality, developing local contacts and accumulating local knowledge. Although a gendarmerie is a militarised force, it is substantially cheaper and leaner than an army, with less developed structure and hierarchy, greatly inferior logistical capabilities and lighter equipment and weaponry. Its main task is territorial control, which can be a fragile area of governance in weak states. Historically, the problem in developing such forces, particularly on a volunteer basis (as opposed to a conscript force) has been a lack of sufficient numbers of volunteers who are willing to reside away from home for long periods of time. Conscription might therefore be the only option effectively available. It is also necessary to develop an administration able to interact positively with local notables, as opposed to taking sides or alienating a substantial part of the population.

A critical aspect of governance, which is, to some extent at least, at odds with the establishment of a monopoly of violence, is the development of a working bureaucratic supervision of administration and police. Historically, in most states bureaucratic types of governance developed much later than the original achievement of a monopoly of violence; but in the contemporary Afghan context there is pressure to carry on both processes in parallel. There is indeed a strong rationale for insisting on a police force and an administration committed to maintaining the rule of law: any system based on the virtue of single individuals is bound to face a crisis sooner or later. Several layers of paperwork-filled supervision are required to ensure that the system works properly and degenerative processes are held in check. Such a system existed in Afghanistan in the 1970s, even if it privileged quick and simple solutions over fairness and 'justice', and stability over rule of law, leaving just a marginal role to the judiciary. That left substantial room for abuse, but it worked in terms of maintaining order.[13]

In the post-2001 context, the failure to set up a professional police force and to disarm the militias straight away compromised the chances of bringing 'rule of law policing' back to Afghanistan. Although the police force was being increasingly re-professionalised after 2004, there was little sign of any deter-mined attempt to re-establish bureaucratic procedures of supervision and control. Issues of corruption and disfunctionality were therefore still unre-solved. In acknowledgement of this problem, efforts to reform and re-train the police were gearing up in the second half of 2007, with major investments in and deployments of trainers and advisers from both the United States and the European Union. Such efforts were however marred by deep disagree-ments over the stress to be given to the shaping forces of the Ministry of Inte-rior, due to the different national traditions of policing in the participating countries, and to the contradictory tasks which the international partners set for themselves. When serious efforts to reform the Ministry of Interior and develop a professional police force started in earnest after 2004, little had been achieved with the disarmament of the militias, and the insurgency was already picking up. The *de facto* abolition of military discipline meant that professional police were able to refuse serving in the more dangerous and remote districts, where indeed the presence of the state was most needed. The expanding insurgency of the Neo-Taliban compounded the situation, further discouraging professional police officers from agreeing to serve in the districts.[14]

Inevitably, the formation of a police force tasked to maintain law and order started being seen as less of a priority than the creation of a militarised force bent on territorial control and able to fight the insurgency. These were not only different, but possibly even contrasting aims—not least because fighting a counter-insurgency and maintaining bureaucratic supervision and the rule of law are in practice somewhat at odds. Establishing a monopoly of violence and guaranteeing the rule of law do not go together well. The political ration-ale was by then increasingly driving the debate on police reform towards privileging a gendarmerie-type force, which the Americans in particular viewed as key to their counter-insurgency efforts; but international con-straints, bureaucratic politics within the international organisations involved, electoral requirements of major donors, etc., continued to make the formation of a civilian police force a necessity. The contradiction was in part resolved, at least in the short term, through the building of a façade of a police force;

although, in practice, at the district level the country in 2007 was still being 'policed' by local militias in uniform. Longer-term options included the creation of two separate forces, a civilian police force focused on law and order, and a gendarmerie tasked with the darker side of state building. The establishment of separate chains of command would allow the former to restrain or at least monitor the activities of the latter. However, the problem of how actually to establish a disciplined paramilitary force remains completely unresolved, as the Americans appeared intent on training existing militias (camouflaged as police). Although several Afghan officials advocated the re-establishment of conscription, politically such an option seemed as distant as ever.[15]

With regard to sub-national administration, by 2005–6 it was becoming evident that rotating governors every few months is not *per se* sufficient to prevent disfunctionalities in the system. In this case too the focus was initially on getting the 'right guys' appointed in the provinces. International partners would pressurise Karzai to appoint 'clean' or unbiased governors sponsored by them, whom however the Cabinet then failed to support adequately. Sometimes, such governors would be effectively sabotaged from the centre in order to discredit them and prepare the ground for their removal. Karzai's decision in 2007 to institute a separate department in charge of appointing and supervising governors was meant to address the issue of professionalisation, but inevitably setting up a new bureaucratic structure from scratch was going to take time. Neither could it be guaranteed that the new structure would work better than the Ministry of Interior itself and be shelved from patrimonial subversion, particularly in the absence of genuine political will at the top.

8

WHAT PREVENTS AFGHANISTAN BECOMING A LANDBRIDGE?[1]

Valey Arya

The strategic importance of Afghanistan rose once again following the 11 September 2001 terrorist attacks on New York and Washington and the subsequent events that unfolded in Afghanistan. Rubin (2006: 17) argues that Afghanistan has changed 'from being a buffer separating South Asia, Central Asia, and the Persian Gulf, to a crossroads or battleground where the conflicts of all of these regions are played out'. Nevertheless, in this paper, I shall try to explore the geopolitical and geo-strategic character of Afghanistan and the subsequent implications for the position of the country as a potential landbridge for commerce and culture—a concept that is being actively promoted by the Afghan government (Spanta, 2006) and is very much desired by many Afghans. But does Afghanistan have the potential to reach that level of development? If it does, what are the threats and impediments in the region, and how can they be turned into opportunities?

Neo-liberalism and critical geopolitics in International Relations, both of which focus on interdependence, cooperation, and regionalism, will form the theoretical framework of this paper.

Current setting

Landlocked Afghanistan is neighboured by Pakistan, Iran, China, and the Central Asian republics of Uzbekistan, Turkmenistan, and Tajikistan. 'Afghanistan's central location in a strategic but tough neighbourhood has had its benefits and drawbacks throughout history' (Thomas, 2006). Currently, as its neighbours are keeping an eye out to see if the struggling government of Karzai can continue to survive in the face of the current insurgency, unmet expectations of the people as well as inadequate international attention—a new smaller version of 'the Great Game' may occur. At present, we have got South Asian Pakistan that is worried by the friendly relations between Afghanistan and India, and Middle Eastern Iran who does not want to see Afghanistan as an ally of the United States.

India wants the friendship of Afghanistan because of its long-lasting dispute with Pakistan and its rivalry with China. At the same time, according to Raja Mohan (2006) writing in the 'India Express', India does not want to displease the United States either. It does not wish to see NATO and US forces leave Afghanistan, as this might help the Taliban to make a comeback, which it fears may increase the regional power of Pakistan.

Despite this, although the US, China and Russia are competing for influence in Central Asia, India seems to be keeping a distance from the new post Cold War geopolitical setting. For example, an Indian delegation to the potentially influential Shanghai Cooperation Organisation (SCO), meeting in Dushanbe in September 2006, was headed by its minister of oil; while Pakistan and Iran were represented by their heads of state. Incidentally, this event was also a good opportunity for Beijing to show Washington that it can be influential in Central Asia and the region.

China keeps watch on developments in Afghanistan because of the latter's relations with Pakistan, Russia, India, the United States, and Central Asian countries. President Karzai's visit to China in June 2006 showed that China is also a very important country in terms of its potential impact on the political and economic future of Afghanistan. There is increasing evidence that the SCO, a Chinese initiative, can be a determining factor in the region. First, SCO has been able to epitomise the unity of Russian and Chinese power, established and emerging superpowers respectively. Moreover, in 2005 SCO called for a timetable for the removal of the US military bases in Central Asia, and consequently, Uzbekistan asked the USA to leave their airbase in Karshi-Khanabad. China and Russia are also concerned about the presence of NATO in Afghanistan as well as the Strategic Partnership Agreement signed between

Afghanistan and the US in May 2005. According to China Daily (cf. Qabool, 2006), although the US is playing the most vital role in Afghanistan from a political and military point of view, wider projects of peace-building and reconstruction make the neighbouring countries very important for Afghanistan—a country that connects South, Central and West Asia and therefore which should theoretically play a more significant role in regional cooperation. China would also like to use Afghanistan for the export of its products, aimed not only at the Afghan market but also those of neighbouring countries.

The situation of Afghanistan can be influential in the stability and security of the Western regions of China. During the visit of President Karzai to China, an agreement was signed for security and economic cooperation. At bilateral talks in the Great Hall of the People in June 2006, President Hu Jintao said that the two countries would fight the three 'evil powers' of separatism, extremism, and terrorism (Dalian China, 2006). Meanwhile, China, as an increasingly salient global economic power, can provide a lot of opportunities and markets for countries in the Central and South Asian regions. Consequently, Afghanistan is also hoping to benefit from Chinese economic growth, and to export more of its products in the future.

Moreover, political scholars and economists believe that the new centre of gravity and global production is going to be in Asia, with the centrality of China and India. In the sixteenth century 78 per cent of world products were made in this part of the world - i.e. across the whole of Asia. Currently only 20 per cent of world products originate from Asia, but by 2020 this is predicted to increase to 43 per cent. This will potentially increase even further, as more economic power will lead to more political capacity, which will in turn lead to more influence and as a result more productive outcomes (Tellis, 2006). In the light of these suggestions, can this region and the world afford to have an unstable Afghanistan that can easily have an impact on the future resurgence of Asia? The answer is, of course, negative. Rationally speaking, regional and global powers will follow an agenda of stabilisation and peace-building in Afghanistan. This can materialise only if Afghans themselves and smaller regional powers pursue a similar agenda. It will be only then that the chances of Afghanistan becoming a landbridge will increase.

Afghanistan gained its new strategic and economic significance following the end of the communist system in the former Soviet Union. The country has once again acquired the status of the crossroad for development in the region. According to Roashan (2006), the huge natural resources of Central Asian states, including Turkmenistan's gas as well as possible trade routes between Central and South Asian nations, make Afghanistan one of the most significant countries that can facilitate trade in the region, open markets in the subcontinent of India to Central Asian countries, and serve as a trade route for products from Central Asia to South Asia and beyond. This may help Afghanistan become a new focal point of commerce in the region.

In addition to Roashan, who believes Afghanistan possesses the potential to become a landbridge, an Afghan commentator who strongly argues for this is Qabool (2006) who writes that as rivalries grow between the US on the one hand and China and Russia on the other, Afghanistan finds itself again in an extraordinarily sensitive strategic location. This new strategic location, which seemed to be lost after the end of the Cold War, calls for the Afghans to come up with an accurate and appropriate definition of their national interests *vis-à-vis* the new geopolitical trends in the region.

Therefore, in the light of what both writers argue, there is an urgent requirement for reconciliation and national unity among the Afghans more than any other time, and at the same time, realisation by all regional actors that stability in Afghanistan is in their favour too.

The ethnic, linguistic, sectarian, and cultural diversity in the population of the country suggests how close the links are with the neighbouring state. Many ethnic groups in Afghanistan have co-ethnics across the country's borders—for example, Pashtuns, Tajiks, Turkmens, Uzbeks and Baluchs. A revitalised Afghanistan could contribute to the chances of peace and affluence in the countries of the region who share a common future with Afghanistan, even though they encompass various nationalities and ethnic groups. That is why Mohammad Iqbal, Pakistan's national poet, once famously called Afghanistan 'the beating heart of Asia'.

It is usually argued that Afghanistan is located in a dangerous neighbourhood. The blame for much of the political volatility and desolation of its people can be traced back to foreign powers trying to realise their own strategic, ideological, and economic interests in the country. The immediate and far-away neighbours of Afghanistan have regularly interfered in its politics and economy. Outsiders have sometimes acted on behalf of their Afghan clients and have assisted and armed them to control large portions of the country (Weinbaum, 2006).

Although (in)famous for resisting foreign invaders, Afghans themselves cannot be cleared of responsibility for much of the misery and destruction that has occurred in recent history. Nevertheless, the infuriating role of outside states, proximate and distant, has exacerbated civil conflicts.

In an often problematic region, external disputes and domestic strife among neighbouring countries can easily spread into Afghanistan. Political unrest in Uzbekistan or Tajikistan, US military action against Iran, extremism in Pakistan, or another war between Pakistan and India could all have a serious impact on Afghanistan.

Both Pakistan and India have been pursuing a policy of gaining an advantage in Afghanistan. Seeking a strategic depth in Afghanistan has been at the top of the Pakistani foreign policy agenda since the late 1980s. It was hoped that Afghanistan would provide a safe haven for Pakistani forces in the case of war with India. Further, a friendly Afghanistan, if not completely obedient, could ensure that India or any other force would not threaten Pakistan from its northwest borders. Advocating the creation of a fundamentalist Islamic state in Afghanistan was not only meant to counterbalance Pashtun irredentism but could also help religious groups in their struggle against India in Kashmir. Moreover, it would also be used as a backyard, by means of which Pakistan could get rid of its growing number of ultra-orthodox radical groups.

Rivalries between Pakistan and Iran are often also played out inside Afghanistan. Other powers have come and gone but these two neighbours have maintained a constant interference in Afghanistan's internal affairs. The Islamic Republic of Iran's discontent with Pakistan is attributed to the latter's military partnership with the United States and close economic and cultural relations with Saudi Arabia—the major rival to Iran in the Middle East. Sectarian attacks between Shi'a and Sunni militants inside Pakistan have provoked Iranian covert operations to support Shi'a groups there. Moreover, both countries suspect the other's involvement in insurgencies among their respective ethnic Baluch populations. The strategic competition between Pakistan and Iran is also fanned by their nuclear programmes—even though Pakistani scientists might have had a role in assisting Iran's nuclear programmes.

Many Afghans are asking whether it is a helpful hand that has been extended to Afghanistan for reconstruction and development by the West and neighbouring countries, or economic and political investment on the part of the aid-giving nations, in order to further their own higher national interests. This is a question that is being asked across the highly politicised contemporary world.

Geopolitics of oil and gas

Recent estimates indicate that Afghanistan harbours huge amounts of gas and oil resources (Nawanews, 2006). If this is proven, the geopolitical milieu of the region could be transformed. At the same time, Afghanistan is also considered a potential landbridge for the transfer of the Central Asian gas to the Indian Ocean.[2]

As far as Afghanistan's own resources are concerned, in March 2006 experts from the US Geological Survey estimated that the country encompasses eighteen times more oil and three times more gas than what had previously been assessed. If proved, this could be a turning point in the process of reconstruction and development, since a new and direly needed source of revenue will be created for the government. Stephen Blank from US Army War College notes that this can also have deep geopolitical implications in the sense that Central Asia is increasingly leaning towards Moscow after the incidents of Andijan in May 2005.[3] Afghanistan as an oil producing country in the US camp will be an asset for the US (cf. Nawanews, 2006).

Currently, there are two major gas pipelines under consideration in the region: the Iran-Pakistan-India (IPI) and the Turkmenistan-Afghanistan-Pakistan-India (TAPI). Naturally, these two projects have resulted in geopolitical manoeuvres—in the sense that the United States is completely against the IPI project and is actively promoting that of the TAPI one, not only because of its anti-Iran foreign policy, but also because the US would like to alienate the Central Asian republics from Russia in order to bring them closer to the western world. Russia is supporting the IPI project, and the Russian company Gasprom has offered to implement it. Even China has shown an interest in joining this venture.

Russia has been making attempts to monopolise Turkmen gas. If this advantage is aquired, it will boost Russia's ambition to create a Eurasian organisation similar to the Organisation of the Petroleum Exporting Countries (OPEC); though Turkmenistan has recently asked Moscow for a higher price for its gas. This has shown that the former can not be a very reliable ally for the latter. On the other hand, India and Pakistan have friendly relations with the USA, and do not want to damage this by promoting a project that is being promoted by Iran and Russia. If India and Pakistan decide to relinquish their support for the IPI, this will be interpreted as a major geopolitical drawback for Iran and Russia.

At the same time, Japan is also attempting to have access to the energy resources of the Central Asian region. Japan initiated the 'Central Asia + Japan' talks in August 2004, to which Afghanistan was also invited. Japan seems to be trying to counter-balance the increasing influence of China and Russia in Central Asia and the Eurasian region by playing a greater geopolitical role. Thus, with regard to the rivalries among the industrial powers in this part of the world, Afghanistan seems to be at the epicentre of these geopolitical and geo-economic calculations. But does Afghanistan have the potential to use its strategic location as a blessing, in contrast to the curse it has previously been, and avail itself of all these opportunities? Despite the pessimism that many people might show, the findings of my research provide a positive and optimistic response.

In the remainder of this chapter, we will explore what the new trade games in the region with the centrality of Afghanistan look like, and what Afghans think about the future development of their country, and, in particular, the concept of Afghanistan as a landbridge.

New trade trends

In 2003 landlocked Afghanistan moved further to achieving its goal of becoming a major trade landbridge between Europe, the Middle East, Central Asia and South Asia, after signing several trade agreements with its neighbours. Pakistan, the gateway for Afghan imports and exports for decades, was excluded because its main regional rivals, India and Iran, were quicker to tap into trade agreements at its expense. The aspirations of Pakistan to open up trade routes with Central Asian states seem to have fallen victim to its confusing policy toward the Afghan government, as well as to its hostility towards India. This can be seen in the hindrances it has created to trade with its western neighbour—such as hiking freight fees for Afghan exports and declining to agree on a new transit-trade deal. According to a western ambassador in Islamabad, 'Pakistan is losing out because its myopic policies place countering India above trade and stability in Afghanistan' (cf. Rashid, 2003: 18).

In early 2003, the Afghan government signed a deal with Iran, which enabled Afghan import-export traders to use the port of Chabahar on the Indian Ocean with a discount of 90 per cent on customs and port fees for non-oil goods, and a 50 per cent discount on warehouse charges. At another meeting in Tehran on 5 January 2003, India, Iran and Afghanistan signed an agreement to give Indian goods destined for Central Asia and Afghanistan similar special consideration and tariff reductions at Chabahar. New Delhi, which is not allowed to trade with Afghanistan through Pakistan, agreed to fund the upgrading of a road connecting the port to the town of Dilaram in southwest Afghanistan via the Afghan-Iranian border post of Zaranj.

In another agreement with Iran, India will build a line linking Chabahar to the Iranian railway network. Iran will extend its railway to the western city of Herat. Iranian officials have said they were planning to develop Chabahar as the major port for Afghanistan and Central Asia.

Afghanistan is also moving rapidly towards open trading routes, and receives concessions from its northern neighbours, the Central Asian republics. Further, Afghanistan has said it would be happy to improve its trade relations with Pakistan. Afghan leaders support the concept of creating multiple trading routes rather than depending on one. President Karzai says he would like to develop similar trade ties with Pakistan: 'We have no preferences, no favourites, as long as Afghanistan can benefit all round' (cf. Rashid, 2003: 19).

Even though Afghanistan has been disadvantaged by its landlocked nature, it has also benefited from it. Jalali (2006: 17) argues that the country has been a trading nation historically, with a strong private sector, and has long served as a 'trade and transit bridge between three main geographic regions: Central Asia, South Asia, and the Middle East'. The expansion of inter-regional economic relations could revitalise Afghanistan's historical role, and so assist its economic recovery. Afghanistan's recent membership of the South Asian Association for Regional Cooperation (SAARC), and the adoption of the 'Kabul Declaration' on regional cooperation at a twelve-nation conference in Kabul in early December 2005, could smooth the progress of the rebirth of the country as a landbridge of economic exchange. In addition to the agreements and arrangements mentioned above, one can also refer to a multilateral agreement in 2004 between Afghanistan, Iran, Tajikistan, and Uzbekistan on the construction of transit routes linking Central Asia with the Middle East through Afghanistan or the aforementioned TAPI project.

During my fieldwork in Afghanistan in the months of April and May 2007, an interviewee noted that a major development taking place in the region is the economic progress of India, Pakistan, Bangladesh and others in the coming ten to fifteen years, which will inevitably lead to higher energy needs. Central Asia has huge energy resources that are waiting to be exploited and exported. India has always said that even if the Iranian IPI pipeline materialises, they would still need that of the TAPI through Afghanistan.

Transportation routes are another necessity. One such project is a highway connecting China to Turkey through Afghanistan, for which the feasibility study is underway. Central Asian countries are also willing to build a railway to Karachi through Afghanistan. There are so many economic opportunities that they can make the political issues seem almost of secondary importance. In the next twenty years, India's trade with Europe alone will be in the region of thirty-eight billion dollars. 'Imagine if half of this passes through Afghanistan. The same thing can apply in the case of Pakistan' (Respondent G).[4] Geopolitical conditions influence international cooperation. The advantages and disadvantages of cooperation are not going to be the same for all countries. According to Jalali (2006), finding a common denominator, such as building intra-regional transport routes, can be the starting point.

Voices of Afghans

In this section, and based on my fieldwork, I would like to reflect on the aspirations and apprehensions of Afghan political leaders and elite regarding the geopolitical identity of their country—their geopolitical visions and other relevant issues. The official position of the Afghan government is that the country does have the potential to become a landbridge connecting South Asia, Central Asia and the Middle East (Spanta, 2006). In addition, the current border separating Afghanistan and Pakistan—the Durand Line—is not recognised by the government, or indeed by many Afghans. Moreover, the government is concentrating on the creation of a strong centralised system as required by the constitution.

As part of my doctoral research, I conducted fifteen semi-structured interviews with Afghan political leaders, cabinet ministers, members of parliament, journalists, and academics representing political and ideological views from across the board. This was during the months of April and May 2007 in Kabul. I have divided the individuals I interviewed into five categories (described below). There were twenty-six main questions covering several thematic issues, but the question relevant to this chapter is whether Afghanistan could become a landbridge between South Asia, Central Asia, and the Middle East, and why it would be beneficial. The five categories of respondents are as follows:

1. Those working with the government,[5] who, whilst they spoke their mind, held opinions in line with the position of the government.
2. Those working with the government who did not want to speak openly about these issues.
3. Those outside the government, but supporting the government position that Afghanistan has potential as a landbridge.

4. Those outside the government who were critical of its policies and visions, including the idea of Afghanistan as a landbridge.
5. Those who were not pro-government, but responded positively to the idea of Afghanistan as a landbridge.

I continue by illustrating in more detail the position of respondents in these categories, using empirical material collected during fieldwork. The quotes chosen are those I judge to be representative of the respondents in each category.

Responses of group 1

(Those working with the government, who, whilst they spoke their mind, held opinions in line with the position of the government).

People falling into this category are actively promoting the concept of the country becoming a landbridge. Respondent A, who is a high-ranking government official, argues that the country is already a landbridge:

If we divide Asia into regions, we have the Asia with energy resources in the north, the industrial Asia in the south and the east as well as the Arab region. They are all connected to Afghanistan. None of these regions can reach the other without passing through Afghanistan.[6]

Respondent A believes that from the socio-political point of view, the potential and the political will is also there, particularly in the North and the South. The North needs to export its energy resources, and the South needs the market in the North for its growing industries. As far as the role of Afghanistan itself is concerned, the government is concentrating on improving relations with the Islamic world and neighbouring countries, as well as promoting the issue of participation in regional organisations, in order to find its place in the family of nations. They all constitute a major part of Afghan foreign policy priorities. Therefore, Respondent A maintains that both the political will and the efforts needed for turning the country into a landbridge are there.

According to Respondent G, as far as relations between Afghanistan and Pakistan are concerned, they have also been trying to work together in the areas of economic cooperation and trade, regardless of the ongoing contentious issue of the validity of the Durand Line. The US has been interested in the concept of a reconstruction opportunity zone, where Pakistan and Afghanistan will have joint economic ventures and projects—in response to which the USA will provide them with free quotas, or duty-free access to its markets.

The important point contained in what the above respondents are saying is that the country does have the potential to connect all these regions together.

Responses of group 2

(Those working with the government who did not want to speak openly about these issues).

This group of people work within the government, but believe the whole concept of making Afghanistan a landbridge is too optimistic and idealistic. Nevertheless, they argue for the need for such a landbridge and for the will for its creation on the part of Afghanistan and some regional countries.

Respondent M, a cabinet minister, has got mixed feelings; and maintains that in terms of geographical location, Afghanistan does have the potential to become a landbridge—particularly between Central Asia and South Asia, but to a lesser degree between the Middle East and South Asia, since they have their connections through the sea. Central Asia has no other alternative—physically nor geographically. Further, before the creation of the USSR, Central Asia had direct contact to South Asia through Afghanistan. However, when it comes to realities on the ground, it is still a matter of debate as to whether Afghanistan has got the political, economic, and social capacity to take on such a role. One could conclude that this group of respondents would speak more critically of the government, were they not high-ranking government officials.

Responses of group 3

(Those outside government but supporting the government policies)

A view that can represent this category of people is that of Respondent O, who believes that due to Afghanistan's strategic location, it has acquired geopolitical significance. Afghanistan possesses the potential to become a hub connecting South Asia, Central Asia and the Middle East, provided that Afghanistan's neighbours restrain themselves from pursuing illegitimate interests in the country, and accept the fact that stability and the independence of Afghanistan will serve their interests too. Respondent O argues that, as a crossroad, Afghanistan possesses an important geostrategic location in this part of the world as a crossroad. It could turn into a transit route for Central Asian products to the ports of the Indian Ocean and the East of Asia. Likewise, South Asian nations could benefit from it for their access to Central Asian markets and the energy resources. Energy is also vitally required by India and Pakistan for their developing economies. Moreover, Afghanistan itself has great potential for trade and investment in all the neighbouring countries from across the three regions.

The above response is a typical viewpoint, normally heard from a mainstream Pashtun elite, regardless of where they work and whether it be inside or outside the government. They strongly believe that Afghanistan should become a landbridge between the three regions, and that it should have a strong central government without any devolution of power to the periphery.

Responses of group 4

(Those outside the government who were critical of its policies and visions, including the idea of Afghanistan as a landbridge).

Most of the people falling into this group represent the disenchanted non-Pashtun political circles, who are very critical of the government policies as well as the presence of US forces in the country under current arrangements.

Respondent K, an ambitious politician, argues that the Pakistani government always accentuates the threat from India when communicating with its public and media, and highlights the need for strategic depth.[7] At the same time, Pakistan has an implicit strategy to influence and control Afghanistan, regardless of the Indian problem. According to Respondent K, in the Afghan year 1368 (1989) Ahmad Shah Masoud was invited to Pakistan by their Army Chief of Staff, Aslam Beg. They raised the issue of having an 'Islamic depth'.[8] This was raised for the first time by General Aslam Beg, who said:

[T]he Muslims [meaning Sunnis] should get united. The Arabs have the money but not the brain. Iran cannot be the axis because they are Shi'ites. The only country that can do this is Pakistan, because it has the army, knows the region, has got the necessary relations, etc. Pakistan should have the leadership of the Islamic world.

Significantly, at this meeting Masoud was given a carpet as a gift, which depicted the map of Pakistan moving towards Central Asia. When Respondent K was asked how he thought this threat could be turned into an opportunity, he described his strategy as follows:

We have formed this united national council composed of fifty-seven political parties and civil society organisations. We have got several proposals in this regard. The first one is that we should resolve the issue of Durand Line with Pakistan. What is important for us is to resolve it and create friendship. How we do it and where the border is going to be is not that important. At least we have this opportunity of having several countries present here who can support us. We don't know whether we are going to have a better opportunity in the future. Even those countries that created this issue are here. They would like to see this resolved at least for their own benefit. We know that Pakistan is not going to stop interfering anyway, but it will have less excuses and pretexts.

Although Respondent K seems to be pessimistic, the ideas he suggests as a strategy for addressing the issues of Pakistan-Afghanistan cooperation—particularly the idea of resolving the issue of Durand Line—will have a positive impact on the geopolitical situation of Afghanistan, and has great potential to contribute to its role as a landbridge.

Responses of group 5

(Those who were not pro-government, but responded positively to the idea of Afghanistan as a landbridge).

This group of interviewees, which includes very influential members of parliament and former government ministers, generally believe that the country has the potential of a landbridge, although they are all very critical of the government.

For instance, Respondent J suggests that the fundamental question is whether the leadership in the country has the ability to take advantage of Afghanistan's geopolitical potential and turn it into a reality—in other words, to avoid a clash of interests and create a convergence of interests. If this can happen, Afghanistan will become the new Dubai of the region.

Respondent L believes that Afghanistan does have the geopolitical advantage, which should be considered as an asset. If the forefathers of the nation could make this region part of the Silk Road, why should Afghanistan not be able to do this in the current globalised world? But he argues there are challenges and obstacles:

We have lost everything during the war—our infrastructures, our legal systems. There are regional and geopolitical conflicts. And this idea was part of our foreign policy objectives after the fall of the Taliban. Before that, Afghanistan was a landbridge, but for narcotics and terrorism—it was their hub. Of course these two issues are still challenges.

Respondent L believes that Afghanistan has some advantages in terms of its geographical location and its membership in regional cooperation organisations.[9] He adds that there is willingness in other regional countries *vis-a-vis* access through Afghanistan. Kazakhstan is interested in having access to Karachi, Chabahar and Gowadar ports through Afghanistan: they need to export their energy to South Asia and import goods from South Asia. This is one of the ways in which Afghanistan can move towards development. He says, 'We should not be distracted by problems across our borders and should stay focussed on this noble cause' (Respondent L).

Nevertheless, the fact remains that the present government in Afghanistan lacks the capacity to realise this ambition. Moreover, the concept of the need for interdependence, and the acknowledgment that the cost of non-cooperation can be higher than that of cooperation, need to be more actively promoted by all parties involved.

Workshop discussions

Having outlined the viewpoints of my interviewees, I would also like to provide a synopsis of the discussions that took place during the geopolitics workshop at the European Centre for Afghan Studies Conference (3 March 2007). The participants discussed the strengths, weaknesses, opportunities and threats Afghanistan is facing regarding its development in general, and, in particular, its potential as a landbridge. Many of the points raised by this mixed group of professionals echo those made in my previous discussion, as well as by my interviewees. As far as Afghanistan's weaknesses are concerned, many referred to the nature of its ethnic makeup in relation to Afghanistan's geographical position: most ethnic groups have larger groups of co-ethnics across the national borders. This situation is a cause of conflict between ethnic groups, and also paves the way for neighbours to interfere. The participants argued that this issue, as well as Afghanistan's history of conflict, has led to a lack of a sense of nationhood among certain ethnic groups.

Many issues were referred to as threats to Afghansiatan and to its position in South Asia: rivalries between India and Pakistan; the issue of Kashmir; Pakistan's strategic interest in a weak government in Afghanistan; the disputed issue of the Durand Line; competition between China and the US and China and India; the history of problems between Afghanistan and Pakistan; Pakistan's internal vulnerabilities (extremism, Talibanism, and lack of control in the Federally Administered Tribal Areas); nuclear weapons; and Pakistan's weak economy.

Regarding the threats in Central Asia, participants referred to Putin's Russia using the region as its sphere of influence in order to embark on rivalries with other powers; Russia and China not tolerating the presence of Western coalition forces in Central Asia and Afghanistan; the existence of authoritarian regimes in neighbouring countries; and extremist groups. Referring to the Middle East, participants highlighted the threat posed by Iranian and Saudi Arabian ideological rivalries, and the concern that they might use Afghanistan as a space to play out these rivalries.

The following recommendations were made on how to turn the threats into opportunities: a more active regional approach by Afghanistan; to not always look at Pakistan negatively, but as a potential friend; greater involvement with SAARC, SCO and other regional organisations; to actively exploit the potentials for oil and gas pipelines for Afghanistan's benefit; to exercise more concerted pressure on Pakistan by the international community regarding the sources of extremism and Talibanisation in Pakistan; to work on resolving the Durand line dispute; to review and modify religious school curricula in Pakistan.

To sum up, one could clearly notice that the workshop discussions fit this chapter's argument very well. Given all the problems raised by participants, as well as the difficulties in resolving them, the concept of Afghanistan as a landbridge can only materialise when Afghans start to unite and develop a strong sense of nationhood. Afghan statesmen should actively pursue foreign policies aimed at building confidence with neighbours and promoting interdependence, cooperation and regionalism with other nations. Further, neighbouring countries should follow suit, stop using extremism as a foreign policy instrument towards Afghanistan, and should cease to play out their rivalries on the Afghan soil.

Conclusion

The geographic location of Afghanistan has been both a blessing and a curse during the course of history. Situated at the point where four of the most densely-inhabited and resource-rich regions in the world meet—between South Asia, Central Asia, the Middle East and the Far East—it has been a civilisational, cultural, and commercial crossroad.

The emergence of Afghanistan as a free, stable, democratic and thriving nation will not only be a unique and unparalleled opportunity for the people of the region, but also for the entire world. Should there be a fundamental transformation of the country, there would be the potential for the first time in centuries of re-establishing strong economic ties that can extend across this vast region.

A regional market that is economically integrated would include nearly half the world's population, a sizeable share of the world's energy supplies, and would provide the basis for pursuing sustainable economic prosperity through closer cooperation. Afghanistan can play a greater fundamental role in the strengthening of the entire region. Successful political and economic transformation of the country after years of war, mayhem and neglect hinges very much upon stronger regional economic cooperation and integration. This is a distinctive opportunity that has the prospect of improving the economic conditions of billions in the region, and of providing greater security for all of the countries of the region and even the world (ANDS/JCMB Secretariat, 2006).

We have a long way to go in fulfilling the full economic potentials of this large region, which at one point was situated at the very centre of the world economy—as symbolised by the Silk Road, which served as the main trade link between Asia and Europe. It was as a result of these age-old trade and transport ties and the associated population movement that Afghanistan turned into a rich cultural, ethnic and linguistic mosaic.

Nonetheless, as Jalali (2006) argues, this country has always suffered from interference from and intrusion by countries in the region. In spite of the presence of international forces in the country and the commitment of the United States, United Kingdom, and NATO to defend the independence, territorial integrity, and sovereignty of Afghanistan, the country is still vulnerable to the influence of those neighbours who can either spoil or support Afghanistan's development.

Strengthening cooperation with neighbours with the vision of mutual benefit will have a significant impact on increasing the stability, peace, and prosperity of war-ravaged Afghanistan. For instance, the advancement of regional trade and cultural relations between the Central and South Asian countries, with Afghanistan as a landbridge, would be one way to do this. This will not only serve the common interests of the people in the region, but will also contribute to confidence-building, resolution of political issues, and easing of tensions. In this regard, Weinbaum (2006) argues that many of Afghanistan's challenges, often considered to be domestic, are also regional in nature, so should be addressed with regional strategies and collaboration. Policies that have sometimes been used to protect the country against intruding neighbours have deprived Afghanistan of the benefits of joining with neighbours to fight common threats and grasp new opportunities.

One can conclude from the viewpoints raised by most of the respondents in this research that it is only by pursuing neoliberal geopolitics and foreign policies that Afghanistan and its neighbours can ensure prosperity and development—not only of Afghanistan, but also its neighbours. This will be possible if Afghanistan and its neighbours focus on interdependence, mutual respect, cooperation, and regionalism—rather than egoistic, narrow-minded, and unilateralist self-interest, not realising that the cost of non-cooperation is always higher than that of cooperation. Afghanistan will become a landbridge if the economic interdependence that comes out in a regional open market provides its neighbours with a greater stake in the stability, prosperity, and development of this country.

9

THE RETURN OF THE REFUGEE WARRIOR

MIGRATION AND ARMED RESISTANCE IN HERAT[1]

Kristian Berg Harpviken

In October 2001, a coalition led by the United States launched an armed attack on Afghanistan's Taliban regime. Forces fighting for the coalition on the ground were almost exclusively Afghan. The vast majority were returning from exile, mainly from the neighbouring countries of Iran and Pakistan, but some from as far afield as Australia, Germany or the United States. In exile, they had been active in various military-political organisations, and many had been engaged in fighting in Afghanistan over the previous two and a half decades. As part of the 'War on Terror', the warriors returning from exile were equipped with money, weaponry, communications equipment, and access to intelligence and strategic advice. Perhaps most importantly, however, the returning warriors knew that this was an opportunity not to be missed: political power in Afghanistan was being reshuffled once again, and those who were part of the armed campaign were likely to benefit the most. Although rarely talked about as such, 'Operation Enduring Freedom' was a massive repatriation campaign, rooted in decades of political and military mobilisation among Afghan refugees.[2]

In this article, I will explore the interface between migration and wartime resistance by drawing on findings from fieldwork conducted in two villages in northwestern Afghanistan (Harpviken, 2009). Both of these villages—Izhaq Suleiman and Sara-e Nau—are located on the outskirts of Herat city, in Enjil district. Both have been heavily affected by successive rounds of armed conflict since 1978. Izhaq Suleiman, the dominant response of the population, as war escalated from 1978 onwards, was to ally with the Soviet-oriented regime of the People's Democratic Party of Afghanistan (PDPA), which they supplied with militia forces. In Sara-e Nau, the majority of the inhabitants joined the armed resistance, and the village became a target for the Kabul regime's military activities. The different choices made by the two villages had deep implications for their migration patterns, the degree of physical destruction they experienced, their relationships to later regimes, their chances of recovery, and—most importantly—the interplay between migration and armed engagement.[3]

Drawing on findings from my Herat fieldwork, I shall examine the role of exile-based warriors through four successive regimes: the PDPA (1978–92), the *mujahideen* (1992–95),[4] the Taliban (1995–2001), and the Karzai government (2001–present). First, however, I will briefly revisit the debate on refugee warriors. In conclusion, I will suggest a few implications both for the study of Afghanistan's wars and for the theorisation of returnee warriorhood.

The debate on refugee warriors

The term 'refugee warrior' was first coined by Astri Suhrke in the mid-1980s: it was inspired by the politicisation and armed organisation that she witnessed while visiting Afghan refugee camps in Pakistan.[5] The concept was introduced through the collaborative work of Aristide Zolberg, Astri Suhrke and Sergio Aguayo, in particular in their book *Escape from Violence: Conflict and the Refugee Crisis in the Developing World* (Zolberg et al., 1989; Zolberg, et al., 1986: 151–69). Since then, the Afghan refugee situation has served as the archetype of refugee warriorhood. Challenging the conventional understanding of refugees as victims, the concept of the refugee warrior emphasises the agency of refugees—their ability, despite severe constraints, to choose and act—even holding a capacity for violent action. The term brought attention to an important, yet previously neglected, aspect of displacement. Zolberg *et al.* (1989: 275) define refugee warrior communities as 'highly conscious [...] with a political leadership structure and armed sections engaged in warfare for a political objective, be it to recapture the homeland, change the regime, or secure a separate state'.

Convinced that refugee warriorism is on the rise, Zolberg *et al.* locate the root cause of the phenomenon in a process of globalisation, in which political and economic inequality are becoming increasingly evident. Driven from their homes by repressive political regimes, radical groups launch armed struggles to gain political power in their state of origin. In these efforts, the support of other states—host countries and great powers—plays a crucial role. While such alliances between states and opposition groups based in exile are nothing new, they have grown more important in the post-World War II era for two reasons. The first is the evolution of an 'international refugee regime that can sustain large-scale civilian populations in exile for years' (Zolberg *et al.*, 1989: 277). Second, what the authors refer to as the 'dominant ideology of democratic nationalism' implies that the existence of a civilian refugee population yields crucial legitimacy to exile-based opposition groups, and by extension, to their supporters.

After the initial introduction of the concept, virtually no work was conducted on refugee warriors for more than a decade.[6] In the first five years of the new millennium, however, a new spate of work on refugee warrior phenomena emerged, including books by Fiona Terry (2002) and Sarah Kenyon Lischer (2005), and an anthology edited by Stephen John Stedman and Fred Tanner (2003). All of these are framed within a wider debate on humanitarianism, in large part inspired by the realisation that the refugee regime sustained Rwanda's war perpetrators in the mid-1990s. Fiona Terry focuses on how militarised groups are assisted in misusing 'humanitarian sanctuaries', which allow militants to hide and permit them a degree of independence, since they are able to live on humanitarian assistance. Sarah Kenyon Lischer takes a broader analytical perspective, comparing the contribution of refugee relief with other factors, including the supportive role of both the host state and other states. For Lischer, the main factor that distinguishes refugee populations that produce violence from those that do not is the supportive role of states. In the conclusion to the volume co-edited with Tanner, Stedman notes two pathways to refugee mobilisation. In some cases, such as Afghanistan during the Cold War, state support would breed mobilisation regardless of the refugee regime. In other cases, such as Rwanda in the mid-1990s, humanitarian naivety was sufficient to enable militants to mobilise successfully.

An alternative approach to refugee warriorism emphasises culture—often referred to as 'ideological factors'. This approach has had negligible influence within the international debate on refugee warriors, but has had its proponents in studies of Afghan refugees (see Guillo *et al.*, 1983; Shahrani, 1995). Here, the starting hypothesis is that migration takes place in accordance with the religious imperative of *hijra*, replicating the Prophet's flight from Mecca to Medina in protest against a ruler who lacked legitimacy in the eyes of God.[7] With a focus on internal legitimisation in the Afghan resistance, Shahrani has argued that religious institutions such as Jihad and *hijra* have played a key role in motivating and directing flight (Shahrani, 1995). Jihad refers to religious struggle, with resistance as one avenue of action; *hijra* refers to religiously motivated flight, modelled on the narrative of Mohammad's flight to Medina (cf. Edwards, 1986). In Shahrani's account, the two are mutually reinforcing, providing a religious justification for a violent response to being driven out by infidels.

Eight years after the Prophet's original departure, Mecca fell to the community of 'refugee warriors' returning from Medina. And, like the first Muslims, argues Shahrani (Shahrani, 1995), Afghan refugees have proven reluctant to distinguish between the decision to flee and the obligation to resist oppression. As in the original narrative, return is an integral part of the religious obligation. The Prophet and his followers, notably, returned as warriors, overthrowing the sitting regime and establishing a legitimate government. Both in the original narrative and in Afghanistan in recent times, this obligation is rooted in the maintenance—even cultivation—of a collective during the time in exile. Indeed, the refugees from Mecca cut all ties with those who did not join the flight, establishing tight bonds with the host population, and forming a new community that would constitute the nucleus of the *Ummah*, the community of Muslims. In general terms, however, ideologies formed in settings that are fairly insulated from the situation in the state of origin, and that are not moulded in the everyday interaction with political opponents, may become particularly inflexible. In the extreme, therefore, they may prevent reconciliation and promote further violent conflict. Such incompatibility of worldviews may be particularly strong in the aftermath of prolonged (or, as in the Palestinian case, multi-generational) exile.

A third approach to the explanation of refugee warriorism emphasises the networks and institutions on which armed organisations are based.[8] In contrast to other conceptualisations of *hijra*, Guillo *et al.* (1983) emphasise not only the religious duty to escape from an infidel regime, but also how the flight is organised collectively, under a traditional leader who activates established networks (see also Grevemeyer, 1988). Social institutions—such as schools, religious congregations or community assemblies—can serve as platforms for political mobilisation. In the study of refugee warriors, there is considerable agreement that camp-settled refugees are more likely to be politically mobilised than self-settled ones (Malkki, 1995). Lischer (2005: 145), for example, suggests that integration in the host country prevents military engagement. By contrast, my own work on Afghans in Iran suggests that a significant degree of military engagement, including host-state support, is possible also among self-settled refugees.[9] Another type of institution that has proved particularly important in the Afghan case is the centre of Islamic learning, the *madrassa*. A massive expansion of the system of *madrassas* in Pakistan transformed them into primary centres for ideological training and recruitment. A large share of the recruits were from the Afghan refugee population. The *madrassas* in Pakistan formed the backbone of the resistance parties in the 1980s, as they did for the Taliban in the 1990s (Dorronsoro, 2005; Harpviken, 1997).

The potential for violent refugee mobilisation has increasingly been recognised by policymakers and practitioners—a realisation which has developed slowly since the 1989 publication of *Escape from Violence* (Zolberg, *et al.*, 1989). However, the implications of refugee warriorism for the reintegration of refugees have not been spelled out. A comprehensive reading of the post-2001 Afghanistan literature on firstly the reintegration of refugees, and secondly the disarmament, demobilisation and reintegration of fighters, reveals no cross-references.[10] Yet, there are strong linkages between the reintegration of returnees, on the one hand, and the demobilisation and reintegration of fighters, on the other. A proportion of returnees will be (current or former) fighters, and, *vice versa*, a proportion of the fighters will be found among the refugees. Nonetheless, it is common to distinguish sharply between fighters and returning refugees. The two are seen as distinct rather than overlapping groups, and the return of refugees, who are all assumed to be 'civilians', is seen to signify a successful peace process.

However, Adelman (2002) has examined the assumption that refugee return is a condition for—or at least a significant indicator of—a viable peace process, and finds that there is no relationship between the two. More dramatically, rapid return may even threaten the viability of peace if returning refugees are actually fighters or are mobilised as fighters. In such a case, the returnees themselves may represent a security threat, and hence undermine a peace process.[11] There is an understandable reluctance to realise that the same person may thus be a returning refugee and a fighter—both victim and perpetrator. The 'refugee warrior' debate has yet to inform the analysis of reintegration. Nonetheless, there is every reason to assume that there is continuity between the exile and the situation upon return: in state sponsorships, in modes of thinking and organisational capacities, and in the courses of action that people collectively pursue.

The PDPA era (1978–1992)

The defection of several thousand soldiers from the 17th Army Division in Herat in March 1979, led by Ismail Khan, then a Senior Captain, was the first major military defeat of Babrak Karmal's PDPA regime. It came about as a reaction to the government's call for local army units to help enforce enrolment in its literacy programme. During the mutiny, a number of PDPA leaders and Soviet advisers were killed. A massive combined air and ground attack by government forces then brought Herat city back under the PDPA's control, with estimates of civilian losses ranging from 5,000 upwards (Roy, 1986: 108). The western part of Enjil was the main scene of fighting in the Herat region. By the early 1980s, both Izhaq Suleman and Sara-e Nau found themselves in a heavily mined and guarded security belt surrounding Herat city. The first village became a 'militia village', providing forces for the government's defence

Figure 1: Location of Izhaq Suleman and Sara-e Nau villages in relation to Herat city.

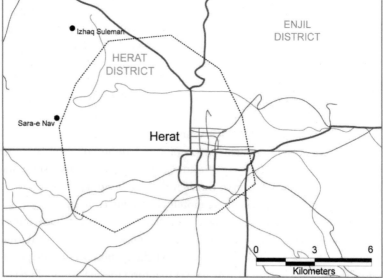

of Herat, although parts of the population joined various *mujahideen* groups. The second village sided with the *mujahideen*. Lines were blurred: families of Sara-e Nau *mujahideen* sought refuge in Izhaq Suleman; members of the militia facilitated access for *mujahideen* incursions in Herat city. The one village was virtually depopulated in the course of the 1980s, while the other remained vibrant.

As many as half of the people I interviewed who had been in exile reported that they had been somehow associated with the *mujahideen*.[12] Not surprisingly among respondents with an exile background, there were fewer *mujahideen* associates in Izhaq Suleman than was the case for Sara-e Nau. Approximately one-third of the heads of households in Sara-e Nau had taken an active part in the armed struggle, and reported that they had spent from six to ten months every year hidden somewhere in the vicinity of the village. All of these had families living in the same neighbourhood in the Iranian city of Mashhad, the nearest major city to the Afghan border, a day's journey by car from Herat. While all maintained links with a variety of parties, they had been fighting under a local commander affiliated to the *Hezb-e Islami* party (led by Younos Khales). The village-based group catered to people of varying ethnic and religious origin, and included both Shi'a and Sunni. Members of the Sara-e Nau *mujahideen* went into exile at various times between 1980 and 1983. The group shifted from *Hezb-e Islami* (Khales) to Ismail Khan and the *Jamiat-e Islami* party in the mid-1980s, though it continued to operate under the same structure and with the same commander.

Habibullah[13] was the head of a household that consisted of some forty people at the start of the war. Constrained by the costs of taking so many people abroad, as well as by concerns related to their housing and land, they were late leavers. Six members of his household fought with the *mujahideen*, both prior to departure and after having settled in Mashhad. Habibullah reflects upon Iran's ambiguous stance as a host country for refugee warriors:

Iran did not give us weapons. When we had an injured soldier and brought him to the border, we had to contact our office in Tehran to get the documents—it could take two to three days. When papers were arranged, we were not allowed to accompany him, but had to leave the injured person with party people in Iran.

The commander of the Sara-e Nau group was among the first to leave the village in 1980, leading a group of twelve families, all relatives. This group travelled straight to Khwaja Rabi in Mashhad, where they received a 'blue card' after six months, which provided access to subsidised food, education and health services. With the family group in safety, the commander spent the major part of each year in Afghanistan, joined by an increasing number of relatives and fellow villagers. Most members of this group returned within weeks of the *mujahideen* takeover in 1992, the commander returning with basically the same set of people that he had left with twelve years earlier.

From Izhaq Suleman, several respondents—all members of the same family line—spent the years from 1984 to 1992 together in Taybad, on the Iranian side of the border with Afghanistan. Most of them had originally fought for commander Safiullah Afzali, who was Ismail Khan's main rival in the Herat region (although both men were associated with the same party, *Jamiat-e Islami*). Upon Safiullah's death in 1986, the *mujahideen* from Izhaq Suleman were reconciled with Ismail Khan. All of the respondents from this network reported a similar pattern—whereby they stayed three months at the front in Afghanistan, then three months in Iran, before returning to Afghanistan to begin the cycle anew. During the periods in Iran, they worked to gather money for the household. At the same time, however, they all reported enjoying a much higher level of support in terms of food, education and health services than did refugees who were not active in the resistance. On this issue, the accounts given by respondents from this particular network were rather consistent, and were generally supported by data from other interviews. Although this cannot be used as the basis for any firm conclusions, it does suggest that Iran actively supported resistance groups operating from its soil, which challenges the common assumption that Iran's need to maintain cordial relations with the Soviet Union prevented it from actively supporting *mujahideen* movements (cf. Grare, 2003; Saikal, 1989).

Individuals' engagement with the *mujahideen* during exile is reflected in where people settled in Iran. The earlier people left, the more likely they were to settle in Khorasan province, which gives relatively easy access by being close to the Afghan border. Those who were active with the *mujahideen* chose Mashhad, the capital of Khorasan, which served as a hub of the Afghan resistance, as their first destination. Thus, people from Sara-e Nau, a *mujahideen* village, often spent their exile in Khorasan, whereas this was rarely the case for people from Izhaq Suleman, a militia village where a smaller share of those leaving, even at the early stages, joined the resistance. By contrast, later in the 1990s, during the reign of the *mujahideen* and the Taliban, refugees seem to have given higher priority to employment opportunities, which were far better in main cities like Tehran and Isfahan than in Mashhad.

Iran served as a base for armed resistance in Afghanistan during the 1980s, but in a manner very different from Pakistan. In Pakistan, the government stood unanimously behind the resistance, and cooperated strongly with a variety of states and international organisations in providing political, military and humanitarian support. Iran, preoccupied with its war with Iraq, took a much more ambiguous stance, largely because it did not want to upset its relationship with the Soviet Union; but also because, unlike Pakistan, it could not draw on Saudi or US support. This did not prevent various resistance organisations from operating out of Iran, but they enjoyed far less support and freedom of movement than those operating in Pakistan. This frustrated resistance leaders in western Afghanistan considerably, and was seen as a major constraint on the effectiveness of the resistance in the area bordering Iran (see Wannell, 1991). Several armed organisations with ambiguous identities, shifting between the militia and *mujahideen* (e.g. the Hezbollah group operating from Jibrail in Enjil district), received considerable support in Iran. For the Iranian government during the 1980s, engaged as it was in an all-out war with Iraq, the main aims of its refugee policy were to capitalise on Afghan labour and build organisations with which it could work in the future, while avoiding upsetting the Soviet Union and risking an additional war on its eastern front. After the end of the Iran–Iraq war in 1988, Iran developed a more active policy, and the country broadened its set of partners to include virtually all non-Pashtun groups.

The constraints placed on Afghan refugees by the Iranian government kept in check the emergence of new Afghan leaders (with some exceptions among the Shi'a); whereas in Pakistan a system was set up that provided all sorts of support to the resistance and the refugees, creating ideal opportunities for refugee entrepreneurs. Iran relied more on traditional leaders and their cohesive networks as a way to keep refugee involvement in the Afghan war as inconspicuous as possible;[14] while in Pakistan, traditional leaders were often replaced by new ones who proved more competent in liaising with Pakistani and international providers of humanitarian and military support. Among refugees in Iran, it seems that those who were associated with the *mujahideen* prior to flight had a relatively clear idea of their destination, and their lives in exile were characterised by stable and cohesive networks. Those engaged with the *mujahideen* also remained well informed about the situation in their areas of origin, since, almost without exception, this was where they fought.

The Mujahideen *government (1992–1995)*

Members of a refugee population who are associated with political or military parties will have a stronger incentive than others to return quickly if there is a regime change in the home country that benefits their party. It is in the early days of a new regime that the best prizes may be won—such as state jobs, political influence, and economic contracts and opportunities. Despite the vast debate on refugee warrior communities, however, little attention has been paid to the effect that rapid repatriation of militarily active refugees may have on political transitions. One prominent voice in the recent 'refugee warrior' debate is concerned that the current international preference for repatriation (over integration or third-country resettlement) fosters more long-term refugee populations that are susceptible to political and military mobilisation (Lischer, 2005: 150–1). The literature on refugee mobilisation, however, pays less attention to the political risks inherent in repatriation, particularly in the context of regime change—such as in Afghanistan in 1992 and 2001.

In the wake of the fall of the Najibullah government in 1992, Ismail Khan's authority in the communities of western Enjil, as in most of Herat province, was virtually indisputable (Giustozzi, 2003: 12). In his core areas, Ismail Khan was the sovereign ruler, whereas in other areas nominally under his authority he depended on alliances with local commanders. There could be tension and conflict over resources and power at the community level; but the fact that there was no real contender for authority at the regional level constrained such local conflicts.

In Enjil, those who had been active in the *mujahideen* parties throughout the war were the first to return after the fall of Najibullah in 1992. In fact, all the respondents who had such a background returned during 1992 and 1993. When asked about the primary reason for returning at this time, almost all identified it as the regime change, using expressions such as the 'victory of the *mujahideen*', 'Ismail Khan was in power' and 'the fall of the communist regime'. By contrast, respondents who had returned later mainly referred to Iranian pressure. The fact that an overwhelming majority of those who returned in 1992 and 1993 said they had done so because of the regime change indicates a strong degree of association with the *mujahideen*. Importantly, in 1992, many Afghans, particularly those in exile, still had confidence in the *mujahideen* leadership. Two to three years later, incompetence and massive fighting between various resistance parties and groups had done severe damage to the reputation of the *mujahideen*, though less so in Herat than in most other places.

In Sara-e Nau, there was only a marginal population that could be considered resident by 1992, all of whom had been displaced for shorter periods during the 1980s. There was little controversy when, in 1992, returning *muja-*

hideen filled the position of *arbab* (village chieftain) and took on a dominant role within the village *shura* (community council): the main *mujahideen* commander from Sara-e Nau, who had been associated with various groups throughout the war but had most recently been a confidant of Ismail Khan, occupied the position of *arbab*, and the *shura* was filled with his close associates. Those who had been internally displaced to Izhaq Suleman were perceived as 'neutral' rather than supportive of the PDPA government, even though some of them had been called on for militia duty. More importantly, the internally displaced did not lay claims to power, but subordinated themselves to the *mujahideen* structure, which was brought home wholesale from exile.

In Izhaq Suleman, too, a majority of the returnees in 1992 and 1993 were *mujahideen*, while the remainder were also in some way associated with them. Those who had been associated with the militia, however, maintained considerable influence within community decision-making—a situation that was possibly facilitated by the killing of their most controversial figure, the militia commander Arbab Saidu, in 1991. In the words of one *mujahideen* commander: 'The relation between the villagers and the government was very good. Arbab Sayed Mohammad [Arbab Saidu], from this village, was with the government, but he also had good relations with the *mujahideen*.' The contact maintained between militia and *mujahideen* during the period that they were officially at war with each other continued after the conflict, laying the foundations for an informal division of power in the *mujahideen* era. While the *mujahideen* had the upper hand in this relationship, several people who had been active with the militia remained influential.

Mujahideen associates from Sara-e Nau all returned within the first few months after Najibullah's fall; whereas in Izhaq Suleman many chose to stay another year in exile before returning. If survival and the local economy had been principal concerns, one would expect the pattern to be the opposite: Sara-e Nau had been virtually demolished, whereas Izhaq Suleman was largely intact. From a security perspective, one can understand that some of the Izhaq Suleman *mujahideen* preferred to wait and see whether a new power balance would develop between the local militia and the returning refugees. The first *mujahideen* to return to the village seem to have had the double advantage of being both well connected to Ismail Khan and on good terms with the local militia. Others, particularly those who were more uncertain regarding their status with the militia, were less eager to be at the forefront in the early—and highly uncertain—days.

It has been established that the *mujahideen* parties had sufficient influence to prevent refugees from returning during the late 1980s, at least from Pakistan (Rizvi, 1990), seeing repatriation as contrary to their political interests. Being able to motivate massive repatriation in the aftermath of a regime change would represent the opposite side of this coin. There was an implicit promise that loyalty to *mujahideen* groups would be rewarded in a future political setup. It has proven difficult to establish, however, the extent to which *mujahideen* parties were directly involved in the organisation of mass repatriation from Iran or Pakistan. There are claims within some reports by humanitarian agencies that such involvement can be established (Jamal and Stigter, 2002; Marsden, 1999), but I have found no substantial description of the phenomenon in the literature. From my own empirical material, it is clear—not surprisingly—that various political parties were active in securing the quickest possible return of key cadre, including local-level commanders. Rank-and-file associates, however, seem to have been encouraged to return only indirectly—by individual commanders and other influential individuals seeking to ensure that as many as possible of their followers returned with them. Fundamentally, the networks on which 'returnee warriors' are based seem remarkably consistent with those that were at work during exile.

The rule of the Taliban (1995–2001)

Following the Taliban's seizure of power in Herat in 1995, Iran continued to work with armed Afghan opposition groups. A descendant of one of the *mujahideen* that had been resident in Taybad, Iran, during the 1980s was enrolled with Ismail Khan's forces in Iran at the very end of 1999, soon after my first interview with him. In December 2002, he said:

After you were here the last time, I went to Iran for some time. I was captured in my house, the Taliban said that you are with the *mujahideen*, they kept me in jail for nine to ten days, then I paid some money to be released, and I left for Iran. I came back three to four months before the fall of the Taliban, having spent six months in Mashhad as a labourer. When I came back, I went to Mazar [with Ismail Khan]; we were ready to attack the Taliban. Also here in Herat, there were people who were ready to attack the Taliban at that same time. I am now working with the military.

This indicates that Iran continued (and became more open about) its support to armed opposition groups during the 1990s. It also shows how the 'exile warrior' engagement is inherited from one generation to the next (the father was incapable of fighting due to a war injury), and that such engagement may pay off eventually in the form of jobs within the new administration.

With the coming to power of the Taliban in 1995, advantages enjoyed by individuals with a *mujahideen* background turned into disadvantages. The Taliban were extremely suspicious of anyone with a *mujahideen* past, though less suspicious of those who had been associated with the so-called communist government. The Taliban acted pragmatically, often allowing former PDPA associates—since these posed no organised threat—to retain their positions within the administration and the army, as well as local power positions (such as *arbab* posts). Known *mujahideen*, by contrast, were often stripped of their positions and kept under continuous scrutiny, since they were assumed to be plotting an armed uprising. Accordingly, those who had enjoyed the largest benefits when returning in 1992 were the hardest hit by the Taliban take-over in 1995. Owing to the risk of persecution, most *mujahideen* supporters tried to keep a low profile, and some departed for the relative safety of Iran. Towards the end of the 1990s, as Iran–Taliban relations turned increasingly sour, Iran actively encouraged and supported the build-up of military capacity in exile.

The Taliban had reason to be suspicious. Following the Taliban's takeover of Herat in September 1995, Ismail Khan and many of his men again escaped to Iran, where they were once more given refuge. Since Iran had become more active in arming the *mujahideen* than it had been during the 1980s, it established several training camps in the Mashhad area, with some sources claiming that Ismail Khan alone had five camps, together with a total of some 5,000 fighters (Griffin, 2001: 80; Rasanayagam, 2003: 169).

In October 1996, Ismail Khan and 2,000 of his fighters were flown from Iran to Mazar-i-Sharif in Afghanistan's central north, to reinforce Abdul Rashid Dostum's forces, who were continuing the fight against the Taliban. Some of my informants were among the forces airlifted to Mazar, having previously been trained and equipped in Iran. The Mazar operation ended badly for Ismail Khan, however: in May 1997 he was arrested and handed over to the Taliban by Abdul Malik, a subcommander of Dostum who swapped sides. Ismail Khan was immediately taken to Kandahar, where he spent the next three years in a Taliban prison, from which he mysteriously escaped in early 2000.

The residents of Sara-e Nau, who had benefited from their loyalty to the *mujahideen* during Ismail Khan's first period of rule (1992–95), quickly discovered that the situation had changed when the Taliban came to power.

Overnight, they were at a disadvantage. By 1999, the *mujahideen*-associated *arbab* had to resign, and a new one—from a family considered to have been neutral during the PDPA era—took over the post. The composition of the *shura* also changed. Although there was no permanent Taliban presence in the village, patrols occasionally visited to ask questions or to search for specific people. A couple of persons who had been with the PDPA in the 1980s, and had later joined the Taliban in Herat, also visited regularly. These had considerable influence on local decisions, though they did not hold formal positions. On a couple of occasions when I was present, one of these men, an employee of the much-feared Taliban intelligence service in Herat, gate-crashed *shura* meetings in Sara-e Nau, creating a rather nervous atmosphere. There was none of the normally quite open debate, and the only decisions taken were those dictated by the unwelcome, but well-treated, guest.

With its past as a militia rather than a *mujahideen* village, Izhaq Suleman fared somewhat better under the Taliban. However, here, too, people known to have been associated with the *mujahideen* were considered a threat by the Taliban, who—if unable to find the suspected individual—would hold relatives, *shura* members or local *mullahs* responsible. A majority of those who had been connected to the *mujahideen* were at some stage traced down and arrested by the Taliban. During an interview conducted in 1999, one man from Izhaq Suleman told the story of his brother, who was then in Iran:

> Now he cannot come back to visit here. He was with the *mujahideen*, then for some time with the Taliban; but then they [the Taliban] suspected him of hiding some arms, and he had to flee to Iran. I myself was put in prison for a month, as they tried to get information from me about my brother. Then they let me out.

None of the residents in Izhaq Suleman supported the Taliban; although when the Taliban pressured some of the village leaders—first and foremost the *mullahs*—to monitor events and to assist with administrative tasks, such as tax collection, the latter adapted to the demands of the new regime as far as it was deemed necessary. In many ways, this was reminiscent of how the local community had dealt with the PDPA regime in the past, although the collaboration with the Taliban was much more limited and did not include military engagement. A handful of locals strengthened their own power considerably through the new arrangements, serving as useful links to the troublesome rulers and invoking the Taliban's authority when acting on their behalf—a classic broker role not unlike that commonly performed by the *arbab*.

The US-led intervention and the Karzai regime (2001–present)

The 2001 regime change in Herat resembled the one that took place in 1992, in that the force spearheading the takeover had largely been built up in exile. However, a significant difference in 2001 was that most members of the returnee force had a firm family presence in the area. Ismail Khan was well prepared for the post-11 September 2001 campaign, having taken most of his exile troops to the inaccessible Ghor province, whence he could drive the Taliban out of northwestern Afghanistan in the wake of the US-led intervention. Once Ismail Khan was back in the vicinity of Herat, 'his armed forces swelled to many thousands', according to Antonio Giustozzi (Giustozzi, 2003: 13),[15] who suggests that Ismail Khan was in command of the largest armed force in Afghanistan during 2002. Combining Iranian support with customs revenue from Afghanistan's main border post, Ismail Khan was able to pay his soldiers generously, securing loyalty and discipline in return. Ismail Khan's organisation brought together an odd amalgam of various solidary groups, which were placed within a hierarchic structure.

In Sara-e Nau, the removal of the Taliban led to a major reshuffle in the *shura*, with people who had stayed in the area during the war, and who had been considered 'neutral' by the Taliban, being replaced by *mujahideen* associates who had spent a long time in Iran. At this time, the position of *arbab* was held by a man who had spent the whole war in the area, some of it in Izhaq Suleman. He had been appointed to this post by the Taliban in 1999 as a replacement for the main *mujahideen* commander in the village. Seeking to pre-empt a reversed *arbab* shuffle now that Ismail Khan was back in control, the incumbent *arbab* put forward a younger relative of his as a candidate for his replacement. This was accepted both by the local *shura* and by the Herat authorities. The old *mujahideen* network, however, continued to make itself felt, and, in late 2003, some thirty men from the village held military positions in Herat, most of them within Ismail Khan's personal guard at the governor's house.

In Izhaq Suleman, the changes in local power relations after the fall of the Taliban were less dramatic. There was some reshuffling of *shura* membership, but the *arbab*, whose family had always cleverly balanced between political groups, remained in his post. As in Sara-e Nau, those who were with the *mujahideen* were enrolled in Ismail Khan's new security apparatus, but in Izhaq Suleman they constituted only a small share of the population.

The 2001 fall of the Taliban had an effect similar to Najib's 1992 abdication in encouraging a rapid repatriation of *mujahideen* from Iran. Much, however, was different. For one thing, many of the Iran-based *mujahideen* were return-ing as part of 'Operation Enduring Freedom', the US-led campaign that ousted the Taliban. Some of my local informants, for example, had been fighting in Herat or elsewhere and had been brought into Afghanistan via Turkmenistan and Uzbekistan. Second, the post-11 September 2001 *mujahideen* returnees were more of an elite than those who returned in 1992–93. Finally, those who returned in 2002 came back to societies with a changed and functioning eco-nomic and administrative structure, and had to find their roles within the new structure rather than define its shape. Nonetheless, by 2002, Herat's political and administrative elite was dominated by recent returnees.

Conclusion

Afghanistan has come to serve as the archetype of refugee mobilisation. Nonetheless, important aspects of refugee warriorhood have received only scant attention, and have at times been misrepresented. For one, Iran has facilitated refugee mobilisation from the early 1980s and at least until 2001, although in a less conspicuous manner than Pakistan. How, and by whom, this has been done on the Iranian side are questions that remain largely unan-swered.[16] There is also the issue of the extent to which resistance groups have actively encouraged and organised flight in order to reinforce themselves in exile. There are singular accounts from refugees to both Iran and Pakistan that '*mujahideen*' groups organised flight, but little is known about the scale of such efforts.

Most importantly, there is the insight that refugees associated with resist-ance groups are early returners, while those lacking such contacts prefer to delay. This has implications for the conflict potential in the aftermath of a regime change, as members of militant organisations may be overrepresented among early returnees. It also has implications for late returnees, who lack the sense of protection that stems from being a member of a resistance group and may be more vulnerable than early returnees, particularly when the state is unable to offer protection. It is high time that the 'refugee warrior' agenda is expanded to include return challenges. Researchers need to look beyond the stovepiped organisation characteristic of peace implementation, whereby some agencies deal with disarmament, demobilisation and reintegration (DDR), while others deal with refugee reintegration. As a first step, we need to understand when, and under what conditions, refugees and other migrants become engaged in organised violence upon return.

Theoretically, the research programme that is emerging is a challenging one. Future studies will need to develop means by which to understand the sequencing of refugee mobilisation.[17] The assumption that refugees are only mobilised once they are in exile needs to be complemented with the alternative option that they are encouraged to flee as an integral part of a mobilisation drive. Also, as argued above, the emphasis on the state, the refugee regime and cultural repertoires needs to be complemented by a focus on organisational processes. How, for example, do pre-existing networks inform mobilisation, and how are such networks transformed in the process (Tilly and Tarrow, 2007)? And how do armed groups maintain coherence when different members are spread across numerous locations (and countries)? An emphasis on the organisational needs to build upon, and incorporate, insights gained through the structural and cultural perspectives. Which organisational forms win out, for example, depends heavily on the actions pursued by states and humanitarian agencies. Likewise, cultural repertoires, such as a call for religious leadership in times of crisis, are important for organisational outcomes. The Afghan case, relatively well documented and with considerable internal variation, offers fertile ground for future studies of refugee—as well as returnee—warriorhood.

SECTION III

A TRANSNATIONAL AFGHAN COMMUNITY?

SECTION III

ARBANASI: A CREATIVE COMMUNITY

10

THE AFGHAN DIASPORA AND ITS INVOLVEMENT IN THE RECONSTRUCTION OF AFGHANISTAN[1]

Ceri Oeppen

Over the last thirty years, millions of Afghans have left Afghanistan. Whilst some might expect that the traumatic nature of refugee flight means that refugees are likely to break links with their country of origin (see for example Waldinger, 2007), it is now increasingly accepted that refugees do not break all ties with their country of origin, simply because they have physically left, or because they have traumatic memories of that country (see Al-Ali *et al.*, 2001; Horst, 2006; Koser, 2007). Improved transport and communication technologies enable refugees (and other migrants) to maintain and even expand ties without relying on geographical proximity. These transnational ties are often characterised by social connections—for example, transfer of information, money or goods between family members; but they may also be political, economic, cultural or religious. A growing awareness of these ties—particularly that money sent by migrants through recorded channels now exceeds official global development assistance (Ratha, 2007)—has led to an increased interest amongst donor governments, aid agencies and academics in the role that the transnational ties of these migrants and refugees could play in the context of development and reconstruction. Monies sent by migrants to family members left in the country of origin (remittances) are the most easily quantifiable way in which migrants and refugees may be involved in development and reconstruction. Other ways include: the transnational transfer of ideas and knowledge, sometimes called social remittances (Levitt, 1998); political lobbying and awareness-raising in host countries; group fundraising and organisation of development projects, as apparent in the migrant home-town associations of many Latin American and African countries; business investment; and trade in 'ethnic' products such as music recordings (see Baily, this volume) and foodstuffs.

The academic idea of 'transnationalism' is a flexible concept, and its breadth and depth are subject to extensive debate in the social sciences. To summarise, Steven Vertovec (1999: 447) suggests that 'most social scientists working in the field [of migration studies] may agree that 'transnationalism' broadly refers to multiple ties and interactions linking people or institutions across the borders of nation-states'. These ties may be symbolic or material, institutionalised or non-institutionalised, or most likely, a mixture.

Awareness of these transnational links between migrants, refugees and their countries of origin, and with each other, has also led to a revived interest in the idea of diaspora. The word 'diaspora' derives from the Greek for being scattered or dispersed (Van Hear, 1998: 5), and has developed a particular social meaning associated with the traumatic dispersal of people: it traditionally refers to the scattering of the Jewish population before the creation of Israel especially, and to some extent to that of the descendents of African slaves in the Americas. Increasingly, however, it is being used as a 'catch-all term' for any migrant or refugee population outside their country of origin. There is significant literature debating the definition and usage of the term diaspora (see for example Clifford, 1994; Cohen, 1997; Safran, 1991), but it is beyond the scope of this chapter to explore the subject in detail, except to note that 'diaspora' is arguably an appropriate term to describe Afghans living outside Afghanistan.

Here the term 'diaspora' is used to refer simply to Afghans living outside of Afghanistan. However, it is worth stressing that 'the diaspora' can never be considered a homogenous 'community' with identical goals and practices. It cannot be assumed that Afghan-Americans, for example, speak for the whole Afghan diaspora when they put forward their views on 'solutions' to Afghanistan's problems: various situations and experiences before and during exile will have differing impacts on people's outlooks. In particular, there may be significant differences between what Van Hear (2003) terms the 'wider diaspora', which in the Afghan case refers to Afghans living in Europe, North America, Australia and New Zealand; and the near diaspora—Afghans living in the neighbouring countries of Pakistan and Iran in particular, but also India and Central Asia. The Middle Eastern region, a destination for Afghan labour migrants, could be considered another category, being neither 'the West', nor within the Central and South Asian region.

There were estimated to be more than five million Afghans living outside of Afghanistan at the end of the twentieth century.[2] Figure 2 indicates the key host countries for the Afghan diaspora: in the near diaspora, Pakistan and Iran; in the wider diaspora, the United States of America, Germany, the Netherlands, Canada, the United Kingdom and Australia, and much of the Middle East—in particular Jordan, Lebanon and the United Arab Emirates.

After the United States (US)-led coalition attacks on Afghanistan in the aftermath of 11 September 2001, donor governments and aid agencies hoped that some members of the Afghan diaspora would become involved in post-conflict reconstruction. On a practical level, their Afghan language skills and cultural knowledge could smooth the way for operations within Afghanistan. On a more symbolic level, some diaspora members' experience and knowledge of donor country norms and politics—in particular the politics of democracy and secularism—led to the hope that diaspora members could be 'bridges' (Shain and Barth, 2003: 450) between donor countries and Afghanistan, helping to implement the goals of the US-led coalition in a culturally sensitive way. Diaspora members can also be an important information source to donor countries, and are often easier to consult with than those inside the post-conflict country. Consequently, they often have a role to play in post-conflict strategic planning. Jazayery (2002) points out that three-quarters of the Afghans involved in the United Nations (UN) sponsored talks on the future of Afghanistan, held in Bonn, Germany in December 2001 were exiles. It is no coincidence that the coalition-backed Afghan Interim Authority formed after the 2001 fall of the Taliban was made up mainly of Afghan diaspora members—including Hamid Karzai, the chair of the interim and transitional authorities and subsequent President of Afghanistan, who had spent much of his life in India, Pakistan and the US. Arguably, these were people donor governments felt more comfortable dealing with.

As in many post-conflict situations, donor countries are also host countries for Afghan refugees and exiles. In such cases, the rhetoric of post-conflict reconstruction is often heavily entangled with the goal of returning refugees for domestic political reasons and of highlighting refugee return as an indica-

Figure 2: The Afghan diaspora, with key populations marked in thousands

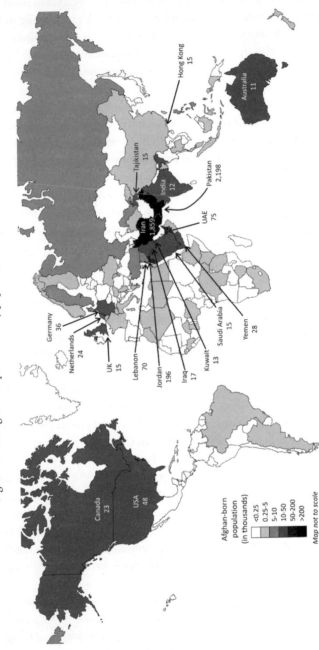

Data are for Afghan-born, based on year 2000 census rounds, as collated in the Global Migrant Origin Database Version 4 (Migration DRC, 2007). Except. data for Pakistan, Tajikistan, India, Uzbekistan and Turkmenistan, which is from UNHC data on Afghan refugee populations, end of 2001 (UMHCR, 2001).

tion of successful peace-building and reconstruction efforts (Black, 2001; Helton, 2002; Turton and Marsden, 2002a). This is problematic when, as Turton and Marsden (2002a) argue, Afghanistan does not have the capacity to absorb large numbers of refugee returnees (see also Rogge, 1994).

One type of return where the potential of the diaspora to contribute to post-conflict reconstruction is more obvious, though not necessarily less problematic, is that of human capital, or 'reverse brain drain' (Nassery, 2003). The return of skilled Afghan professionals has been promoted by donor governments, as the following statement from the Swedish Government's assistance strategy for Afghanistan illustrates (Ministry of Foreign Affairs/Sida, 2002: 15):

Swedish support should pay particular attention to initiatives focussing on the repatriation of Afghans with special skills who have the potential to play an important role in the reconstruction of the country (e.g. teachers, health care personnel, administrators, engineers and technicians, economists, agronomists).

To encourage the return of Afghan professionals, European Union governments have funded the International Organisation for Migration (IOM) to operate programmes of assisted return, including programmes aimed specifically at Afghan professionals living in Europe. In addition, the World Bank has established the Afghanistan Directory of Expertise, and also coordinates the Afghanistan Reconstruction Trust Fund Expatriate Services Programme— both of which aim to link Afghan professionals with skills gaps in Afghanistan. The IOM's programmes have assisted the return of over 800 professionals between 2002 and 2007 (IOM, 2008). However, whilst these schemes may provide added support to those Afghans already considering returning to Afghanistan, the benefits offered are insufficient to persuade the majority of Afghan professionals to return, even temporarily.

Whilst bearing in mind the strategies and goals of donor governments and international organisations, it is also important to remember that Afghan diaspora members are not passive actors in this situation. For many Afghans, the fall of the Taliban offered an important opportunity for the materialisation of transnational ties, and an opportunity to get more involved in Afghanistan again after many years of exile. It became easier to travel to Afghanistan and to send money. Also, despite significant remaining obstacles, particularly insecurity and corruption, it became relatively easy to invest in private sector enterprise and to set up humanitarian projects within Afghanistan; whereas the previous focus of such activities had mainly been refugee camps in Pakistan.

However, the capacity of Hamid Karzai's government to reach out to the diaspora is extremely limited. Nonetheless, some symbolic efforts have been made, particularly by the Embassy of Afghanistan in Washington DC, to encourage involvement. Their website describes the diaspora as 'central to the rebuilding of Afghanistan', and highlights their positive role in establishing charitable organisations, institutional capacity building and investing in business (Embassy of Afghanistan, 2007).

There are a number of collective actors with variable and multiple motivations for an interest in the nature of the Afghan diaspora's involvement with Afghanistan, including diaspora members themselves, Afghans in Afghanistan, donor governments, aid agencies, refugee host governments, and the Afghan government. Each group, and individuals within each group, will have differing priorities and views on how the diaspora should be involved; for example, some Afghans living in the USA may have very different ideas from some of those living in Pakistan. Clearly, this can be problematic; the risks and benefits of diaspora involvement, from the point of view of different actors, are not clear-cut. Also, in the Afghan case there is only limited scholarly work on the subject, which makes evaluating the potential benefits of diaspora involvement difficult.

This chapter has, thus far, provided an impression of the different actors involved. However, in order to understand the risks and benefits of Afghan diaspora involvement in Afghanistan, some issues have to be addressed in more detail. This chapter continues by firstly exploring different positions on whether the diaspora should be involved in reconstruction in Afghanistan at all; and secondly, through examining some of the existing ways in which Afghans in the diaspora are involved in reconstruction via transnational links with Afghanistan. These observations are based partly on available literature, but primarily on the author's fieldwork with Afghans in the San Francisco Bay Area of California and London, so consequently focus on the activities of the wider diaspora.

Should the Afghan diaspora be involved in reconstruction?

The efforts of various donor countries, international organisations and the Afghan government to reach out to the Afghan diaspora may suggest that diaspora involvement in Afghanistan is generally seen by institutional actors as a positive thing. This is not always the case. In fact, perhaps more commonly, diasporas are seen as a negative force, which fund and perpetuate conflicts. Benedict Anderson pithily states that migration 'disrupts' place-based nationalist feelings with 'often explosive' results, because the migrant, or 'long-distance nationalist', who finds it 'tempting to play identity politics by participating (via propaganda, money, weapons, any way but voting) in the conflicts of his imagined *heimat*' is not accountable for their actions in the country of origin (Anderson, 1992: 13). In other words, it is easy to support a political movement's goals if you do not have to live with the consequences of their actions. For example, some professional women in the diaspora supported the Taliban as a Pashtun nationalist movement, and hosted visits from Taliban representatives looking for diaspora support; but they admitted in interview they would not like to live under Taliban rule themselves.[3]

Nevertheless, Anderson (*Ibid.*) overstates the lack of accountability somewhat. Whilst it may be true that individuals living abroad are not necessarily going to feel the direct effects of their transnational actions, in the case of newer diasporas they often have family or other contacts remaining in the country of origin, who may be affected. However, Anderson is not the only commentator who points out the negative aspects of diaspora involvement. Others have highlighted the role diasporas may have in supporting and prolonging conflict, both ideologically and materially (see for example Byman *et al.*, 2001; Collier *et al.*, 2003; Lyons, 2004).

In the Afghan case, the diaspora has clearly had an integral role in funding and providing other means of support to various armed groups at different stages of the conflict. The role of Afghan refugee settlements in and around Peshawar, Pakistan as a resting place and headquarters for *mujahideen* groups during the struggle against Soviet occupying forces is an obvious example in the near diaspora; but the wider diaspora also played a role, through fundraising and organising opportunities for resistance leaders to visit Western countries to try to gain political and financial support from both the diaspora and non-Afghan sympathisers (Ansary, 2002; Naby, 2005).

However, the causes and perpetuation of conflict are usually extremely complex; and it is difficult to measure the precise impact of this kind of diaspora involvement, especially that of the wider diaspora. Shain and Barth (2003) suggest that a key way in which diaspora members can have influence is through affecting foreign policy decisions in their 'host' country. In the Afghan case it is clear that certain members of the diaspora (often Western educated) do have disproportionate influence, particularly in the US. Naby (2005) suggests that Afghan-Americans such as Zalmay Khalilzad[4] have been integral to shaping a pro-Pashtun strategy in Afghanistan since 2001 (see also Hanifi, 2004).

It is likely that some individuals will always have disproportionate influence based on social and human capital; but the question remains whether diaspora members' influence is welcomed by donor governments and international organisations in the post-conflict situation because of a real knowledge of what is best for Afghanistan, or because they have foreign language skills and know how to operate in a Western context. Certainly, the position of wider diaspora Afghans and their ability to access high-status titles in the Afghan government or well-paid employment in international aid agencies has caused resentment and distrust amongst those Afghans who stayed throughout the fighting (Sharifzada, 2004). During a short research trip to Kabul in March 2008, the author witnessed a number of examples of negative feelings towards returnees.[5] At the same time, however, some diaspora members distrust those who stayed in Afghanistan, especially many of those currently holding government positions, labelling them warlords, criminals or drug smugglers.[6]

For many Afghans, particularly from the wider diaspora, travel to Afghanistan has been difficult. Many have not lived in the country for over twenty-five years and are not directly aware of changes that have taken place over that time. In any case, for the urbanised and educated Afghan elite in the wider diaspora (those most likely to have an influence on host country foreign policy), the Afghanistan they lived in was not representative of that inhabited by the majority of Afghans, a fact acknowledged in Afghan-American memoirs (see for example Ansary, 2002; Daoud, 2002; Hosseini, 2003). For these Afghan elites in the diaspora, there may be a particular interest in returning to the so-called 'golden age' of Afghanistan as a burgeoning democracy under the leadership of Zahir Shah in the 1960s and early 1970s.

Whilst it is true that this era did lead to educational and political infrastructure development, most benefits were confined to the urban middle and upper classes; and the associated inequalities, reliance on foreign governments and the undermined capacity of the labour market to absorb educated youth, have been directly implicated in the growth of the Communist parties in Afghanistan (Roy, 1994). Maybe, as suggested by a young Afghan research participant in California, the (now elderly) bureaucrats who oversaw that era are not necessarily well-placed to govern Afghanistan's future. In addition, their employment experience over the last twenty-plus years in exile may not be in line with the kind of high-status managerial positions they expect to achieve on return. An Afghan-American interviewee (who worked in recruitment for a large Non-Governmental Organisation (NGO) in Afghanistan) told of how he had employed a fellow Afghan-American on the basis of his degree qualification, achieved in the 1970s, from the University of Kabul. It was not until the employee arrived in Afghanistan that the NGO realised he had been working as a taxi driver since leaving Afghanistan and had never put his educational qualifications into practice.

Afghan-Americans, particularly those living in Virginia and Maryland, have been influential in United States policy towards Afghanistan (Naby, 2005); but due to their geographical proximity, Afghans in Pakistan and Iran are probably more involved in smaller-scale, more frequent transnational political involvement. As mentioned above, diasporas are not a homogenous group. Clearly, different groups and individuals will have different goals. The Afghan diaspora has been represented as particularly fragmented along ethnic and political lines; and although these differences should not be overstated (Monsutti, this volume), it is clear that fragmentation can limit the ability of the diaspora to put together cooperative projects. This is obviously an issue for many diasporas. On the other hand, problems also occur when there is one dominant group operating in the diaspora, as they may put undue pressure on diaspora members to contribute to their chosen goals—as in the relief operations of the Liberation Tigers of Tamil Eelam (Bivand Erdal, 2006). It may be that the fragmented nature of the Afghan diaspora means that Afghans are less vulnerable to this kind of 'forced transnationalism' (see also Al-Ali, et al., 2001).

The issue of representation, or who speaks for the diaspora, was frequently raised in discussion with Afghans in the diaspora. For example, Afghans in California feel that too often their views are ignored in favour of those of Afghans living closer to Washington DC; meanwhile, some Afghans in London feel that the Afghan-American voice is heard over all others. In discussion with Afghans in both California and London, another issue was frequently raised, one that has perhaps not been adequately addressed by migration or development scholars: the question of responsibility. Should Afghans living in the diaspora, who may be struggling with the processes of integration in the host country, have the additional task of further transnational involvement in Afghanistan? Given that many of them already make transnational transfers in the form of remittances, do they have the resources (time and financial) to get further involved in reconstruction or development projects? Indeed, during fieldwork with Afghans in California and London, research participants expressed concern about the resources required for active transnational involvement in development and reconstruction; and some Afghans in London expressed a fear that the UK government's interest in diaspora involvement in reconstruction was an attempt to shift responsibilities away from the government and onto Afghan shoulders. This unintended reaction to the attempts of the UK Department for International Development to engage in dialogue with diaspora groups is mainly due to a wider mistrust of the UK government amongst Afghans in London—a mistrust that stems at least partly from what some Afghans see as an unrealistic promotion of return by the UK Home Office.[7]

However, whilst there is empirical evidence to suggest that transnational transfers can be a burden on refugees and migrants (see for example Hammond, 2006; Riak Akuei, 2005), there is a substantial body of literature outlining the positive impacts of migrant transnational transfers on reconstruction and development in their country of origin and in the near diaspora (see for example GCIM, 2005; Horst, 2006; Hugo, 2003; Newland, 2004). In the Afghan case there is no macro level data on the impacts of these transfers; but case studies have indicated the importance and volume of remittances, and the desire of Afghans in exile to contribute something in the way of financial, political or humanitarian action towards those left behind. The next section describes some of the ways in which Afghans in the diaspora are involved in transnational activities that may contribute to reconstruction in Afghanistan.

The transnational activities of the Afghan diaspora

The Afghan diaspora is widely dispersed around the world, as Figure 2 indicates. As the conflict in Afghanistan evolved and changed, people left at various stages in response to events that affected different social and political groups in different ways. At the same time, some countries became more or less feasible as host countries, as foreign governments' sympathies towards Afghan refugees changed in response to their own domestic or foreign policy concerns. Multiple reasons for flight and multiple reception contexts have led to a complex, dispersed and heterogeneous diaspora. In many cases Afghan families have members in several different countries of the wider diaspora, near diaspora, as well as in Afghanistan itself. This can, and usually does, result in transnational social networks linking various sites of the diaspora and the 'home' country.

Of interest to this chapter are the transnational *activities* that link Afghans in the diaspora to Afghanistan itself, since arguably these may have the greatest impact on reconstruction in Afghanistan. This is not to discount the potential impact of symbolic transnational ties or feelings of transnational consciousness; rather, the outcome of these kinds of ties may only become apparent in the longer term, particularly if the Afghan diaspora communities become more established entities in 'host' countries.

Perhaps the most obvious way in which the diaspora can contribute to Afghanistan is through the transnational activity of sending remittances. During fieldwork, Afghans in California and London frequently mentioned that *all* Afghans were sending money to either Afghanistan or relatives in neighbouring countries. Whilst I did encounter those who claimed to send none, fieldwork suggests that the vast majority did. However, neither the Ministry of Finance in Afghanistan nor international financial regulatory bodies are able to provide accurate figures on inflows of remittances. This is partly due to a lack of data recording capacity in Afghanistan but also because most remittances are sent using a so-called 'informal' money transfer system called *hawala* (for more information on *hawala* see Monsutti, 2004, 2005).

Nonetheless, estimates have been made; for example, Thompson (2006) estimates a remittance flow of $1–1.5 billion from the diaspora through *hawala* into Afghanistan in 2004, an estimation based on empirical research with *hawala* agents in multiple sites in Afghanistan. However, the majority of what is known about remittance sending comes from research in the diaspora. For example, studies in Iran have shown that young single men are sending 70 to 80 per cent of their income as remittances (Stigter and Monsutti, 2005), which amounts to about $500 to $1,300 per year (Abbasi-Shavazi and Glazebrook, 2006; Stigter and Monsutti, 2005). *Hawala* agents in Vadean's (2007) study suggest that Afghans in Hamburg, Germany, are sending €200 per month per household. Agents in Hanifi's (2006) study suggested that in a typical month the average amount sent from Virginia in the USA to Afghanistan and Pakistan by each customer was over $200, with these amounts increasing in the month of Ramadan, where the total amount agents send may equal the sum sent in all other months together (Hanifi, 2006). Vadean and Hanifi's findings present a similar picture in Hamburg and Virginia to that observed during fieldwork amongst Afghans in California: estimated amounts, alongside knowledge of the size of the Afghan diaspora, suggest that remittances are a substantial monetary transfer into Afghanistan; and therefore are arguably a significant factor in reconstruction, as well as essential to the day-to-day survival of many.

However, remittances are not the only type of transnational transfer. Writing about their research with Bosnian and Eritrean refugees, Al-Ali, Black and Koser (2001) make the useful categorisation of transnational activities into economic, social, cultural, religious and political types, and highlight that these activities can have a home-country focus or a host-country focus. Figure 3 gives selected examples of transnational activities that some Afghans in California and London are involved in.

There are likely to be significant differences between the transnational activities of Afghans in the wider and near diaspora. Transnational activities require resources; and generally, though by no means always, those in the wider diaspora have greater resources to 'invest' in transnational activities. It could also be generalised that those with greater resources are less likely to have family remaining in Afghanistan: many Afghans living in California had been outside Afghanistan for upwards of twenty-five years; and in that time, they had achieved a level of financial stability—although often nothing compared to the lifestyle they had enjoyed as the upper class of Kabul—which had allowed them to support family members remaining in Afghanistan to leave. Consequently, they are less likely to have regular remittance responsibilities, although many still send money to more distant family members in response to specific celebrations (e.g. weddings) and crises (e.g. to cover medical bills or funeral costs). Despite fewer family responsibilities, most, however, still felt a strong emotional connection to Afghanistan, and expressed feelings of guilt about leaving.

Indeed, a recurring theme that emerged during interviews with Afghan professionals in California and London was the guilt many felt about receiving their education at the expense of the Afghan government and then leaving before the country could receive any benefit from that investment. As a result, a lack of transnational activities directed towards kin did not necessarily mean a lack of transnational activities; rather, it often meant a focus on more general philanthropic transnational transfers. For example, transnational activities amongst Afghans in California often took the form of charitable donations, such as fundraising events to buy equipment for schools or hospitals in Afghanistan; making regular contributions to NGOs working in Afghanistan; or sponsoring a widow or orphan there. It is difficult to make similar generalisations about Afghans in London, as the situation is more mixed, with both newer and more established groups of Afghans who have various levels of resources.

For Afghans in Pakistan and Iran, geographical proximity means that transnational activities are likely to be more frequent and more intense, often because Afghans in the near diaspora are more likely to have family remaining in Afghanistan, and so may be more likely to go back and forth regularly

Figure 3: Examples of Afghan transnational activities, California and London[2]

	Social	Economic	Cultural	Religious	Political
Home country focus	Travelling to Afghanistan. Involvement in social and educational projects in Afghanistan.	Sending remittance to Afghanistan. Fundraising for projects in Afghanistan. Investing in business in Afghanistan.	Fundraising for heritage and/or cultural projects in Afghanistan.	Fundraising for reconstruction of mosques and *madrassas* in Afghanistan.	Returning to work in the Afghan government.
Host country focus	Using social networks and/or the internet to find a spouse from Afghanistan or the diaspora.	Import-export business. Money from renting property in Afghanistan. Employment as a consultant in reconstruction projects.	Inviting musicians from Afghanistan and the diaspora to perform. Watching Afghan satellite television.	Inviting craftsmen from Afghanistan to make tiles etc for new mosques in the host country.	Raising awareness about the situation in Afghanistan. Arranging visits from Afghan politicians. Discussing Afghan politics in print and online media.

across national borders. In addition, transnational activities are more likely to be part of an ongoing family livelihood strategy, rather than a philanthropic exercise (see Abbasi-Shavazi and Glazebrook, 2006; Stigter and Monsutti, 2005).

Return migration is not always considered a transnational activity; but in the Afghan case it is appropriate to regard it as one, as return often takes place on a short-term or circulatory basis (Monsutti, 2006). The unstable security and economic situation in Afghanistan makes return highly problematic, and it is understandable that most of those with alternative opportunities will choose to return on a temporary basis in order to keep their options open—if they return at all. Indeed, temporary return may be a more attractive option to Afghans in the diaspora who want to contribute to the future of Afghanistan; and given the skills gaps, the return of human capital to government ministries, NGOs and the private sector should have a positive impact on reconstruction. However, Afghans in California who returned found it extremely difficult to stay in Kabul, never mind the rest of the country. The destruction of their in-country social networks made it difficult for them to operate effectively in either business or government environments, and many went back to California, frustrated by how the country had changed in their absence. Similar issues may affect second generation returnees who do not have the right social networks, having been brought up in exile (Saito, 2007). Nevertheless, successful return is possible; and there have been some returnees, particularly entrepreneurs in the private sector, who have managed to start or resurrect successful businesses, bringing much-needed investment. Some of these companies, such as Afghan Wireless, a mobile phone company, have integrated corporate social responsibility into their business plans. Whilst these returnee entrepreneurs will probably have a positive effect on reconstruction, they are in the minority. Afghanistan remains an uncertain investment environment; and although many Afghans spoken to in California and London express a desire to return and invest in Afghanistan, few are in a position to take that risk.

However, for some there is more to it than money or a wish to help Afghanistan: although most Afghan professionals in California and London are employed, they often do not feel that their position in the labour force is commensurate with their family background, education and status in the Afghan community; many who were of working age in the 1970s worked in the Government or Civil Service and a return to a position in the present Government, or a managerial position in a high-profile NGO, could be seen as a return to their 'natural' status in society.

In reality, transnational activities such as return, sending remittances, investment and fundraising will have a varying degree of influence on reconstruction processes, and they are dependent on a variety of factors. Further, this influence can be problematic: the reliance on diaspora to fill key roles in the government and NGOs, at the expense of employment opportunities for those who stayed, has caused resentment. International remittances, whilst essential to some peoples' survival, are not a catch-all solution to the lack of sustainable livelihoods in Afghanistan; and are not available at all to those who do not have relatives abroad. Philanthropic projects set up by the diaspora are in most cases small-scale and often lack coordination. However, despite the problems it is clear that the diaspora do have an important role to play, and many want to be involved. Moreover, the sheer size of the diaspora and the human capital contained within implies that the diaspora will be an important factor in Afghanistan's future.

Conclusion: encouraging positive diaspora involvement

In the introduction to this chapter various actors were introduced: Afghans in the diaspora, Afghans in Afghanistan, donor governments, aid agencies, refugee host governments and the Afghan government. All can play a role in encouraging positive diaspora involvement. This chapter has described a number of ways in which the diaspora is already involved: many of these involvements are small-scale and involve transnational transfers from individual to individual, or via small collectives. This chapter has also demonstrated that diaspora involvement is not problem-free: it should not be assumed that common language or heritage means that the Afghan diaspora automatically knows what is best for the future of Afghanistan. Nevertheless, it is clear that the diaspora is responsible for a substantial amount of money going into Afghanistan. In addition, many Afghans in the diaspora want to be involved, and to contribute to their *watan* (homeland); feelings of guilt at leaving, of their status and skills being undervalued in exile, and initial optimism after the 2001 fall of the Taliban, have all led to a revitalised commitment to Afghanistan amongst Afghans in California, and are likely to do the same elsewhere in the diaspora.

These feelings have not necessarily translated into a desire to return. For the majority, the security and economic difficulties of life in Afghanistan, as well as for some the lack of in-country social networks, mean that return is not an option. The conflict in Afghanistan is over twenty-five years old, and it is unrealistic to expect that Afghans have been in stasis, simply waiting to repatriate. Instead, they have been living their lives, and as a result, have started the process of integration. Since 2002, however, there has been a strong push for return amongst host governments of the near diaspora and some countries of the wider diaspora, particularly European countries. The Afghan government has also encouraged return, though only of educated and skilled Afghans. This emphasis on return amongst policy makers is at odds with the actual transnational activities of the Afghan diaspora, which, although including temporary return, have mainly been in the form of remittances, fundraising, awareness raising and some investment. Arguably, policy makers should turn their attention to encouraging and facilitating these activities rather than pushing for return as a solution.

In discussions with Afghan diaspora members during fieldwork in California and London, many welcomed host government support of transnational projects, and some actively sought it out. They did stress, however, the importance of Afghan ownership of diaspora projects, even if supported by host governments or international aid agencies. In London in particular, there was a mistrust of the host government—a fact to which policy-makers will have to be extremely sensitive if they want to collaborate with the diaspora in reconstruction projects.

Finally, it is important to note that the diaspora cannot be a catch-all solution for reconstruction in Afghanistan. Whilst there is growing evidence of the significant positive impact of some diasporas, for example the Indian or Taiwanese diasporas (Lowell and Gerova, 2004), the relationship and situation of these countries and their diasporas are not comparable with that of Afghanistan. As Newland (2004: 33) argues regarding diasporas and poverty reduction in general, whilst 'problems such as poor infrastructure, corruption, lack of access to credit, distance from markets, lack of training in entrepreneurial skills, disincentives to savings and so forth' are still apparent, there is only so much the diaspora can do—an argument Afghans in the diaspora repeat, citing the further problems of insecurity and lack of infrastructure.

11

THE CIRCULATION OF MUSIC BETWEEN AFGHANISTAN AND THE AFGHAN DIASPORA

John Baily

In 2006 the Arts and Humanities Research Council, as part of its research programme on Diasporas, Migration and Identities, gave me a grant to investigate Afghan music in London, and to look into London's musical connections with Kabul and the Afghan diaspora—specifically with Hamburg (home to a very large Afghan colony)—and Dublin (with a very small one). The London research completed a paradigm for the comparison of far and near sites of Afghan settlement: Peshawar (Pakistan) and Mashhad (Iran) on the one hand, and Fremont (California) and London on the other (Baily, 1999, 2005a).

In this chapter I address some of the general questions about the circulation of music between Afghanistan and the Afghan diaspora that my recent study raises.[1]

The circulation of music in Afghanistan in the 1970s

From the late 1940s, the radio station in Kabul gradually became the centre for innovation and patronage in the creation of a new popular music suitable for radio broadcasting. One of the key figures in this development was Ustad Ghulam Hussein, who was in fact a performer of Indian classical vocal music.

It is likely that Indian film music—available to Afghans via the few cinemas and 78 rpm records—served as a model for what Afghan popular music could become. Work at the radio station had far-reaching consequences: in a country where there was no university department of music, no conservatories, no music as part of the school curriculum, and no national sound archive, it was the radio station that became the centre of musical activity and creativity. It employed a large number of musicians, singers and instrumentalists, male and female, as well as a number of composers. It ran various orchestras and ensembles, each with its own leader. The radio station provided new possibilities for musicians to be recruited from amateur backgrounds.

It is important to point out that in Afghan society in the recent past (and even today), an important distinction was made between professional musicians, drawn from hereditary musician families, and amateur musicians, who took great care to distance themselves from the hereditary professionals (Baily, 1988: 101–3). The radio station bestowed a degree of modernity, anonymity and respectability on the musicians, which enabled a number of originally amateur and middle-class performers to become professional, 'full-time economic specialists', as Merriam (1964: 124) puts it.[2]

Perhaps the best example of a new singer of popular songs is Ahmad Zahir, whose music is still remarkably popular and widely emulated today. Ahmad Zahir was from an elite social background, the son of a former Prime Minister of Afghanistan. In the 1960s Ahmad Zahir was much involved in creating and performing modernised Afghan music, using western instruments rather than 'traditional' ones.[3] Ahmad Zahir himself played an electric organ rather than the harmonium, and had in his groups instruments such as a trap set (drum kit, often called *jaz*), Boehm flute, saxophone, and trumpet.[4] A number of similar figures emerged from upper class families—amateurs who became professional singers in the context of the radio—such as Dr Fitrat (whose professional radio name was *Nashenas*, meaning 'Unknown'). Equally striking was the promotion of women singers—perhaps most notably Farida Mahwash (Madadi and Baily, 2001). In 1975 she was given the honorific title of *ustad* by the Afghan government, somewhat to the surprise of male musicians, who considered the title *ustad* to be reserved for men.

By means of a modernised music, the process of modernisation in Afghanistan was promoted and encouraged. In a far-sighted paper, Slobin discussed the role of radio in Afghan musical life:

Radio Afghanistan is one of the few unifying factors in a country unusually marked by ethnic and linguistic fragmentation [...]. For the Afghan villager or nomad [...] the radio has drastically reduced the restrictions on the scope of his imagination [...] he shares in the music of the Kabul studio, one of the few manifestations of an emerging pattern of national values and expression that may eventually comprise a pan-ethnic, distinctively Afghan society (Slobin, 1974: 248).

Following Slobin's lead, I have argued that radio music was much involved in the creation of an Afghan national identity (Baily, 1994), as a centripetal force which gave members of the various ethnic groups making up the Afghan population something of a *pan*-Afghan identity—a fact which remains relevant today.

In 1981, in an article on popular music in Afghanistan (Baily, 1981), I proposed the following representation for the circulation of *kiliwali*, or popular, music, see Figure 4.

This shows the two-way flow of music as information between the centre and the periphery of the urban network, looked at from the perspective of the provincial city of Herat in the 1970s, when I was doing my major fieldwork. Moving from the centre to the periphery, new popular songs were learned from Radio Afghanistan and recreated in Herat, played by small local ensembles—professional and amateur—and typically consisting of a singer, and accompanied by harmonium, *rubab*, *dutar* and *tabla*. In the 1970s the audio-cassette was just becoming common, and cassettes imported from Kabul were also a source of new songs in Herat. But the radio provided the quickest access to the latest hits.

At the same time, when moving from the periphery to the centre, we have a process of Herati songs (many but not all of them traditional songs of

Figure 4: Centre and periphery of the *Kiliwali* network

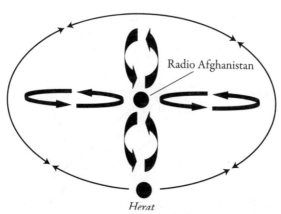

Radio Afghanistan

Herat

unknown authorship—i.e. 'folk songs') being turned into popular radio songs performed with radio ensembles. The singer Abdul Wahab Madadi, from Herat, recorded a large number of such songs: when I visited the radio archive in 1976, I found he had well over 100 songs there, many originating from Herat. Iran also served as a source of new popular songs, which were often transmitted to Kabul by Herati musicians who listened to Iranian radio or had access to Iranian popular music cassettes. The regional musics of other parts of Afghanistan were likewise absorbed into the radio station's repertoire.

There was also direct communication between different sites in the periphery. In Herat, for example, items of repertoire from Mazar-i-Sharif in the north,[5] and from the Logar Valley in the south,[6] were very popular. These borrowings were in part the result of visits by musicians to other parts of the country. The singer Bolbol Herawi, with Rahim Khushnawaz (*rubab*), Gada Mohammad (*dutar*) and Naim Khushnawaz (*tabla*), all from Herat, had spent some time as a band in Mazar-i-Sharif in about 1971; Salaam Logari (vocal and harmonium) and his band played at the spring country fairs in Herat in 1974 (Baily, 1982). In the 1970s many Ramazan concerts in Herat brought in musicians performing popular music from Kabul, such as Zaland and Khyal in 1974, and Afsaneh, Shamsuddin Masrur and Aziz Ghaznawi in 1977.

The picture for art music would be rather different, with a uni-directional flow of music information from Kabul to provincial cities, see Figure 5, and with no links between provincial cities. However, there were major links with the Indian Sub-continent, the primary source of the art music performed in

Figure 5: Centre and periphery of the art music network

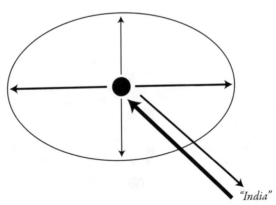

"India"

Kabul, and these were not just one-way connections; for example, the Afghan classical singer Ustad Mohammad Hussein Sarahang, a representative of the Patiala *gharana* (a stylistic school of North Indian vocal art music), was very well known in India, and was a frequent visitor there to give concerts. His photograph can be found in Neuman (1980: 211).

Changes since 1978

In retrospect, the 1960s and 1970s are looked upon by many Afghans as a 'golden era' in their recent music history. The circulation of music as represented in Figure 4 has been dramatically changed by a number of factors since the pro-Soviet communist putsch of Taraki in 1978:

a) The civil war, which started in 1978 and continued until the defeat of the Taliban government in 2002, with a continuing insurgency;

b) The increasingly anti-music ideology as the moderate Sufi-orientated Islam of Afghanistan was replaced by more fundamentalist tendencies derived from Saudi Arabia, culminating in the Taliban's ban on musical instruments, and hence, of music;

c) The mass migration of Afghans out of the country, and new travel possibilities allowing people to move around much more freely than before;

d) Technological changes, with new electronic musical instruments, new media and the internet.

We may ask: in what ways is music as information being moved about today in the 'Afghan world community'? And where are today's centres of creativity?

Mass movements of people

As a result of the communist coup in 1978, a mass exodus to Pakistan and Iran began. Several million Afghans went into exile in these adjacent countries. There were also substantial migrations to Europe, especially Germany, and the USA, and later to Canada and Australia. It is probably correct to say that those who went to the more distant western countries were the better educated middle-class Afghans (see Oeppen, this volume), particularly those from Kabul, many of whom had worked for western organisations such as USAID, US Peace Corps, The British Council, and many other agencies of Western governments.

This mass movement of people inevitably included singers and instrumentalists, amateur and professional. The musicians who went West were mostly of amateur origin. One can identify three generations: the big stars of the 1960s-1970s, such as Khyal, Zaland, and Mahwash; a younger group of originally amateur musicians from Kabul, who were active there in the Communist era, such as Farhad Darya and Wahid Qassemi; and a new generation of Afghan musicians raised, if not born, in the West, such as Qader Eshpari, Habib Qaderi, and Ehsan Aman.

In contrast, the hereditary professional musicians tended to relocate in sites close to Afghanistan—in Pakistan and Iran. Thus, musicians from Kabul's Kucheh Kharabat, the musicians' quarter, went to Peshawar and Quetta, while musicians from Herat went to Mashhad. Rather few hereditary musicians from the Kharabat escaped to the West; but in this respect London is unusual in having five musicians from Kharabat families. The *tabla* player Ustad Asif Mahmoud led the way.

These migratory movements placed the Afghans in contact with other kinds of music—in Pakistan, Iran, and in the West. The interactions led to various instances of interculturalism: in Pakistan, Afghan music became reconnected with its Indian roots, and in Iran with its Iranian roots; while in the West the Afghan musicians had the opportunity to take forward the Ahmad Zahir project to both modernise and westernise Afghan music, with Western electronic instruments like keyboards and drum machines, and with the development of simple harmonic progressions. California was an important site for the development of this new kind of Afghan music, as exemplified in the work of Qader Eshpari, who claims to have been the first to programme the keyboard with the three basic Afghan rhythms: *Geda*, *Dadra* and *Mogholi*, which in Western terms are 4/4, 6/8 and 7/8 (Baily, 2005a, 2005b).

Live performance

The various communities making up the Afghan diaspora have their own local singers and accompanists. In London one can identify half-a-dozen such individuals: they perform mainly at wedding parties and on festive occasions such as concerts held during the two *Eids*, *Now Ruz* (Afghan New Year, 21 March), and the UK New Year (1 January). They fulfil a ritual function, since music is an essential part of such festivities. In London I would name Belqiss, Hashmat, Mahmud Kamen and Obaid, amongst others. But such local singers are not of great appeal for concerts: they are too well known by the local audiences. For concerts, singers are usually brought from abroad, from elsewhere in the periphery.

An Afghan concert is a big event. It is usually held in a banqueting suite with an elaborately decorated stage, very loud amplification and one or more mobile video cameras recording the event for release in DVD format. Singers are generally brought from outside the UK, and sometimes with an accompanist, such as a keyboard player. In the space of three months I attended concerts in London by Faiz-e Karezi (Germany), Seema Tarana (Canada), Habib Qaderi (USA), Ehsan Aman (USA), Shahna (The Netherlands) and Asad Badie (Austria). They performed very much in the style of the new Afghan music, dominated by keyboards, drum machines, and drum pads; though the singers themselves tended to play the harmonium on these occasions. Tickets cost between £15 and £20. It is clear that considerable amounts of money are involved in organising these events, which are promoted as business enterprises. There is the hire of the hall, lighting and PA system, security, travel and accommodation of visiting artists, and their payment.

Much of the music played at such concerts is dance music; which brings us to an important distinction between two types of event, which I designate the 'family concert' and the 'open concert'. To attend a family concert one has to be a member or guest of a family group. The groups sit around large circular tables for ten, and it is a fairly restrained event. There will be dancing, but usually only for small numbers of dancers at a time. It is very much a middle-class family event, the guests smartly dressed and well behaved.

The open concert, in contrast, is open to anybody who can buy a ticket. Here the audience is seated in long rows, and the area in front of the stage is dominated by large numbers of young men dancing together—perhaps a hundred or even two hundred at a time. Many of these young men are asylum seekers and illegal immigrants, cut off from their families, living in hostels or cheap flats provided by local councils. Given that they represent the various ethnic groups that make up the London Afghan community, and given the rivalries that exist between such groups, it is not surprising that arguments sometimes flare up: fights are not unknown, hence the need for several security men to maintain order. The point of the family concert is to cut out the 'riff-raff'. The audience at such concerts, open and family, consists almost entirely of Afghans: they are not for people outside the Afghan community, who simply do not know that such events are taking place, for they are not part of the 'world music' scene in London.

During my fieldwork in Fremont in 2000, I found that a number of famous singers from Kabul, who were now in exile in Pakistan, had toured in the

USA—tours that were organised by Afghan businessmen. Rahim Bakhsh, Haji Hamahang, Amir Mohammad and Alem-e Shauqi were Kabuli singers who had made such visits, and videos of their concerts in the USA were on sale.

After the fall of the Taliban in 2001, traditional musicians from Afghanistan were on occasion sent abroad as cultural ambassadors. A group was sent from Kabul to London to play at a big concert of Central Asian music, organised by the Aga Khan Trust for Culture—an elaborate show that was staged in the English National Opera's Coliseum Theatre. The USA Embassy in London arranged a concert for *rubab* player Ghulam Hussein and his band to play fusion music with an American jazz group. There have also been visits by Afghan singers living abroad to Kabul to give concerts. Singers Farhad Darya, Wahid Qassemi and Qader Eshpari have done this. These are big events, held in the Kabul stadium, where under Taliban rule public floggings, amputations, and executions took place.

Farhad Darya has perhaps been the most significant visitor. In one of his projects he arrived with a high-powered television crew which accompanied him to various parts of the country, where he was filmed performing with local musicians. The result was a DVD called *Salaam Afghanistan*, published in the USA. Farhad Darya has used some of his resources to work with an orphanage in Kabul, and has produced an elaborate music DVD with the children, released under the title of *Kochah*.

Recordings

In the 1970s there were several companies in Kabul recording and selling commercial audio cassettes, with labels such as Afghan Music and Music Center. In Herat there was a local 'cottage industry' for recording and marketing local performers and performances, using very basic equipment and selling unlabelled cassettes. The production of CDs by Afghan-owned businesses in the West probably started in the 1980s, to provide music for Afghans living in exile. There seem to be two main centres for the production of compact discs. One is Alexandria, in Virginia, home to companies such as Afghan Music Production. The other is Hamburg, which has a wealthy Afghan business sector. In 2006 I visited Keyhan Music in Hamburg, which has both a large shop selling CDs and DVDs, and a twenty-four–track studio out in the suburbs. However, very few CDs are published in the UK.

Some of the CDs are releases or re-releases of old recordings, either copied from audio cassettes originally published by Kabuli companies like Afghan

Music, or from the original quarter-inch masters. There are many CDs of Ustad Sarahang, Afghanistan's greatest singer of *ghazal*s and Indian classical music in the later twentieth century.[7] Many of these are domestic recordings made at private parties where Sarahang was invited to sing. Likewise, there are numerous CDs of Ahmad Zahir, some of which are also of domestic origin.

In addition, there are CDs of many singers from the past singing traditional genres—either 'albums' devoted to a particular artist, or compilations. However, there are many more CDs of new Afghan music—vocal (male or female) and accompanied by keyboards, drum machines and drum pads—and it is these which crowd the racks in the shops where the CDs are sold.

The typical outlet for Afghan music in Fremont is what is called locally an 'Afghan Market'. This type of store typically stocks a wide range of ingredients for Afghan cuisine, including halal meat and freshly baked Afghan bread. They sell Afghan national costumes for young girls to dress in on festive occasions, books, ornaments and wall-clocks in the shape of Afghanistan. Such stores usually also stock a large selection of music audio-cassettes, CDs, VHS cassettes and DVDs, many of which are of Indian film music, which remains very popular with Afghan audiences. I observed a number of similar shops in the Steindamm area of Hamburg. A CD in Fremont in 2000 sold for about $10, and a CD in Germany in 2006 for €5.

In 2006 I found only one such store in London—Sure Bazaar in West Ealing; but it changed hands in the middle of the year, and the new (Afghan) proprietors do not sell music.[8] In London most CDs would seem to be sold at concerts, where it is common for a trader to set up a stall at the back of the hall. However, in Southall there is the Afghan Music Centre in the Himalayan Shopping Centre, which sells CDs, DVDs and music cassettes of Afghan music from Germany, USA and Pakistan.[9]

In Afghanistan itself there is the continuation of the long-standing popularity of Indian film music, and Ahmad Zahir remains a big seller. The audio-cassette remains important, as does the VHS video cassette; but CDs, DVDs and VCDs also abound, selling for around $1 each. There are studios in Pakistan where a few singers from Afghanistan have made their recordings; but Pakistan also produces a large number of pirated copies of CDs made by Afghan companies in the West. Similarly, CDs of big stars like Habib Qaderi, Qader Eshpari, Wahid Qassemi and Amir Jan Saburi are copied for sale in Afghanistan, with no concern about issues of copyright.

One may note the separate domains of 'world music' Afghan CDs, and CDs recorded and circulated within the Afghan community. Magazines in the UK like *fRoots* and *Songlines* will offer reviews of 'world music' Afghan recordings, but not of those made by Afghans for consumption in the Afghan communities, for they have no contact with the encapsulated world of Afghan-made recordings. Likewise, few Afghans buy recordings of Afghan music made for the world music market; and accordingly, few of the latter seem to have been pirated for sale in Afghanistan, which perhaps reflects rather different aesthetic criteria held by Afghans on one hand and by world music 'buffs' on the other.

Radio

In London the BBC World Service Afghanistan Stream has invested a lot in music. Some of my fieldwork was directed towards the weekly programme *Studio Haft* (Studio 7), presented by Haroon Yousofi—a well-known radio personality and one of the best-informed Afghans about the life of Afghan music around the world. Each week there is a special guest connected to the studio in London via satellite. The guest is announced beforehand on the programme's website and Afghans from all over the world phone in to indicate they would like to speak to the special guest. When the programme is broadcast, a succession of these people are phoned back from London, and they talk to Haroon and the guest. It was quite an experience to sit in the studio, the other side of the table from Haroon, and witness the Afghan global community talking to itself about music.

Haroon's wife Amina Yousofi, who also works for the BBC, has her own women's radio programme, *Zamzama*, where women from Afghanistan phone in on their mobile telephones to talk to Amina, who encourages them to sing over the phone (unaccompanied). Afghan women all over the world are thus able to hear the voices of ordinary women in Afghanistan. The BBC has various other music programmes, and the Music Jukebox, a computerised system, which selects programmes from a vast data store of tunes.

Back in Afghanistan, Radio Afghanistan is a pale shadow of its former self. Very little investment has been made to improve its facilities and to upgrade its management. After years of neglect, the crucially important audio archive of music tapes only recently began a process of digitisation. Further, Radio Afghanistan was for several years the site of contestation over whether women's voices could or could not be heard on radio: after the fall of the Taliban there was a complete ban on women singing on state-run radio and television, and on the stage or concert platform. Women could announce, read the news, recite poetry, and act in plays; but they could not sing. This ban was the subject of intense argument within the radio and television organisations, which are under the control of the Ministry for Information and Culture. However, in January 2004, a few days after the ratification of the new constitution for Afghanistan by a *Loya Jirga* (National Assembly), Kabul TV, the state television station, broadcast old video footage of the female singers Parasto and Salma performing. Explaining the reasons for this dramatic break with the recent past, the Information and Culture Minister stated, 'We are endeavouring to perform our artistic works regardless of the issue of sex'. However, the action provoked an immediate backlash from the Supreme Court, which was opposed to women singing and dancing as a whole. Despite these statements, the radio and television persisted with its new policy.

At the same time, in Kabul there are many so-called 'independent' local FM radio stations, which are actually funded by Western nations aspiring to bring Western ways to Afghanistan. These local radio stations play a lot of music. They also broadcast female singers at a time when Radio Afghanistan was not able to do so. It was partly to compete with these local FM stations for audience share that the BBC stepped up its music output.

Television

Television broadcasting in Afghanistan began in about 1979, and in due course local TV stations were opened in provincial cities such as Herat. During the Coalition era (1992–96) the service was severely disrupted; and from 1996–2001, with the Taliban in power, there was no television at all, although the studio equipment and transmission systems were preserved.

Television services resumed at a very restricted level after 2001. Many households in Kabul have satellite dishes to receive BBC, CNN and other international news channels. The independent Tolo TV station opened in Kabul in about 2003, with a strong emphasis on programmes for young people: it broadcasts programmes such as *Setareh Afghan* (Afghan Star), modelled on Western programmes like Pop Idol. It soon established itself as a controversial institution; the female presenter Shaima Rezayee was murdered by fundamentalists in 2005, and her colleague Shakeb Issar had to flee for his life after presenting footage of Western female singers. He was granted political asylum in Sweden, and is now Tolo TV's Europe entertainment correspondent. Other channels are Ariana Afghanistan TV, which broadcasts by satellite from Los Angeles and is watched by Afghans across the world, and one confusingly also called Ariana TV, which has recently started broadcasting from Kabul.

Internet

Internet has become an important medium for the circulation of Afghan music, especially for the younger generation of Afghans, amongst whom computer literacy is common. Inevitably, most of the music that is broadcast in this way is the new Afghan music.

At the time of writing, some key Afghan sites for music are:[10]

a) www.afghanmtv.com
b) www.afghansite.com
c) www.afghansongs.com
d) www.afghanhits.com
e) www.afghana.com

YouTube is also a very popular site for sharing videos (www.youtube.com). This site has recently been utitilised by the new singers to publicise their songs even before they are released on CD, VCD or DVD—presumably following the example of some Western popular music acts. The new singer Valy used the internet in this way: he recently released his videos on YouTube. In an international poll conducted by Ariana TV (in Los Angeles) during the second anniversary of its launch, Valy's song *'Bia Tu'* was voted Song of the Year. Valy has his own website, and other Afghan sites have been selling and broadcasting his songs.

MySpace is also used by Afghans, but is less popular than YouTube. In addition, the social networking site Facebook is used by Afghans, and singers like Valy have their own profiles and regularly interact with their fans. Users create online groups and fan-clubs for their artists, which hundreds of Afghans join; in such groups they interact with one another and discuss their favourite musicians and songs—not always in the most positive of terms.

Redrawing the musical map

Figure 6 represents how I see the flow of Afghan music as information in 2006. Compared with Figure 4, the size of the network has expanded enormously: the centre of the Afghan global community may still be Kabul, but now the periphery includes geographically and culturally distant cities like

Figure 6: The flow of Afghan music, 2006

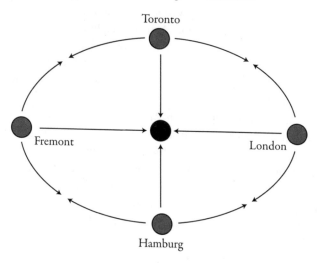

London, Hamburg, Fremont, Toronto and Melbourne, as well as cities in Pakistan and Iran.

Where are the centres of creativity equivalent to the 1970s' Radio Afghanistan in Kabul? From one point of view, there has been little significant creativity in Afghan music since the 'golden era' of the 1960s-1970s, at least in terms of repertoire. Certainly there has been a 're-instrumentation' of Afghan music, with traditional instruments such as harmoniums, *tablas, rubabs, dutars, delrubas* etc. being replaced by keyboards, drum machines and drum pads. Here, creativity is perhaps more a matter of modernisation (with the new types of instrument) and westernisation (with some use of harmonic progressions). There are also new ways of presenting music: the elaborate concert with its stage show, CD covers and posters are all building a new kind of image—one which is much influenced by Western popular music.

However, if we regard this modernisation as creativity, then it is evident that the equivalent to Kabul's role in the past as 'the centre of creativity' is now a multi-sited centre located in the periphery, particularly in Western countries such as the USA and Germany. Accordingly, Figure 6 indicates that the flow of music today is now mainly from the periphery into Kabul and Afghanistan. There is also a lot of circulation between the various sites in the periphery—especially between those located in, again, the West. This picture follows a more general pattern of economic flow—from the diaspora into Afghanistan. Here I do not refer simply to economic aid from the wealthier countries that are trying to support Afghanistan, but also to the remittances that Afghans abroad send to support their families back home.

In terms of music, the Afghan diaspora is very different to those of the Pakistanis or Indians—Pakistan and India being two other countries close to Afghanistan with large diasporic communities in the West. Their centres of musical creativity remain located in Pakistan and India, even though their diasporic communities may also foster innovation—by utilising 'the possibility of a distinctive creative, enriching life in host countries with a tolerance for pluralism' (Cohen, 1997: 26). Diasporic music is 'expected' to be centred on the homeland. But this is not the case with the Afghans. The fact that their musical creativity comes from outside indicates the unique situation of the Afghans in today's world. One cannot expect Kabul to function as a centre, because the very institution that fostered such activity in the past—the radio station—is no longer fully functional.

The role of music in the Afghan diaspora

What is the significance of music in the Afghan diaspora? Is it just entertainment, or does it have a deeper role? Certainly, music provides a connection with the past; and for the older generation of Afghans in exile, its importance is partly related to nostalgia. Adeleida Reyes quotes a remark about Vietnamese music in Orange County, California: 'They never come up with anything new because they are trying to keep the memory of home alive so they use the same songs' (Reyes, 1999: 143). The same may be true for the Afghan diaspora. It is common for people to be particularly attached to the music they heard between the ages of 15 and 25; and for older Afghans who knew Afghanistan in that 'golden age' before the Communist coup of 1978, older music may serve a therapeutic role.

This brings us to the vexed and over-worked notion of identity. In my experience, identity (*haviat*) is not a term invoked very much by Afghans. It is an explanatory concept we ethnomusicologists like to impose on our data. I have invoked such ideas myself, as in my paper on radio music and national identity (Baily, 1994); and I have interpreted the new Afghan music from Fremont as creating a new Afghan-American identity (Baily, 2005a).[11] Afghan people like to listen to Afghan music because it is what they are used to, they are brought up with it, it is familiar, and they hear stories from the older generation about it. That does not mean they extract a self-conscious feeling of identity from it. However, Afghans do talk about keeping and maintaining their culture (*farhang*), and about showing their culture to others; so identity is perhaps implicit here. The discourse of Afghan culture-brokers is more likely to be couched in terms of 'identity', as shown in the following statement (made in English) made by an Afghan community leader in Fremont:

Music brings unity to the people, old and young together, *and helps us not to lose our identity* [my emphasis]. We Afghans have some differences, but the concerts are the only times when we forget about everything, all people from different parts, different sects, we come and buy our tickets and go to the concerts (Baily, 1999: 12).

This is an optimistic and somewhat naive view of music, identity and social cohesion. Concerts can lead to dissent as well as to unity. Perhaps the most interesting data to come from the London research concerns dance. What is happening when 100–200 young Afghan men are dancing *en masse* in front of a stage from which very loud dance music is being played? Is this a chance for young Afghan migrants living in very impoverished and difficult circumstances to experience their Afghan culture anew, in a sense to even perform their Afghan idenity? Is this the outcome of the 'pan-ethnic, distinctively Afghan society' posited by Slobin (1974) for the radio? Or are the dancers subverting traditional Afghan culture? Their presence on the dance floor challenges traditional values which consider dance to be appropriate in particular ritual circumstances (like weddings) but to be strictly rationed and performed with restraint.

12

AFGHAN MIGRATORY STRATEGIES AND THE THREE SOLUTIONS TO THE REFUGEE PROBLEM[1]

Alessandro Monsutti

The normality of movement

This chapter is based on data collected since the mid-1990s in Afghanistan, Pakistan and Iran, and then in Western countries, especially among the Hazaras, a marginal group originating in the centre of Afghanistan.[2] Beyond some specificity, their migratory networks express more widespread social features, and reflect old patterns of mobility.

Afghans give different and usually multiple reasons for their decision to migrate: perhaps an outbreak of fighting, the danger of bombing or compulsory conscription, or a threat from a personal enemy; or perhaps the search for work or opportunities to trade, the need for medical treatment, or the undertaking of a pilgrimage. My main aim here, however, is not to highlight these motives in a context of diffuse insecurity but to describe how transnational networks and ongoing mobility are at the core of strategies developed by many Afghans. A study of individual trajectories and family strategies shows that few Afghans have stayed exclusively in their country since the Communist *coup d'état* of 1978 and the Soviet intervention of 1979, and also that many have returned at some point for at least a short visit. The leaving and coming back has been constant.

Whilst Afghans are, and have been since the 1990s, the largest refugee population in the world, we are a long way from the pathetic imagery of the victim compelled to leave his or her homeland in the face of a towering threat, with the vague hope of one day being able to return. Although Afghan migratory movements reached an unprecedented scale during the war (a peak of 6.2 million Afghan refugees in 1990), they have existed for a long time in one form or another—and have remained in the memory of the members of many Afghan communities. Nor do they necessarily have the traumatic significance that is often attributed to them by humanitarian actors: individual mobility and the dispersion of families or mutual support groups are not always experienced as destructuring phenomena in and of themselves. Seen from this angle, the concepts of 'economic migrant', 'political refugee', 'country of origin', 'host country', 'voluntary' or 'forced' migration, or even 'return', appear singularly reductionist in the Afghan context. All these categories overlap with the combined presence of political, cultural, economic and ecological factors.

Based on ethnographic evidence, this chapter will propose three main theses: firstly, the normality of movements and the prior existence of transnational networks in the region; secondly, the resilience and inventiveness of the Afghan population, illustrated especially by the remittance system; and thirdly, the relevance of migratory movements and transnational networks for the reconstruction of Afghanistan (both the economy and social life). My intention is to contrast Afghanistan's migratory strategies with the three so-called durable solutions to the problem of refugees promoted by the United Nations High Commissioner for Refugees (UNHCR): voluntary repatriation in the country of origin; integration in the host country; resettlement in a third country. They are based on the idea that solutions are found when movements stop. But mobility may be seen as a key livelihood strategy (Horst, 2006; Monsutti, 2005; Van Hear, 1998, 2002). Therefore, policy-wise, a more comprehensive solution is needed—one which takes into account the full range of strategies and responses developed by the Afghan population, including the back-and-forth movements between Afghanistan, Pakistan, Iran and beyond (Stigter and Monsutti, 2005).

Through the action of the Afghanistan Comprehensive Solution Unit, the UNHCR has become progressively aware of the necessity of developing a new paradigm supplementing the historical mandate of protection and assistance (see for example UNHCR, 2003, 2004). Such a perspective reflects both a changing political context (with the Soviet withdrawal and the end of the Cold War, the subsequent conflict between factions, the rise and fall of the

Taliban and the establishment of a government backed by the international community in Kabul) and a progressive learning from social realities (mobility as an asset and not only as a problem).

Beyond the unprecedented wave of return

Migration is part of the Afghan social and cultural landscape: the seasonal movements of nomads who bring their herds to better pasture lands, but who take the opportunity to trade with sedentary farmers; the mountain people who go to urban centres or to lowlands in order to find a menial job; and pilgrims, soldiers, or refugees. Afghans have had a long history of migration in its various forms.

Nevertheless, the war which tore Afghanistan apart after the Communist coup of April 1978 and the Soviet invasion of 1979 has given a more dramatic dimension to those movements of populations. Large numbers returned after the Soviet withdrawal (1989) and the capture of Kabul by resistance forces (1992), but over the following years this trend was partially reversed as more outward flows accompanied the new outbreaks of fighting, especially in the Mazar-i-Sharif and Kabul regions.

The attacks on the World Trade Center and the Pentagon of 11 September 2001 and the subsequent intervention of an international coalition led by American forces, bringing about the fall of the Taliban in late 2001 and the establishment of a government in Kabul backed by the international community in winter 2001–2002, set the stage for a new era filled with hope for peace and prosperity: the prospect of a restoration of normality has caused an unprecedented wave of repatriation. According to official figures, more than 5 million Afghans have returned to their country, mostly from Pakistan and Iran, either with the assistance of the UNHCR or spontaneously. Another half a million internally displaced people have returned to their village of origin. Afghanistan has been one of the largest repatriation campaigns in the history of the UNHCR.

But following a new deterioration of the security situation, the pace of repatriation has dropped since 2005. Even without including 1.3 million Afghans living outside the camps, Pakistan—as well as Iran—are still asylum countries with one of the largest number of refugees worldwide. By the end of 2006, both countries together hosted 20 per cent of the world's refugee population (UNHCR, 2007: 6–7). Many of the remaining Afghans have been living outside their country of origin for more than two decades, and more than 50 per cent were born abroad. The UNHCR acknowledges that they have become used to different living conditions, and that many originate from areas currently affected by insecurity and poverty. Voluntary repatriation, which takes place within the framework of tripartite agreements signed by UNHCR and the Governments of Afghanistan, Pakistan and Iran, is nevertheless still considered to be the preferred durable solution by UNHCR.

The level of repatriation initially showed a degree of confidence in the renascent state, but also reflected the expectations created by donor pledges about the rebuilding of the country, and the deterioration of living conditions in the places of refuge. To a certain degree, the level of repatriation was also affected by the Iranian and Pakistani authorities, who were increasingly implementing policies to encourage Afghans to return home.

The sustainability of such a large return movement has been questioned by many. Turton and Marsden (2002b), for instance, assess the repatriation operation, reintegration opportunities, and the role and interests of the international community. They stress the fact that many registered returnees may be 'recyclers', repatriating to Afghanistan, getting the assistance package and then going back to Pakistan or Iran. Some others may be seasonal migrants with no intention of staying in Afghanistan on a long-term basis. They also drew attention to the difficulties returnees faced in resettling, leading to a 'backflow' of returnees to Iran and Pakistan and further movement within Afghanistan.

Return to Afghanistan does not necessarily mean the end of displacements, and may prompt onward passage, following a pattern of multidirectional cross-border movements. Channels of pre-established transnational networks exist between Afghanistan, Pakistan and Iran, as the movement of individuals to seek work, to escape drought or to flee war has been a common experience in the whole region. Despite the high levels of repatriation, the number of Afghans living abroad is still considerable (see Oeppen, this volume). Families and individuals continue to move, and it seems unlikely that the back-and-forth movements will stop while such movements constitute a key livelihoods strategy. Many Afghans have been shifting from one place to the next for years—some never returning to their place of origin, others only on a temporary basis before deciding to return into Iran, Pakistan or further afield. Young men in particular, who have not travelled before, are still choosing to leave Afghanistan. This suggests that displacement is not only caused by conflict, but may also be conceived as a necessary stage in the men's existence—a rite of passage to adulthood and a step towards manhood (Monsutti, 2007b).

With the passing of time, the Afghans have woven very efficient migratory networks based on back-and-forth movements and on the dispersion of members of kin groups between Afghanistan, Iran, Pakistan, and beyond. The migratory movements are highly organised, and resultant transnational networks became a major, even constitutive, element in the social, cultural and economic life of Afghans. One of the most striking aspects of this migration is the huge flow of capital drawn towards Afghanistan. Once the migrants are in Pakistan, Iran or elsewhere, Afghans have to solve the technical problem of sending money they have saved to their family in Afghanistan. Official channels became progressively available after 2002, but the problem was especially acute in the 1980s and 1990s, when no banks were operational.

Migration to Afghanistan's neighbouring countries, and the very significant sum of remittances sent home, can be seen not only as a response to war and insecurity but also as an efficient economic strategy for households and a crucial contribution to the economy of the country as a whole. There is a clear pattern of multidirectional cross-border movements that indicates the ongoing, cyclical nature of migration, and which blurs the boundaries between refugees and voluntary migrants (Hanifi, 2000; Monsutti, 2004, 2005; Stigter and Monsutti, 2005).[3]

Refugee motivations and vintages

Several authors have argued that typologies are integral to any general theory of migration and refugee displacement. Migration then tends to be conceived through the lens of motivations, with forced migration being a specific and somehow extreme case, where the agency is minimal. Kunz, for instance, starts with the following definition of the refugee: 'With a different past and with motivations at variance with those affecting voluntary migrants, the refugee moves from his homeland to the country of his settlement against his will. He is a distinct social type' (Kunz, 1973: 130; see also Kunz, 1981), whose aim is one day to rediscover community ties by returning to his homeland. Kunz's central distinction is between voluntary and involuntary migration (characterised by push and pull factors respectively) and he uses a classical decision model to identify the diverse combinations of motives and external circumstances. Thus, he speaks of the 'anticipatory refugee movement', where refugees move to the host country in anticipation of a worsening situation at home; and the 'acute refugee movement', where they flee, often in difficult conditions, a context of violence and insecurity. In both cases, it is true, 'push

factors' are the decisive ones, but the urgency gives them much greater promi-
nence in 'acute movement'. Pull factors may then often play a role in the choice
of an (at least temporary) host country.

Inspired by such a model, Connor (1987a; 1987b; 1989) focuses on the
many Afghans who have settled outside the refugee villages within the urban
fabric of Pakistan. Her work on the 'self-settled refugees' in Peshawar starts
from the assumption that choice of residence is influenced by the refugee's
past history and cultural framework, including geographical and ethnic origin, social position (educational level, occupational experience) and political
involvement (membership of a resistance movement), time of departure from
Afghanistan, and reasons for the decision. Connor seeks to close the gap
between studies of voluntary migrants and refugees, and to move beyond the
idea that the route taken by the latter is always 'forced, chaotic, generally ter-
ror-stricken'. Following Kunz, she argues that a general theory of refugees
must formulate causal typologies and include the notion that different
'vintages' of refugees share a number of distinct characteristics (Connor,
1987b: 155). She shows that Afghans left their country after events related in
some way to their own particular sociology; they did not flee *en masse*.

The results of her research are expressed in percentages of the motivations
to migrate correlated with the year of departure. Her conclusion, which it is
certainly possible to agree with, is that Afghans left their country after events
related in some way to their own particular sociology. Her mapping of Afghan
refugees in Peshawar is most interesting, but the significance of her information on the reasons for departure from Afghanistan is open to some doubt. In
fact, the results are rather disappointing. It comes as no surprise that the
bombing and fighting, together with general pressure from the Soviet army
and the Communist government, were the main reasons driving Afghans into
exile (rural populations were more likely to suffer bombing and massacre,
whereas city dwellers had more to fear from wrongful arrest). However, the
percentages given by Connor do not take account of the inevitable overlap in
motives. Moreover, her chronological section focuses particularly on the
moment of departure: she does not notice that people do not necessarily stop
moving in Peshawar, says nothing about back-and-forth movements, and takes
no interest in refugee movements within a diachronic perspective. She gives
the impression that Afghans left at a precise moment and for precise reasons.

But in reality, motivations and causes overlap. People may leave Afghanistan for protection-related reasons, but seek work in Iran or Pakistan. While
abroad, they have the chance to improve their income and access compara-

tively better medical facilities, and in this time they reassess their priorities. The motivation to support the household is often combined with more personal reasons, such as those mentioned above for young men.

Categorisation by 'date of departure' does not allow us to draw out medium-to-long-term strategies. In seeking to group refugees by the 'vintage' category and by socio-cultural and ethnic factors, Connor (1989: 927–29) neglects the planned 'multi-location' of domestic units and kinship groups, as well as the complementarities of places of residence and occupations. Driven by poverty as much as by war, Afghans have been constantly on the move. They have woven an intricate web of transnational relations, so it is pointless to try to specify the moment at which the decision to leave Afghanistan was taken.

Migration is also a way of spreading risk within a household (with more than one son) or between households (of various brothers). It is a coping strategy to cover basic needs and repay debts through remittances. The migration of individual members of a household may allow their family to stay in their area of origin. For single migrant workers, the availability of pre-established transnational networks facilitates the migration and influences the place of destination. Most Afghans living and working in Iran have brothers staying behind with their parents in Afghanistan, and they see their migration as a coping strategy that allows their family to receive remittances to pay for daily needs, and to accumulate capital for investment in land and housing.

Factors which induce migration cannot be reduced to the explicit motivations of social actors. Further, the factors that induce migration are not necessarily the same as those which perpetuate it. Migrants weave networks of contacts that make it easier to move between different countries. Addressing the causes of migration does not constitute a guarantee to bring it to an end, since the factors which sustain migratory flows come to form more or less stable systems.

Transnational networks and social strategies

A recent and growing body of literature proposes a novel approach to migration and mobility. Several scholars have applied the concept of transnational social networks to the study of specific refugee groups (see for example Al-Ali et al., 2001; Chatelard, 2002; Shami, 1996). Without negating the legal specificity of the term 'refugee' or minimising the hardships they face, these authors borrow methodological and theoretical concepts developed mainly for the study of labour migration. This approach stems from the concern that refugees are not always merely victims but can also be people adapting to the world system, much like other migrants. Refugees and other migrants share a number of social features, and individuals may belong to several categories at one time or successively. Social networks almost always include people who can be labelled as labour migrants or as refugees.

This new approach is also influencing research on Afghan refugees. A number of texts have been published on the Afghan diaspora settled in Western countries (Centlivres, 2000; Centlivres et al., 2000; Omidian, 1994; Omidian and Lipson, 1992; Shalinsky, 1996),[4] and the networks existing between distant locales and scattered people are increasingly studied (Monsutti, 2004, 2005).[5] It appears that the migratory trajectories of Afghans are not definitive or linear. It would be more accurate to describe them as a series of multidirectional displacements. This phenomenon has become an encompassing aspect of the Afghan way of life, and it implies an intense circulation of people and goods across international borders.

In order to describe the interplay of local and global forces and to understand how Afghan migrants are linked to the world system, three methods of observation and analysis seem relevant: an open and flexible use of the proven concept of a network; a focus on the production and distribution of commodities; and multi-sited ethnography and transnational studies. The concept of a network has been defined by Barnes more than fifty years ago in a very simple and still workable way:

The image I have is of a set of points some of which are joined by lines. The points of the image are people, or sometimes groups, and the lines indicate which people interact with each other. We can of course think of the whole of social life as generating a network of this kind (Barnes, 1954: 43).

This definition has been reformed and adapted to the globalisation context by Hannerz (1992), who has reduced the importance of individuals in the network, and attached considerably greater scope to the strategies of groups such as households, lineages, neighbourhood circles, and even tribal segments. Emmanuel Marx (1990) has established the usefulness of the concept of network for understanding the experience of refugees whose social ties are expanding in different locales. The study of such networks should not concentrate only on permanent institutionalised relations, since passing ties also hold essential information about social practices. In the Afghan case, this means going beyond the apparent weight of official kinship relations and ancestral, tribal or ethnic affiliation, in order to bring out the actual relations of cooperation implemented by the people in a context of insecurity and mobility.

The focus on networks and people remains nevertheless insufficient. Studying objects and their social meanings, and describing the production and distribution of a set of services and commodities, have proven to be a fruitful approach. Exchanges do not only satisfy material needs, but also produce and reproduce social ties. The relation between commodity flows and social ties is then reciprocal.

These two cogent methodological devices are encompassed in the concept of multi-sited ethnography defined by Marcus (1995: 116–10) who talks of 'tracking' strategies and who proposes different ways to apply his program: 'follow the people', 'follow the thing', 'follow the metaphor', 'follow the plot, story, or allegory', 'follow the life or biography', and finally 'follow the conflict'. As Rouse states in his research on Mexican migration in the United States:

[t]hrough the continuous circulation of people, money, goods, and information, the various settlements have become so closely woven together that, in an important sense, they have come to constitute a single community spread across a variety of sites, something I refer to as a 'transnational migrant circuit' (Rouse, 1991: 14).

Research which follows such an agenda will bring outputs other than the typology perspective, which is about motivations and distinguishes vintages among refugees and migrants. Here, the study does not focus on any one location nor on the moment of departure, but considers—both diachronically and synchronically—the migratory circuit as a whole.

Multi-sited research on multi-sited strategies

Therefore, it seems worth tracking the strategies rather than reconstructing the motivations, asking *how* rather than *why* people migrate. Adopting such a perspective, fieldwork is not carried out within a bounded territory but rather follows mobile people. The limit of the social group which is studied is not defined at first. The itinerary of an initially small number of persons and their effective social ties is reconstructed step-by-step during the research.

The effective relations of solidarity may be studied by describing three complementary phenomena: firstly, the spatial mobility of individuals, their transnational routes and the associated migrant smuggling rings; secondly, the transfer of goods and money, and the trading activities across international borders; and finally, the circulation of information through visits, telephone, letters and e-mail. This corresponds to Rouse's (1991) study of how people, money, information and commodities circulate. In this chapter I continue by addressing the first two.

I have conducted research in Afghanistan, Pakistan, Iran and the wider diaspora. The different locations have distinct advantages and drawbacks to the people that live there.

1) *The village of origin*. Afghanistan is a devastated country. Insecurity, poverty, and the lack of schools and hospitals are all major handicaps. Yet it is the 'homeland', and many refugees have kept family ties and land in Afghanistan. People live there among their own: the women, children and old people are not isolated. This makes it possible for men to leave their family when they go to Pakistan, Iran or the Arabian Peninsula. The cost of living is low, at least in the countryside.

2) *The refugee camps and cities of Pakistan*. In Pakistan, Afghans were able to move freely (at least in the 1980s and 1990s), but the professional activities available to them were scarce. Many Afghans have obtained a Pakistani identity card or even a passport. Certain cities serve as hubs if expulsions are under way in Iran; or if there is major fighting in Hazarajat, people know that there will always be a relative to welcome them in Quetta, for example. On the other hand, Quetta does not offer many occupational outlets.

3) *Iranian urban centres*. Iran presents a striking contrast with Pakistan. The labour market seems to offer more possibilities: it is quite easy to find a relatively well-paid job (building industry, construction of roads, quarry, agriculture etc.) by drawing upon family or tribal networks; although Afghans are mainly employed as unskilled workers and find that many activities are forbidden to them. On the other hand, living conditions generally remain precarious in Iran. Since its position on the international scene prevented Iran receiving the kind of international aid that Pakistan did, proper camps have been very thin on the ground. Meanwhile the constant danger of expulsion, harassment and police violence means that it is difficult for Afghans to settle with their family on a permanent basis.

A growing number of Afghans also went to Europe, North America, or Australia. In the 1980s and early 1990s, most of them were from upper and middle urban classes. But many rural people found their way to the West during the time of the Taliban. For instance, some Hazaras are now present in Washington DC, New York and New Jersey, where they are taxi drivers or are active in the catering industry. Many others preferred to go eastwards and tried their chance crossing illegally between Indonesia to Australia on small fishing boats (Monsutti, 2007a).

My travels from Pakistan to Afghanistan and Iran, and from Europe to North America, Australia and New Zealand, allowed me to study some worldwide transnational social networks. Contrary to the idea that people who have settled in Western countries and become acquainted with democracy and human rights may play a mitigating role in quelling the conflict in their home country (Weiss Fagen and Bump, 2006), the ethnic faultlines are sometimes exacerbated in the wider Afghan diaspora, because previous agricultural and commercial cooperative complementarities disappear. Although the Afghan migratory networks have acquired a transnational dimension, they seem to divide along ethnic lines: Pashtuns, Tajiks, Hazaras, Uzbeks and others rarely rub shoulders along the way. In both Afghanistan and host countries, competition among the various components of society has become more pronounced. Forced migration has led to a process of urbanisation and detribalisation. It may foster a broader identity with reference to the Afghan nation, but concrete day-to-day existence is based on narrow social ties. There is a line of tension between an abstract sense of Afghan-ness developed in exile, whilst everyday life tends to be fragmented by the group of origin.

Too great a stress on the ethnic dimension does, however, mask the reality of solidarity networks, which are usually organised around aspects such as lineage, marital ties or residential proximity, at a sub-ethnic level. Regional origin also often carries greater weight than ethnic affiliation. At the macro social level, several faultlines are especially visible: the mistrust with which minority groups view Pashtuns, who themselves tend to feel that their claims are insufficiently acknowledged by the Afghan authorities; and probably more importantly, the difference between urban and rural populations; the tense relations between the Sunni majority and the Shiite minority; and the wide gap between Afghans who have lived in the West and those who have remained in Afghanistan or neighbouring countries—for example the conflicts of interest between diaspora elites and internal commanders. At the micro social level, operational solidarity groups are based on a set of overlapping criteria (kinship and residential proximity, but also religious affiliation, educational level, and so on), which cannot be simply reduced to the dimension of ethnicity, tribe or lineage.

Linking mobile people through money transfers[6]

Money transfers are a matter of interest for at least four reasons: (1) they reveal the existence of social networks linking faraway places; (2) they are economically important for the areas from which the migrants originate; (3) they sustain migration as a strategy of domestic groups; and (4) they stimulate and orient future movement, since migrants pass on information about the possibilities in various regions.

In the 1990s, when an Afghan worker in Iran (*kargar*) wished to send his savings to his family in Afghanistan, he could not use the official banking system since he was unlikely to have any identification papers; and, in any case, the banking system was not operating in Afghanistan. He therefore entrusted his money to a businessman specialising in informal remittances, and who was known locally as a *hawaladar* (from the Arabic *hawala*, 'transfer' and by extension 'letter of credit, cheque'). Half-merchant, half-banker, his expertise in the transfer of funds has kept money and goods flowing without interruption between Iran, Pakistan and Afghanistan—a role that has a long history but which has acquired unprecedented dimensions during the war. Both *kargar* and *hawaladar* must belong to the same lineage or come from the same valley. If the relationship was less close than that, a middleman was needed.

The *hawaladar* passed on a letter to his partners, stating the details of the transaction; and gave another one to the *kargar*, which he sent to his family in Afghanistan via a friend going back home. The commission charged is very low (most of the time less than three per cent), since the *hawaladar's* profit is earned from the trade itself, and depends on the distance of the deadline for repayment, and the closeness of the relationship between the *kargar* and the *hawaladar*. The *hawaladar* might use this money to buy some merchandise (plastic shoes, shirts, cloth, water coolers, etc.) and export them, or directly send the money through the official banking system to Pakistan, where one of his partners (always a close relative) retrieved the money.[7] He used it to make a profit through currency exchange and finally bought some goods (wheat, rice, cooking oil, sugar, tea, but also shoes, cloth, cooking pots, etc.). He dispatched them by lorry to the family village in Afghanistan, where a third partner ran a shop. The goods were sold and the proceeds were used to reimburse the *kargar's* family.

In the absence of any external guarantee from the State, an atmosphere of trust was essential to ensure that the transaction was respected. Such trust could only arise if the interaction occurred regularly and over a long period of time. Members of each social and ethnic group dealt with members of other groups only when strictly necessary, such as to cross borders or travel in hostile areas. Despite the trauma of war and exile, the Afghans had thus managed to deal with, and even take advantage of, their geographic dispersion and the resulting economic diversification by developing new transnational cooperation structures.

Beyond their economic dimension, money transfers play a crucial role in producing and reproducing social relations, despite the context of dispersion and (very often) war. Although the emigration of young men may pose long-term problems for the reconstruction of Afghanistan, it is still a survival strategy that has proved its effectiveness.[8] The *hawala* system has enabled many families inside Afghanistan to feed themselves, whereas humanitarian aid mainly focused on refugees during the Soviet occupation, then gradually dried up during the 1990s before making a chaotic reappearance after the fall of the Taliban in 2001. International aid has certainly helped many Afghans to cope with periods of acute crisis, but the multiplication of rival NGOs and a lack of coordination mean that the overall results have been often rather poor (Donini, 1996). Remittances through the *hawala* system are considerably larger, and arguably much better distributed, than the total sum of humanitarian aid.

We have seen that economic exchange and social ties may be conceived in correlation. Often, commodities and people circulate in opposite directions; and this is precisely the case in the remittance system among the Afghan migrants. It is a complex interlace of solidarity and competition, trust and mistrust, whose study enables us to understand how Afghan society has not sunk into Hobbesian chaos despite war and migration. Dispersion and mobility may be seen as an asset with a social, economic and political dimension.

Beyond the three solutions to the refugee problem

The migration of Afghans is neither definitive nor temporary; it is more appropriate to speak of recurrent multidirectional movement. Few Afghan refugees have never made a return trip after their initial departure; and there are few domestic units within Afghanistan without at least one member abroad. Migration and exile are therefore not usually followed by sheer integration into a host country or permanent return to Afghanistan: movement is continual and eventually leads to the constitution of a genuinely transnational community. Drawing upon the example of the Hazaras, we have seen how the Afghans have established a 'circulatory territory', to borrow an expression from Tarrius (1995: 15–35). By maintaining a certain dispersion of family members, they take advantage of spatial and economic diversification; while at the same time they diminish the risks associated with insecurity and poverty.

Shifting away from a focus on the moment of departure and the motivations of refugees to leave their country of origin, the multi-sited study of ongoing mobility and domestic strategies has shed new light on one of the largest movements of people in the late twentieth century. Having initially followed the same people in three places (Afghanistan, Pakistan, Iran) and then beyond (Western countries), and having studied the transnational networks (the movement of people, of goods and money, and of information), I base the three claims on ethnographic evidences: firstly, the normality of movements and the prior existence of transnational networks in the region; secondly, the incredible resilience and inventiveness of the Afghan population, who have largely relied on themselves to face the most trying conditions in war and exile, especially illustrated by the *hawala* system; finally, the relevance of migratory movements and of transnational networks for the reconstruction of Afghanistan (economic and social).

This chapter is based on a research conducted since the mid-1990s, after the end of the Cold War, and among a particular population. Nevertheless, similar results could have been reached following the same methodological approach in the 1980s and among other mobile groups, in Afghanistan or elsewhere (for the Somali example see Horst, 2006). The refugees are not mere victims: they have social, economic and political assets that they are able to mobilise. Mobility is one of them, which blurs the boundary between the categories of refugees and migrants: refugee camps were part of larger social networks organised on a diversified allocation of tasks between members of domestic units. Some people stayed behind in the place of origin for fighting or looking after the fields; some went to the Afghan Refugee Villages in Pakistan and received food rations and housing; and some went further to Iran, Kuwait, the United Arab Emirates or Saudi Arabia to earn a livelihood in order to benefit the whole dispersed family through the *hawala* system.

Policy options regarding Afghan migration have generally been framed within the 'conflict–refugee' approach, which presumes that Afghan refugees arrived in Pakistan or in Iran in order to escape war, and that they will return once the fighting is over. Research with a multi-sited perspective breaks from this view by approaching the subject more broadly—from the perspective of 'transnational networks' and acknowledging the complexity of experiences. The reasons for migration cannot be reduced only to exposure to armed conflict. Whilst violence and insecurity provided the backdrop to migration from the late 1970s onwards, the precise ways in which people were affected varied between individuals, families, social classes and geographical origin. Furthermore, the decision to leave Afghanistan was not unrelated to prior economic expectations about the destination as well as pre-existing connections. It is common to observe complex patterns of movement, including repeated departure and repatriation. Pre-existing social networks, which cannot be reduced solely to kinship, tribe, ethnicity, religion or political affiliation, have been critical in protecting, facilitating and sustaining Afghans on the move. Many examples of people travelling back and forth between their place of origin in Afghanistan, Pakistan or Iran have been documented, despite the fact that, since late 2001 and the fall of the Taliban, Afghans have been increasingly vulnerable to police harassment in their host countries.

The refugee perspective that informs the current policy paradigm is too simple a framework to incorporate the multiple dimensions and complexity of the Afghan migration experience. It is unrealistic to expect that a complete cessation of all conflict and political uncertainty within Afghanistan will automatically lead to the return of all people of Afghan origin who are currently living in Pakistan and in Iran. It would be more accurate to see migration between Afghanistan, Pakistan and Iran as an ongoing historical phenomenon, whose scale dramatically increased with war but which will continue, as it did before, even in the absence of military and political crises. Such a phenomenon could be acknowledged by regional governments in order to move away from the present-day framework and to pay more attention to the actual strategies of Afghans and the obstacles they meet.

Afghan movement partially blurs the boundary between forced and voluntary migration, since the social strategies of people labelled as refugees and those of economic migrants are often similar. Given that ongoing migration was an efficient survival strategy for so many people, that it may be seen as a tool of reconstruction, and that it is a constitutive feature of Afghan social life, there is a real necessity to look beyond the three 'durable' solutions to the refugee problems usually recommended and promoted by UNHCR: voluntary repatriation to the country of origin, integration in the host country or resettlement in a third country. Such a formal framework is not sufficient for managing the present situation, as it is based on the idea that solutions are found when the movements of a population come to an end. A more comprehensive solution based on an understanding of social practices and of strategies developed by the people labelled as refugees is necessary.

Based on its experience in the region and the evolution of the political situation, the UNHCR itself is aware of the limitations of its own action, and has acknowledged the necessity of defining a new approach:

Return to Afghanistan is a much more complex challenge than previously recognised. This is attributable not only to the challenges inside Afghanistan but also to the changing nature of population movements and social and economic shifts induced by protracted exile. [...] There have been three major causes of population movements from Afghanistan—political conflict and violence, natural disasters, and economic migration. Many Afghans cross borders to look for seasonal employment, to trade, to access services, and to maintain social and family connections. These networks may have become a critical component in the livelihood systems of many Afghan families, including returnees (UNHCR, 2004).

The absorption capacity inside Afghanistan is limited, and the national economy needs the inflow of cash and commodities financed by migrants. Full repatriation is neither feasible nor desirable. Implemented at all costs, it could destabilise the fragile equilibrium of the renascent Afghan state and have negative effects on the neighbouring countries.

Even if the causes of migration are addressed to the greatest extent possible in Afghanistan, and if the government of Kabul is gradually able to provide more effective, authoritative and democratic guidance, migration will undoubtedly continue because of population growth, the underdevelopment of the country, persistent lack of rule of law, and potential natural disasters, as well as the corresponding demands of Pakistani and Iranian economies. As we have seen, it would be naïve to see in the pervasiveness of mobility and transnational networks the ideal breeding ground for national unity and peace-building in Afghanistan. But it would be equally narrow-minded to overlook the fact that it is an important aspect of social strategies, and may be a factor in the reconstruction of Afghanistan and in the future stability of the whole region.

NOTES

1. BEYOND 'THE WILD TRIBES': WORKING TOWARDS AN UNDERSTANDING OF CONTEMPORARY AFGHANISTAN

1. In particular, Anthropology, Human Geography, Development Studies, History, Economics, Political Science, and Sociology.
2. Including the Afghan Education Trust, Afghan Research and Evaluation Unit, Afghan Student's Association UK, Afghan Women's Council, Afghan Youth Fund, Afghanaid, Amnesty International, BBC World, British Agencies Afghanistan Group, British Library, British Red Cross, Refugee Council, Royal Geographical Society, WOMANKIND and representatives from a variety of Afghan refugee community organisations based in the United Kingdom.
3. We recognise that the noun 'Afghan' is problematic in itself as an identifier. Before the current boundaries of a state called Afghanistan were established, 'Afghan' tended to be used to refer to people of Pashtun ethnicity only. However, over the years the term Afghan has been accepted by the majority of people who live in Afghanistan as a national descriptor. In this volume the term Afghan is used to refer to people who consider themselves Afghan or of Afghan descent.
4. It is worth noting that by 'Afghans' these texts refer to Afghan *men*. Although sometimes containing chapters that mention women—as in chapter II.7, 'Marriages, condition of women, funerals etc' (Elphinstone, 1815)—these colonial-era authors were unlikely to have had any contact with Afghan women.
5. There are notable exceptions—for example, the in-depth work of the Afghanistan Research and Evaluation Unit, and a handful of individual researchers, as some of the work in this volume illustrates. Nevertheless, without (and even with) the logistical and security support of an established organisation it is extremely difficult for individual academic researchers to do this kind of work in Afghanistan.
6. Fieldwork interview by Oeppen, April 2007, California, USA.
7. For further information see Brettell (1993).

2. CHALLENGES TO RESEARCH IN AFGHANISTAN AND ITS DIASPORA

1. This paper is the result of participants' contributions during the workshop 'Challenges to research in Afghanistan' at the Launch Conference of the European Centre for Afghan Studies (ECAS) at the School of Oriental and African Studies (SOAS) on 3 March 2007, as well as a literature review. Furthermore, it incorporates contributions from some of the contributors to this book. All inaccuracies and omissions are entirely my responsibility.
2. See Introduction for further discussion.
3. Here some variation is allowed in 'very specific and exceptional research contexts', and specific guidelines are available from the ESRC (2005).
4. This could be why most research projects are currently conducted in major cities, e.g. Kabul, Kandahar, Herat etc., rather than in more remote provinces—in order to have access to contingency plans, and to a more comprehensive infrastucture that can aid organised research.
5. Arya, V. Personal communication, January 2008
6. Arya, V. Personal communication, January 2008
7. Arya, V. Personal communication, January 2008
8. First, during the Soviet invasion and the ensuing Communist government from 1979 to 1992; secondly, at the onset of the *mujahideen* war and the fight for the city of Kabul up to 1996; and thirdly, with the appearance of the Taliban, and arguably up to the present day.
9. This need for sensitivity on my part was probably in a small way similar to that which many Afghans in exile must feel in a similar situation.

SECTION I: AFGHAN HISTORY, SOCIETY AND CULTURE

3. BRITAIN IN THE FIRST TWO AFGHAN WARS—WHAT CAN WE LEARN?

1. For an authoritative and comprehensive account of the First Afghan War, see Kaye (1851).
2. For a full account see Kaye (1851, vol. I:441).
3. *Hansard*, Commons, Vol. LI col. 1330 (1840).
4. For an evaluation of the cost of the Iraq war alone, see Bilmes and Stiglitz (2006).
5. For an account of *Pashtunwali*, see Elphinstone (1815:158–79).
6. Whose task was to guide the ruler of Afghanistan, and represent the desires of the British Government in India to him.
7. In the recent Asia Foundation Report, *Afghanistan in 2006*, a poll showed that 77 per cent of Afghans identified corruption as a major problem, and that 60 per cent believed that it had increased over the previous year (p. 15). Similarly, trust in the judicial system stood at 39 per cent (Asia Foundation, 2006:29).
8. In Kabul, the rate of inflation (consumer prices index) peaked at 24 per cent in 2003/4, before falling back to the current level of 9.2 per cent (International Monetary Fund, 2006).

9. See for example Tzemach (2006).
10. Hensman's (1881) accounts, contemporary to the events described, capture perfectly the sense of the aimless policy and aporia on the part of the British. For a full account of these events and the conflict, see also Hanna (1899).

4. THE SITUATION OF WOMEN AND GIRLS IN AFGHANISTAN

1. Available to download from: www.womankind.org.uk. Statistics and data in this article, unless otherwise stated, are drawn primarily from these reports.
2. Also available to download from: http://www.womankind.org.uk/takingstock-downloads.html
3. For more information on The North Atlantic Treaty Organization's (NATO's) International Security Assistance Force (ISAF) see: http://www.nato.int/ISAF/index.html [Viewed 02/2008].
4. There are currently sixty-eight women in Afghanistan's parliament (of 249 MPs)
5. See interview with the Afghan Independent Human Rights Commission in the British Afghan Women's Society / WOMANKIND Worldwide's DVD, 'Tradition, War and Freedom' (2006).
6. It is estimated that at present there are only 8—10 shelters operating in the country (one in Herat, one in Balkh, four in Kabul and two in central Afghanistan)
7. Women's NGOs have contributed to the prevention of human rights abuses through their ongoing work, including data collection, protecting individual rights at a community and household level through local level awareness raising and advocacy, grassroots peace education work, and their successful work at national level in preventing the re-establishment of the Department for Vice and Virtue in Afghanistan.
8. See AWID (2006). This research clearly indicated that 'whilst public awareness of women's rights violations internationally may have increased, funding for women's organisations to guarantee those rights has not... The situation for so many women's organisations doing critical work to guarantee the rights of women on the ground is so incredibly challenging that their very survival is at stake' (AWID, 2006:105–6).
9. Two prominent female journalists were murdered in Kabul in June 2007, threats to female MPs such as Malalai Joya are well documented, attacks on girls schools in Afghanistan are on the rise (Human Rights Watch, 2006), and the murder of Safia Amajan in Kandahar in October 2006 is a chilling reminder of the threats to those women who defy Taliban orders not to educate girls and women.
10. European Network of NGOs in Afghanistan—a European network facilitated by the British Agencies in Afghanistan Group (BAAG).
11. Formed by a group of BAAG and ENNA members in March 2007 with the following aims: raising the voice of Afghan women and girls and women's local civil society groups at a European level; sharing programmatic experience and knowledge; developing a common understanding of advocacy and support strategies to promote women's and girl's human rights; and building the capacity of local and international NGOs, donors and policy makers to better monitor, protect and

promote women's and girl's human rights in Afghanistan. The group recently submitted a paper on rule of law to the Rome Conference on Rule of Law in Afghanistan (July 07), outlining details of concerns.

12. According to the UN, where imprisioned women cannot arrange for a family member to look after their children, the children are put in prison with them. And they are not given extra food for the children (UN, 2004:19).

13. For example, in the capital, Kabul and the western city of Herat, enrolment rates for girls can reach 50 per cent; whilst in insurgency-hit Uruzgan and Zabul provinces in the south, more than 90 per cent of girls cannot go to school (see IRIN, 2007).

14. Such as *nafaqa*, the monetary support of widowed or otherwise destitute female family members by male relatives.

15. Seventy per cent of Afghanistan's population lives on less than US$2 per day (UNDP, 2004).

16. The *wolesi jirga* passed a bill on 31 January 2007 that would grant immunity to all Afghans involved in war crimes during the last quarter century; see Synowitz (2007) for more details.

17. For more information, please contact: awrc.kabul@ceretechs.com.

18. www.afghanwomensnetwork.org.

19. www.awec.info/project.html.

20. For more information, please see our website: http://www.womankind.org.uk/afghanistan.html.

21. This approach is currently being piloted by AWEC in Mazar-i-Sharif with WOMANKIND support, and is having excellent results in tackling violence against women at a household and community level.

5. THE POLITICAL ECONOMY OF NORMLESSNESS IN AFGHANISTAN

1. This article (in particular the section 'A Critical Appraisal of the Thesis of Normlessness') has grown out of a workshop organised by the author at the inaugural conference of the European Centre for Afghan Studies (ECAS) and would not have materialised without the lively attendance of its participants. In particular I would like to thank Antonio Giustozzi, Jonathan Goodhand, Kristian Berg Harpviken, Alessandro Monsutti, Gabriele Rasuly-Paleczek and Angela Schlenkhoff for their valuable and thoughtful comments. All inaccuracies and omissions are entirely my responsibility. Interviewees' names are fictive. This research was partially funded by EMergence In the Loop (EMIL), a European Union Sixth Framework Programme project.

2. For the use of the notion 'traditional' see also Canfield (1988:186).

3. The argument made here is about the co-formation and -existence of norms and normlessness and not about the emergence of a space completely emptied of social norms.

4. This statement naturally evokes the questions of 'What is *the* norm?' and 'Do general norms exist?' The following examples imply that norms exist which are accepted by a majority. However, no explanation is given from a Foucaultian per-

spective of who exactly these majorities are and who the enforcers were of a particular social norm.

5. In essence, this alternative was never different from the time of former Afghan governments, as the two main cleavages of Afghan statehood—between urban and rural areas and between elites and ordinary people—kept on persisting (cf. Roy, 1994; Rubin, 1992).

6. See for example Human Rights Watch (1998).

7. Interview with Maulawi Abdul Kabir, a former Taliban *mullah*, 22 October 2006, Kabul.

8. Interview and observation with Gulzeb Khan, a former Taliban *mullah*, 17 October 2006, Kabul.

9. Interview with John Smith, an international businessman working in Afghanistan, 3 October 2007, Kabul.

10. For a similar argument see Roy (1998), who points out that during the Jihad ethnical and religious radicalism have been imported to Afghanistan by Arab volunteers.

11. Interview with John Smith, an international businessman working in Afghanistan, 3 October 2007, Kabul

12. Personal observation on many occasions, particularly in Kabul.

13. It has not escaped my notice that polls in Afghanistan, as in any other conflict-torn context, are problematic and doubtful.

14. The question how neo-*qawm* differ in detail from *qawm* has to my knowledge not yet been fully answered empirically.

15. Findings from the author's own interview data collected during various field research trips between April 2003 and September/October 2007. See also Rasuly-Paleczek (1998).

16. Interview with George Powell, a senior member of an International Organisation, who in autumn 2007 worked in and around Kandahar, 1–2 October 2007, Kabul.

17. For Weber (1978: 314), the monopoly of power is integral to the definition of a state. If applied to the case of Afghanistan, then Afghanistan has always been a 'failed' state.

18. Personal observations in the summers of 2003 and 2004.

19. By the same token it should be noted that the social phenomenon of normlessness has loomed in Afghanistan also before the time of the Jihad, namely in the monarchic period though on a scale incomparable to that of today.

20. With regard to this paragraph, see the journal *Iranian Studies* (2007, vol. 40, 2), a special issue on Afghan refugees.

21. It might be worth exploring whether such innovation predominantly appears along the fringe zone of spheres of normlessness and spheres where norms prevail: cf. Goodhand (2005) and Rasuly-Paleczek (2004).

22. Personal communication with Gabriele Rasuly-Paleczek; see also Rasuly-Paleczek (2004).

23. See for a similar argument for the case of Colombia, Richani (2002).

24. For how such evidence can be made fruitful for social simulation purposes, see Geller and Moss (2008).

6. KEEPING THE PEACE; GENDER, JUSTICE AND AUTHORITY: MECHANISMS FOR COMMUNITY BASED DISPUTE RESOLUTION IN AFGHANISTAN

1. The author wishes to acknowledge the research team: Zia Hussain; Shelly Manalan; Fauzia Rahimi; Jamila Wafa and Shafiq Ziai for their dedication, attention to detail and resilience, under what were often difficult conditions, in conducting the fieldwork for this research and their contribution to the analysis of the data.

2. AREU is currently continuing this research, collecting data in Kabul to capture the processes for dispute resolution among an urban community and within business communities. Following this, data will be collected in the rural areas of one further province.

3. *Qawm* often translated as tribe, essentially means a kinship group which can range considerably in size and scope.

4. Community is an often used but rarely defined term. Drawing on Agarwal's (1997) definition, a community can be based on residency, e.g. the village community, or on social grouping, e.g. a religious community or a *qawm* community. A person can simultaneously be a member of several different communities, for example a member of a particular *qawm* within a village, which also spreads across several villages. It is recognised that communities are not homogeneous, but instead heterogeneous—in terms of power, resources and interests.

5. Customary law can best be described as a non-codified system of laws or rules which are recognised by the community using them as a legitimate form of justice.

6. The case can also be made for certain criminal cases to be resolved solely by community based dispute resolution mechanism, such as petty theft, see Barfield, Nojumi and Their (2006).

7. For a wider discussion of different conceptualisations of power based on coercion as opposed to power based on authority see (Lukes, 1974; Skalnik, 1999).

8. In Nangarhar these men are also referred to as *jirgamars*.

9. For a fuller discussion on how the status of white-beard is attained please see AREU case study papers on community based dispute resolution in Bamiyan and Nangahar provinces (Smith, 2009; Smith and Manalan, 2009).

10. Other terms are used throughout Afghanistan for similar bodies, such as *shura*. However, in the areas where we conducted research the term *shura* was used to describe institutions with more fixed membership and of a more formalised nature, such as district level *shuras* of various kinds who had representation from each village and the community development councils of the National Solidarity Programme.

11. The terms *jirga* and *jalasa* are used interchangeably in this paper, dependent upon whether dispute resolution processes are being discussed in relation to Bamiyan

or Nangarhar; *jirga* being the term used in Nangarhar and *jalasa* being used in Bamiyan.

12. While using the Pashtu and Dari terms *jirga* and *jalasa* throughout this paper, when pluralised the standard English form of pluralizing is used with *jirga* becoming *jirgas* and *jalasa* becoming *jalasas*.

13. Traditionally nomadic *Pashtun* group

14. *Shinwars* are one of the largest *qawms* living in Nangarhar province.

15. Indeed a practice found within *Pashtun* customary law, *teega* or *dabara*, specifically serves the purpose of controlling the dispute, by all parties agreeing not to fight over these issues for a specified period of time. For example, during the *Mujahideen* war in one of the villages where research was conducted, a *teega* was put on all disputes for the duration of the war.

16. It was extremely unusual for disputants to go to the police. Of the many cases explored through the course of the research, in only one example did a party in a dispute go directly to the police with his grievance, and this was in regard to a relatively minor dispute regarding the selling of meat from a cow that had been sick.

17. It is important to note that this stability relates more to the position of *woliswal* rather than the individual holding that post. Nixon (2008), researching issues of sub-national governance in Afghanistan, found that for the eight districts he studied the *woliswals* had been in post for on average only eight months.

18. Appointed or chosen village leader.

19. *Bad* is not practiced in all areas of or among all groups in Afghanistan; indeed it is primarily only practiced by Pashtuns. The degree to which it may be used as a method of dispute resolution, even within Pashtun areas, also varies.

20. For a detailed description and analyses of these differences and the reasons for them see AREU's cases study papers on community based dispute resolution in Bamiyan and Nangarhar (Smith, 2009; Smith and Manalan, 2009).

21. Not her real name

22. Among this particular Pashtun *qawm*, women may be sold if they are suspected to have behaved in a sexually deviant way, or to have committed some other deviant offense.

SECTION II: SECURITY AND GOVERNANCE

7. DILEMMAS OF GOVERNANCE IN AFGHANISTAN: BETWEEN PATRIMONIALISM AND BUREAUCRATISATION

1. With institutionalisation (institution building) in this chapter I simply refer to the process of embedding values and norms in state organisations, in order to reduce uncertainty and increasingly shape expectations.

2. With bureaucratisation I refer here to the process of making state institutions responsible not to an individual (the ruler), but to impersonally applied rules, and of staffing them with salaried professionals who do not own the institutions themselves.

3. Khalq was one of the two wings of the *Hezb-i Demokratik-e Khalq* (People's Democratic Party), a pro-Soviet group which took power in April 1978. A bitter rivalry existed with the other wing of the party, *Parcham*, led by Babrak Karmal.
4. Interviews with Afghan police officers, Kabul, October 2007.
5. Interviews with Afghan police officers, Kabul, October 2007.
6. Interviews with Afghan police officers, Kabul, October 2007.
7. Interviews with local elders and expatriate NGO workers, 2006–2007.
8. Disarmament Demobilisation and Reintegration or DDR, and Disarmament of Illegal Armed Groups or DIAG
9. And W. Azoy, personal communication, October 2007.
10. For more information about this period see Giustozzi (2000).
11. Interviews with tribal notables and former Taliban officials, 2005–7.
12. Personal communication with UN officials, Kabul and Mazar-i Sharif, May 2005.
13. Interviews with police officers, NGO workers and foreign travellers, October 2007.
14. Interview with senior official at the Ministry of Interior, October 2007.
15. Personal communication with UN officials and diplomats, October 2007.

8. WHAT PREVENTS AFGHANISTAN BECOMING A LANDBRIDGE?

1. This chapter is based on my PhD thesis, which explores whether Afghanistan can become a landbridge between South Asia, Central Asia and the Middle East. The findings in this paper are based on review of primary and secondary documents, interviews conducted in Afghanistan in April and May 2007 and a workshop attended by Afghans and non-Afghans at the launch conference of the European Centre for Afghan Studies at the School of Oriental and African Studies, London on 3 March 2007.
2. Please refer to Rashid (2008) for more information on how the US tried to negotiate with the Taliban to build a pipeline across Afghanistan when they were in power.
3. The Uzbek government resorted to violence in suppressing the uprising by the radical groups—a move that was seriously criticised by Western governments and human rights groups.
4. I have used pseudonyms for my interviewees to preserve their anonymity.
5. Please note that members of parliament were not considered as government officials.
6. One could dispute the last point as the Middle East can access South Asia through sea as well.
7. Pakistan's military leaders have considered using Afghanistan's territory for retreating in the case of an Indian offensive, i.e. to use it as their backyard depth.
8. By Islamic depth, the general seems to have meant that Muslim nations should become united under the leadership of Pakistan to create a depth against other powers.
9. Under the chairmanship of Dr. Rangin Dadfar Spanta, the Foreign Minister of Afghanistan (2006–), the seventeenth Meeting of Council of Ministers of the

Economic Cooperation Organization (ECO) was held in Herat, Afghanistan, on 20th October 2007. ECO membership includes countries from the Middle East, Central Asia and South Asia: Afghanistan, Azerbaijan, Iran, Kazakhstan, the Kyrgyz Republic, Pakistan, Tajikistan, Turkey, Turkmenistan and Uzbekistan. Moreover, Afghanistan is part of the Central Asia + Japan initiative. On June 6th 2006 the Afghan Foreign Minister visited Japan to take part at the Second Ministerial Meeting of 'Central Asia + Japan Dialogue'. In relation to Afghanistan's centrality, the second conference on regional economic cooperation, held in Delhi in November 2006, recommended the setting up of a 'Centre for Regional Economic Cooperation' in Kabul, dedicated to in-depth and rigorous pursuit of authoritative, constructive, practical and specific initiatives for regional development. Afghanistan is also a member of the Central Asian Regional Economic Cooperation (CAREC) and the South Asian Association for Regional Cooperation (SAARC).

9. THE RETURN OF THE REFUGEE WARRIOR: MIGRATION AND ARMED RESISTANCE IN HERAT

1. This study forms part of the project 'Going Home To Fight? Explaining Refugee Return and Violence', funded by the Research Council of Norway's programme on Poverty and Peace (POVPEACE) for the period 2008–11. I would also like to acknowledge the support of the Centre for the Study of Civil War (CSCW) at PRIO, and I am grateful for input from the participants at a workshop in the CSCW working group on Transnational and International Facets of Civil War on 31 May 2006. Most importantly, I am deeply grateful to all those Afghans who have volunteered their time to be interviewed for this study, but who will remain anonymous in this article. Full responsibility for the contents of the article, of course, remains with the author.

2. In this article, I will be focusing on refugees, in line with the established literature on refugee warriors. It is important to note, however, that factors driving armed mobilization among both internally displaced persons (IDPs) and other types of migrants may be similar to those behind refugee mobilization.

3. The most intensive period of fieldwork in both villages took place in 1999, when the Taliban was in power, but I have also undertaken several shorter visits during the subsequent years, most recently in April 2006. The study is based on a combination of open-ended interviews, structured interviewing and ethnographic data. For a comprehensive discussion of the methodology, see Harpviken 2006.

4. Herat fell to the Taliban in September 1995, one year earlier than the Afghan capital, Kabul.

5. Astri Suhrke, personal communication.

6. The only exceptions known to this author are Adelman (2002) and Goodson (1990).

7. On the general concept of *hijra* and its relevance to present-day migration, see Aldeeb Abu-Sahlieh (1996) and Shami (1996).

8. For a more comprehensive treatment, see Harpviken (2009).

9. One main difference—borne out by the comparison between Afghans in Iran and Afghans in Pakistan—is that, in camp settlements, it is likely that there is a signifi-

cant international presence and reporting. When self-settlement is the main pattern, it is likely that such a presence is either marginal or non-existent (Harpviken, 2009).

10. This reading included the central policy and planning documents related to refugee reintegration and disarmament, demobilization and reintegration (DDR), as well as relevant academic publications available in English. I make no claim that the review encompassed all relevant documents, but I am confident that it covered the most important documents from the key actors. The review was conducted in late 2006.

11. This goes beyond the question of 'absorptive capacity', which focuses on the capacity of the community to assist and accommodate returnees, first and foremost in the economic domain.

12. The majority of the 143 respondents had spent time in exile.

13. All informants have been given fictive names to protect their anonymity.

14. At the same time, among the Shia, Iran encouraged the emergence of new types of leaders educated in their religious schools, with close ties to leaders of the Iranian revolutions. The challenging of traditional leaders created massive armed conflict throughout most of the 1980s, particularly within the Hazarajat region (Harpviken, 1997).

15. A few days after the onset of the US-led attack on 7 October 2001, a team of US Special Forces were in Uzbekistan, prior to their deployment with Ismael Khan (Woodward, 2002: 331).

16. This is not surprising. For similar problems in ascertaining the nuts and bolts of Pakistani support to the Taliban, see Giustozzi (2007).

17. The literature on process tracing and narrative analysis provides the methodological foundations: see Abbott (2001) and George and Bennett (2005).

SECTION III: A TRANSNATIONAL AFGHAN COMMUNITY?

10. THE AFGHAN DIASPORA AND ITS INVOLVEMENT IN THE RECONSTRUCTION OF AFGHANISTAN

1. The author gratefully acknowledges the input of participants at the workshop at the launch conference of the European Centre for Afghan Studies (ECAS), School of Oriental and African Studies, 3 March 2007, and in particular the support of workshop co-organiser Gary Bell. However, the author is responsible for the content of this chapter and any errors are her own.

2. Author's own estimate based on information from the Global Migrant Origin Database (Migration DRC, 2007) and the United Nations Refugee Agency data (UNHCR, 2007). This is a conservative estimate, as data from the Global Migrant Origin Database is based on place of birth and therefore will not include children of Afghan parents born outside of Afghanistan, the so-called second generation.

3. Fieldwork in California, 2006–7.

4. Zalmay Khalilzad is of Afghan descent but moved to the US for his doctoral studies after studying at the American University of Beirut. He has been hugely influ-

ential in shaping US foreign policy, in his previous position as US ambassador to Afghanistan (2003–2005) and currently as ambassador to the United Nations. His power and influence have led to strong contrasting reactions amongst Afghans in the wider diaspora. Some see him as an example of successful integration, whilst others see him as a traitor (fieldwork observations, California 2006–07).

5. When I started telling people that I was interested in the development role of the diaspora, the response I repeatedly received (from Afghans who had not lived in the wider diaspora) was a query as to why I was not investigating the negative role of the diaspora. Returnees were referred to as cowards and 'dog-washers'—people who had low-status, menial jobs in the diaspora but have returned to claim superior jobs and status, simply because of English language skills.

6. Fieldwork observations, California and London, 2006–7.

7. For many Afghan asylum seekers and refugees in the UK, the Home Office has come to represent 'the Government', since the vast majority of their interactions with the Government are those during their initial reception experiences and whilst navigating the asylum process.

11. THE CIRCULATION OF MUSIC BETWEEN AFGHANISTAN AND THE AFGHAN DIASPORA

1. The foundation of my knowledge of Afghan music comes from two-and-a-half years' fieldwork in Herat, and to a much lesser extent Kabul, in the 1970s. My first foray into the Afghan diaspora was in 1985, when as a Royal Anthropological Institute Film Training Fellow at the National Film and Television School, I spent three months in Peshawar, Pakistan, researching and then shooting the film *Amir: An Afghan refugee musician's life in Peshawar, Pakistan*. Since then I have conducted fieldwork on Afghan music in Peshawar, Mashad (Iran), New York, Herat and Fremont (California). After the defeat of the Taliban, I made four visits to Kabul, where I set up a music course for the Aga Khan Music Initiative in Central Asia, which has now grown into a significant school for the teaching of Kabul's distinctive art music. My work with Afghan music has become a large-scale and long-term study of music and migration, though clearly I never planned it as such.

2. Our knowledge of the muscal activities at the radio station in Kabul has been greatly enlarged by the recent PhD thesis of Ahmad Naser Sarmast (see Sarmast 2004).

3. Of course, instruments like the hand-pumped harmonium and *tabla* drums are not indigenous to Afghanistan but have been imported from India, presumably from the mid-19th century. But they have been in use for long enough for them to appear 'traditional' to many, perhaps most, people of Afghanistan.

4. It is worth noting that Kabul's first rock festival was held in 1975 (Dupree 1976).

5. Described as *Mazari, Uzbeki, Katarghani*.

6. Described as *Logari*.

7. The *ghazal* is a very important poetic form in Persian literature, consisting of a series of couplets following an aa ba ca da... rhyme scheme. *Ghazal* also refers to a musical form for performing such poetry.

8. The name Sure Bazaar is copied from that of a famous street in the old city of Kabul, the Shor Bazar. The musicians' quarter was close to this bazaar, and several instrument makers had their workshops in Shor Bazar—notably Joma Khan Qader, the *rubab* maker.

9. I am indebted to Angela Schlenkhoff for this information about the Afghan Music Centre.

10. The nature of the Internet means that this information is likely to be subject to change over time.

11. My work with the Gujarati Khalifa Jamat in the UK (Baily 2006) is a further example of music and identity. Here the argument is that there may be differences between 'official community identity' within the community, and a less conscious sense of one's identity which may conflict with the official version.

12. AFGHAN MIGRATORY STRATEGIES AND THE THREE SOLUTIONS TO THE REFUGEE PROBLEM

1. A first version of this paper was published in *Refugee Survey Quarterly* 27(1), 2008. It is re-edited here, slightly revised, with the kind permission of Oxford University Press.

2. Data was collected during several field research trips to Afghanistan, Pakistan, Iran, Europe, North America, Australia and New Zealand; and which were conducted since 1993 on Afghan transnational networks and migratory strategies, in particular for a project entitled *Beyond the Boundaries: Hazara Migratory Networks from Afghanistan, Pakistan and Iran toward Western Countries*, supported by a research and writing grant from the MacArthur Foundation (Chicago) between 2004 and 2006. It also draws upon a series of team studies carried out by the Afghanistan Research and Evaluation Unit (Kabul), funded by the United Nations High Commissioner for Refugees (UNHCR) and the European Commission.

3. This author considers in a historical perspective the political economy of the whole region of which Afghanistan is a part. He argues that all the Afghans who left their country in the 1980s and 1990s cannot be univocally labelled as refugees, as they have followed ancient patterns of economic migration.

4. There are other ongoing research projects and further publications are forthcoming, for instance by Angela Schlenkhoff and Ceri Oeppen on Afghans in the UK and the USA respectively.

5. See Monsutti (2004; 2005a; 2005b). There is also a series of reports on transnational networks published by the Afghanistan Research and Evaluation Unit (accessible on their homepage: www.areu.org.af).

6. For further description of the Afghan remittance system, see Maimbo (2003) and Monsutti (2004, 2005).

7. Although a similar system as that of the 1990s still occurs, many money transfers from Iran now go directly from Iran to Afghanistan, without the need for Pakistan as a hub.

8. It is true that, in the Afghan case, the *hawala* system would be even better if it included banking facilities to convert money into loan and investment funds, which could be used to rebuild infrastructure.

REFERENCES

Abbasi-Shavazi, Mohammad Jalal; and Glazebrook, Diana, 'Continued protection, sustainable reintegration: Afghan refugees and migrants in Iran', *Briefing Paper*, Kabul: Afghanistan Research and Evaluation Unit, 2006.

Abbott, Andrew, *Time matters: on theory and method*, Chicago: University of Chicago Press, 2001.

ABC News, *Life in Afghanistan*, http://abcnews.go.com/International/PollVault/story?id=1363276 (viewed 02/2008), 2005.

ABC News/BBC World Service, *Afghanistan: Where things stand*, http://news.bbc.co.uk/1/shared/bsp/hi/pdfs/07_12_06AfghanistanWhereThingsStand.pdf (viewed 02/2008), 2006.

Adelman, Howard, 'Refugee repatriation', in Stedman, Stephen J.; Rothchild, Donald and Cousens, Elizabeth M. (eds), *Ending civil wars: The implementation of peace agreements*, Boulder: Lynne Rienner, 2002, pp. 273–302.

Agarwal, Bina, 'Bargaining' and gender relations: Within and Beyond the household', *Feminist Economics* 3, 1997, pp. 1–51.

AIHRC, *Peace, reconciliation and justice in Afghanistan: action plan of the government of the Islamic Republic of Afghanistan*, http://www.aihrc.org.af/actionplan_af.htm (viewed 02/2008), 2005.

Akeroyd, Anne V., 'Ethics in relation to informants, the profession and governments', in Ellen, Roy F. (eds), *Ethnographic research: A guide to general conduct*, London: Academic Press, 1984, pp. 133–54.

Al-Ali, Nadje; Black, Richard; and Koser, Khalid, 'The limits to 'transnationalism': Bosnian and Eritrean refugees in Europe as emerging transnational communities', *Ethnic and Racial Studies* 24, 4, 2001a, pp. 578–600.

Al-Ali, Nadje; Black, Richard; and Koser, Khalid, 'Refugees and transnationalism: the experience of Bosnians and Eritreans in Europe', *Journal of Ethnic and Migration Studies* 27, 4, 2001b, pp. 615–34.

al-Marashi, Ibrahim, 'Iraq's security and intelligence network: A guide and analysis', *Middle East Review of International Affairs* 6, 3, 2002, pp. 1–13.

Al-Rahman Khan, Abd, *The life of Abdur Rahman (Volume II)*, London: John Murray, 1900.

Aldeeb Abu-Sahlieh, Sami A., 'The Islamic Conception of Migration', *International Migration Review* 30, 1, 1996, pp. 37–88.

Ames, Genevieve M.; Cunradi, Carol B.; Moore, Roland S.; and Stern, Pamela, 'Military culture and drinking behavior among U.S. navy careerists', *Journal of Studies on Alcohol and Drugs* 68, 3, 2007, pp. 336–44.

Amnesty International, 'Afghanistan: police reconstruction essential for the protection of human rights', ASA11/003/2003, Amnesty International, 2003.

Amnesty International, *Lives blown apart: crimes against women in times of conflict*, Oxford: Alden Press, 2004.

Anderson, Benedict, 'The new world disorder', *New Left Review* 193, 1992, pp. 3–13.

Anderson, Ewan W.; and Hatch Dupree, Nancy (eds), *The cultural basis of Afghan nationalism*, London: Pinter, 1990.

ANDS/JCMB Secretariat, *A Vision for regional cooperation: progress since the Kabul conference (conference proceedings)*, Second Regional Economic Cooperation Conference on Afghanistan, 18–19 November 2006, New Delhi, 2006.

Ansary, Tamim, *West of Kabul, East of New York*, New York: Picador, 2002.

Asad, Talal, *Anthropology and the colonial encounter*, London: Ithaca Press, 1973.

Asia Foundation, 'Afghanistan in 2006: a survey of the Afghan people', Washington DC: The Asia Foundation, 2006.

AWID, 'Where is the money for women's rights? Assessing resources and the role of donors in the promotion of women's rights and support of women's organisations', Washington DC: Just Associates, 2006.

Azoy, G. Whitney, *Buzkashi, game and power in Afghanistan*, Long Grove: Waveland Press, 2003.

Baily, John, 'Cross-cultural perspectives in popular music: the case of Afghanistan', *Popular Music* 1, 1981, pp. 105–22.

Baily, John, *The annual cycle of music in Herat*, London: Royal Anthropological Institute, 1982.

Baily, John, *Music of Afghanistan: Professional musicians in the city of Herat*, Cambridge: Cambridge University Press, 1988.

Baily, John, 'The role of music in the creation of as Afghan national identity, 1923–73', in Stokes, Martin (eds), *Music, ethnicity and identity: the musical construction of place*, Oxford: Berg, 1994, pp. 45–60.

Baily, John, 'Music and refugee lives: Afghans in eastern Iran and California', *Forced Migration Review* 6, 1999, pp. 10–13.

Baily, John, 'So near, so far: Kabul's music in exile', *Ethnomusicology Forum* 14, 2, 2005a, pp. 213–33.

Baily, John, *Tablas and drum machines: Afghan music in California*, DVD, London: Goldsmiths, 2005b.

Baily, John, 'Music is in our blood': Gujarati Muslim musicians in the UK', *Journal of Ethnic and Migration Studies* 32, 2, 2006, pp. 257–70.

Baitenman, Helga, 'NGOs and the Afghan war: The politicisation of humanitarian aid', *Third World Quarterly* 12, 1, 1990, pp. 62–85.

Barakat, Sultan, 'Setting the scene for Afghanistan's reconstruction: The challenges and critical dilemmas', in Barakat, Sultan (eds), *Reconstructing war-torn societies, Afghanistan*, New York: Palgrave, 2004, pp. 1–16.

Barfield, Thomas, 'Weak links in a rusty chain', in Sharani, Nazif M and Canfield, Robert L (eds), *Revolutions and rebellions in Afghanistan: anthropological perspectives*, Berkeley: University of California Press, 1984, pp. 170–83.

Barfield, Thomas; Nojumi, Neamat; and Thier, J. Alexander, *The clash of two goods. State and non-state dispute resolution in Afghanistan*, http://www.usip.org/ruleof-law/projects/clash_two_goods.pd (viewed 02/2008), 2006.

Barnes, John A., 'Class and committee in a Norwegian island parish', *Human Relations* 7, 1, 1954, pp. 39–58.

BBC, *New Afghan governor pledges order*, http://news.bbc.co.uk/1/hi/world/south_asia/3653516.stm (viewed 02/2008), 2004.

BBC, *Scores killed in Afghan violence*, http://news.bbc.co.uk/1/hi/world/south_asia/4992462.stm (viewed 02/2008), 2006a.

BBC, *UK troops 'to target terrorists'*, http://news.bbc.co.uk/1/hi/uk_politics/4935532.stm (viewed 2/2008), 2006b.

BBC, *Afghan deployment 'beyond 2009'*, http://news.bbc.co.uk/1/hi/uk_politics/6636113.stm (viewed 02/2008), 2007a.

BBC, *'Lack of vehicles' in Afghanistan*, http://news.bbc.co.uk/1/hi/uk/6614255.stm (viewed 02/2008), 2007b.

Beeston, Richard, 'Al-Qaeda threatens new terror offensive', *The Times*, London, 12 September 2006.

Bilmes, Linda; and Stiglitz, Joseph E, 'The economic costs of the Iraq war: an appraisal three years after the beginning of the conflict', *John F Kennedy School of Government Faculty Working Papers Series*, RWP 06–002, Cambridge MA: Harvard University, 2006.

Bivand Erdal, Marta, 'Contributing to development? Transnational activities among members of the Tamil diaspora in Norway', Master's thesis, University of Oslo: Department of Human Geography, 2006.

Black, Richard, 'Return and reconstruction in Bosnia-Herzegovina: missing link, or mistaken priority?' *SAIS Review* 21, 2, 2001, pp. 177–99.

Brand, Laurie A, 'Displacement for development? The impact of changing state-society relations', *World Development* 29, 6, 2001, pp. 961–76.

Brettell, Caroline B, *When they read what we write: the politics of ethnography*, London: Bergin and Garvey, 1993.

Burke, Jason, 'The New Taliban', *The Observer*, 14 October 2007.

Burnes, Alexander, *Travels into Bokhara: being the account of a journey from India to Cabool, Tartary and Persia (volume I, II and III)*, London: John Murray, 1834.

Byman, Daniel; Chalk, Peter; Hoffman, Bruce; Rosenau, William; and Brannan, David, *Trends in outside support for insurgent movements*, Santa Monica, CA: RAND, 2001.

Canfield, Robert. L., 'Afghanistan's social identities in crisis', in Digard, Jean-Pierre (eds), *Le fait ethnique en Iran et en Afghanistan*, Paris: Éditions du Centre National de la Recherche Scientifique, 1988, pp. 185–99.

Cassell, Joan; and Jacobs, Sue-Ellen, 'Introduction', *A special publication of the American Anthropological Association*, 23, Arlington: AAA, 2006.

Centlivres, Pierre, 'Exil et diaspora Afghane en Suisse et en Europe', *Cahiers d'études sur la Méditerranée orientale et le monde turco-iranien* 30, 2000, pp. 151–71.

Centlivres, Pierre; Centlivres-Demont, Micheline; and Gehrig, Tina, 'La diaspora afghane: le paradoxe apparent de l'identité et de l'intégration', in Centlivres, Pierre and Girod, Isabelle (eds), *Les défis migratoires: actes du collogque CLUSE, Neuchâtel 1998*, Zurich: Seismo, 2000, pp. 272–78.

Chant, Sylvia, *Women headed households: diversity and dynamics in the developing world*, London: Macmillan, 1997.

Chatelard, Géraldine, 'Iraqi forced migrants in Jordan: conditions, religious networks, and the smuggling process', *Working Paper*, 49, Florence: Robert Schuman Centre for Advanced Studies, Europena University Institute, 2002.

Christensen, Aasger, *Aiding Afghanistan. The background and prospects for reconstruction in a fragmented society*, Copenhagen: Nordic Institute of Asian Studies, 1995.

CIA, *The World Factbook*, https://www.cia.gov/library/publications/the-world-factbook/ (viewed 04/08), 2008.

Clifford, James, 'Diasporas', *Cultural Anthropology* 9, 3, 1994, pp. 302–38.

Cockburn, Caroline, 'The gendered dynamics of armed conflict and political violence', in Moser, Caroline O. N. and Clark, Fiona C. (eds), *Victims, perpetrators or actors? Gender, armed conflict and political violence*, London: Zed Books, 2001, pp. 13–29.

Cohen, Robin, *Global diasporas: an introduction*, London: University College of London Press, 1997.

Collier, Paul; Elliott, V. L.; Hegre, Håvard; Hoeffler, Anke; Reynal-Querol, Marta; and Sambanis, Nicholas, *Breaking the conflict trap: civil war and development policy*, Washington DC: World Bank/Oxford University Press, 2003.

Colville, Rupert, 'Afghan refugees: is international support draining away after two decades in exile?' *Refuge* 17, 4, 1998, pp. 6–11.

Connor, Kerry M., *An analysis of residential choice among self-settled Afghan refugees in Peshawar, Pakistan*, Lincoln and Omaha: University of Nebraska, 1987a.

Connor, Kerry M., 'Rationales for the movement of Afghan refugees to Peshawar', in Farr, Grant M. and Merriam, John G. (eds), *Afghan resistance: the politics of survival*, Boulder: Westview Press, 1987b, pp. 151–90.

Connor, Kerry M., 'Factors in the residential choice of self-settled Afghan refugees in Peshawar, Pakistan', *International Migration Review* 23, 1, 1989, pp. 904–32.

Coon, Carlton S., *A North Africa story: The anthropologist as OSS agent, 1941–1943*, Ipswich, MA: Gambit, 1980.

Cordesman, Anthony H, *Lessons of Afghanistan*, Washington DC: CSIS, 2002.

Dalian China, *SCO 'committed to peace, prosperity'*, http://2003.dl.gov.cn/i18n/en/affair/news/16287_51325.jsp (viewed 02/2008), 2006.

Daoud, Zohra Yusuf, 'Miss Afghanistan: a story of a nation', in Mehta, Sunita (eds), *Women for Afghan women: shattering myths and claiming the future*, New York: Palgrave Macmillan, 2002, pp. 102–11.

Docherty, Leo, *Desert of death: a soldier's journey from Iraq to Afghanistan*, London: Faber and Faber, 2007.

Donini, Antonio, *The policies of mercy: UN coordination in Afghanistan, Mozambique and Rwanda*, Providence: Watson Institute for International Studies, 1996.

Dorronsoro, Gilles, *Revolution unending: Afghanistan, 1979 to the present*, London: Hurst, 2005.

Dupree, Louis, *Afghanistan*, Oxford: Oxford University Press, 1973.

Dupree, Louis, 'It wasn't Woodstock, but. The first international rock festival in Kabul', *American Universities Field Staff Reports, South Asia Series* 20, 2, 1976, pp. 1–11.

Dupree, Louis, 'Functions of folklore in Afghan society', *Asian Affairs* 1, 10, 1979, pp. 51–61.

Dupree, Louis, 'Tribal warfare in Afghanistan and Pakistan: a reflection of the segmentary lineage system', in Ahmed, Akbar S. and Hart, David M. (eds), *Islam in tribal societies: from the Atlas to the Indus*, London: Routledge & Kegan Paul, 1984, pp. 266–86.

Dupree, Nancy Hatch, 'Afghan women under the Taliban', in Maley, William (eds), *Fundamentalism reborn? Afghanistan and the Taliban*, New York: New York University Press, 1998, pp. 145–66.

Dupree, Nancy Hatch, 'Cultural heritage and national identity in Afghanistan', in Barakat, Sultan (eds), *Reconstructing war-torn societies, Afghanistan*, New York: Palgrave MacMillan, 2004, pp. 177–89.

Durand, Henry M, *The first Afghan war and its causes*, London: Longmans, Green and Co., 1879.

Editors Forced Migration Review, 'Overcoming challenges related to data collection and measurement', *Forced Migration Review* 27, 2007, pp. 28–29.

Edwards, David Busby, 'Marginality and migration: Cultural dimensions of the Afghan refugee problem', *International Migration Review* 20, 2, 1986, pp. 313–28.

El Bushra, Judy, 'Fused in combat: gender relations and armed conflict', in Afshar, Haleh and Eade, Deborah (eds), *Development, women and war: feminist perspectives*, London: Oxfam, 2004, pp. 151–71.

Elphinstone, Mountstuart, *An account of the Kingdom of Caubul and its dependencies in Persia, Tartary and India*, London: Longman, 1815.

Embassy of Afghanistan, *Afghan Diaspora*, http://www.embassyofafghanistan.org/diaspora.html (viewed 11/2007), 2007.

Enloe, Cynthia, *Maneuvers: the international politics of militarizing women's lives*, Berkeley: University of California Press, 2000.

Esmat, Sohaila, *In pictures: return to Afghanistan (a photo essay for the BBC)*, http://news.bbc.co.uk/2/shared/spl/hi/pop_ups/03/south_asia_return_to_afghanistan/html/5.stm (viewed 02/2008), 2003.

ESRC, 'Research ethics framework', February, Swindon: Economic and Social Research Council, 2005.

Evans, Anne; and Osmani, Yasin, 'Assessing progress: update report on subnational administration in Afghanistan', *Issues Paper Series*, Kabul: Afghanistan Research and Evaluation Unit, 2005.

Ewans, M., *Afghanistan: a short history of its people and politics*, New York: Perennial, 2002.

Farr, Grant M.; and Merriam, John G. (eds), *Afghan resistance: the politics of survival*, Boulder: Westview Press, 1987.

Gall, Carlotta; and Sanger, David E, 'Civilian deaths undermine allies' war on Taliban', *New York Times*, New York: 13 May 2007.

GCIM, 'Migration in an interconnected world: new directions for action, Report of the Global Commission on International Migration', Geneva: Global Commission on International Migration (GCIM), 2005.

Geller, Armando, *Macht, Ressourcen und Gewalt, Zur Komplexität zeitgenössischer Konflikte, Eine agenten-basierte Modellierung*, Zurich: VDF, 2006.

Geller, Armando; and Moss, Scott, 'Growing *qawm*: An evidence-driven declarative model of Afghan power structures', *Advances in Complex Systems*, 11, 2, 2008, pp. 321-355.

George, Alexander; and Bennett, Andrew, *Case studies and theory development in the social sciences*, Cambridge, MA: MIT Press, 2005.

Gilsenan, Michael, 'On conflict and violence', in MacClancy, Jeremy (eds), *Exotic no more: Anthropology on the front lines*, Chicago and London: The University of Chicago Press, 2002, pp. 99–113.

Giustozzi, Antonio, *War, politics and society in Afghanistan, 1978–1992*, London: Hurst, 2000.

Giustozzi, Antonio, 'Respectable warlords? The politics of state-building in post-Taleban Afghanistan', *Crisis States Programme*, Working Paper 33, London: London School of Economics, 2003.

Giustozzi, Antonio, *Koran, kalashnikov and laptop: the neo-Taliban insurgency in Afghanistan 2002–2007*, London: Hurst, 2007a.

Giustozzi, Antonio, 'War and peace economies of Afghanistan's strongmen', *International Peacekeeping* 14, 1, 2007b, pp. 75–89.

Giustozzi, Antonio, 'Bureaucratic facade and political realities of disarmament and demobilisation in Afghanistan', *Conflict, Security and Development* 8, forthcoming,

Glatzer, Bernt, 'Is Afghanistan on the brink of ethnic and tribal disintegration?' in Maley, William (eds), *Fundamentalism reborn? Afghanistan and the Taliban*, New York: New York University Press, 1998, pp. 167–81.

Goodhand, Jonathan, 'Research in conflict zones: ethics and accountability', *Forced Migration Review* 8, 2000, pp. 12–15.

Goodhand, Jonathan, 'Afghanistan in Central Asia', in Pugh, Michael and Cooper, Neil (eds), *War economies in a regional context*, Boulder: Lynne Rienner, 2004a, pp. 45–89.

Goodhand, Jonathan, 'Aiding violence or building peace? The role of international aid in Afghanistan', in Barakat, Sultan (eds), *Reconstructing war-torn societies, Afghanistan*, New York: Palgrave MacMillan, 2004b, pp. 37–59.

Goodhand, Jonathan, 'Frontiers and wars: The opium economy in Afghanistan', *Journal of Agrarian Change* 5, 2, 2005, pp. 191–216.

Goodson, Larry P, 'Refugee-based insurgency: The Afghan case', PhD thesis, University of North Carolina at Chapel Hill: Department of Political Science, 1990.

Gough, Kathleen, 'Anthropology and imperialism', *Monthly Review* April, 1968, pp. 12–27.

Grare, Frédéric, 'The geopolitics of Afghan refugees in Pakistan', in Stedman, Stephen J. and Tanner, Fred (eds), *Refugee manipulation: War politics and the abuse of human suffering*, Washington: Brookings Institution Press, 2003, pp. 57–94.

Grevemeyer, Jan Heeren, *Die Afghanen: Widerstand und Flucht*, Berlin: Edition Parabolis, 1988.

Griffin, Michael, *Reaping the whirlwind: The Taleban movement in Afghanistan*, London: Pluto Press, 2001.

Guillo, Alain; Puig, Jean-Jose; and Roy, Olivier, 'La guerre en Afghanistan: Modifications des deplacements traditionnels de populations et emergence de nouveaux types de circulations', *Ethnologica Helvetica* 7, 1983, pp. 139–53.

Gusterson, Hugh, 'Anthropology and the miliatry—1968, 2003 and beyond?' *Anthropology Today* 19, 3, 2003, pp. 25–26.

Hammond, Laura, *Obliged to give: remittances and the maintenance of transnational networks between Somalis 'at home' and abroad*, 10th International Association for the Study of Forced Migration conference, 18–22 June 2006, York University, Toronto, 2006.

Hanifi, M Jamil, 'Editing the past: colonial production of hegemony through the "*Loya Jerga*" in Afghanistan', *Iranian Studies* 37, 2, 2004, pp. 295–322.

Hanifi, M. Jamil, 'Anthropology and the representations of recent migrations from Afghanistan', *Rethinking refuge and displacement: selected papers on refugees and immigrants*, 8, Arlington: American Anthropological Association, 2000.

Hanifi, Shah Mahmoud, 'Material and social remittances to Afghanistan', in Westcott, Clay and Brinkerhoff, Jennifer (eds), *Converting migration drains into gains: harnessing the resources of overseas professionals*, Manila: Asian Development Bank, 2006, pp. 98–126.

Hanna, H. B, *The second Afghan war 1878-79-80 (volume I, II and III)*, London: Archibald Constable and Co., 1899.

Hannerz, Ulf, 'The Global ecumene as a network of networks', in Kuper, Adam (eds), *Conceptualizing society*, London: Routledge, 1992, pp. 34–56.

Harding, Luke, 'Opposition Warlords Prepare for Their Big Chance', *The Guardian*, 19 September 2001.

Harpviken, Kristian Berg, 'Transcending traditionalism: The emergence of non-state military formations in Afghanistan', *Journal of Peace Research* 34, 3, 1997, pp. 271–87.

Harriss, John; and De Renzio, Paolo, 'Missing link' or analytically missing? The concept of social capital, an introductory bibliographic essay', *Jounral of International Development* 9, 7, 1997, pp. 919–37.

Haver, Katherine, 'Duty of care? Local staff and aid worker security', *Forced Migration Review* 28, 2007, pp. 10–11.

Helton, A. C., *The price of indifference: refugees and humanitarian action in the new century*, Oxford: Oxford University Press, 2002.

Hensman, Howard, *The Afghan war of 1879–80*, London: W.H. Allen, 1881.

Hoffman, Danny, 'Frontline anthropology: Research in time of war', *Anthropology Today* 19, 3, 2003, pp. 9–12.

Horst, C., 'Transnational dialogues: developing ways to do research in a diasporic community', *Transnational Communities Working Paper*, WPTC-02–03. 2002.

Horst, C., 'Money and mobility: transnational livelihood strategies of the Somali diaspora', *Global Migration Perspectives*, 9, Geneva: GCIM, 2004.

Horst, Cindy, *Transnational nomads: how Somalis cope with refugee life in the Dadaab camps of Kenya*, Oxford: Berghahan, 2006.

Hosseini, Khaled, *The kite runner*, New York: Riverhead Books, 2003.

Hugo, Graeme, *Circular migration: keeping development rolling?* http://www.migrationinformation.org/Feature/print.cfm?ID=129 (viewed 12/04), 2003.

Human Rights Watch, 'Afghanistan: The massacre in Mazar-i Sharif', *Human Rights Watch Report*, 10, 7, 1998.

Human Rights Watch, 'Lessons in terror: attacks on education in Afghanistan', *Human Rights Watch Report*, 18, 6(c), 2006.

Human Rights Watch, 'Afghanistan: country summary', New York: Human Rights Watch, 2007a.

Human Rights Watch, 'The human cost: the consequences of insurgent attacks in Afghanistan', *Human Rights Watch Report*, 19, 6(c), 2007b.

ICG, 'Reforming Afghanistan's police', *Asia Report*, 138, Bruxelles: International Crisis Group, 2007.

International Monetary Fund, 'IMF executive board approves US$119.1 Million PRGF Arrangement for the Islamic Republic of Afghanistan', *Press Release*, 06/144, Washington DC: IMF, 2006.

IOM, 'Return of qualified Afghans Programme', *Fact Sheet March 2008*, Kabul: IOM, 2008.

Iranian Studies, 'Special issue, 'Afghan Refugees'', *Iranian Studies* 40, 2, 2007, pp. 133–303.

IRIN, *Afghanistan: record numbers enrol in new school year*, http://www.irinnews.org/Report.aspx?ReportId=70844 (viewed 02/2008), 2007.

Islamic Republic of Afghanistan, *Constitution of the Islamic Republic of Afghanistan (unofficial translation into English)*, http://www.reliefweb.int/library/documents/2003/afg-afg-03nov.pdf (viewed 02/2008), 2003.

Jalali, Ali A, 'The future of Afghanistan', *Parameters* 36, 1, 2006, pp. 4–19.

Jalali, Ali A., 'The legacy of war and the challenge of peace building', in Rotberg, Robert I. (eds), *Building a new Afghanistan*, Washington DC: Brookings Institution Press, 2007, pp. 22–55.

Jamal, Arafat; and Stigter, Elca, 'Real-time evaluation of UNHCR's response to the Afghanistan emergency', Geneva: United Nations High Commissioner for Refugees, 2002.

Janata, Alfred; and Hassas, Reihanodin, 'Ghairatman—Der gute Pashtune, Exkurs über die Grundlagen des Pashtunwali', *Afghanistan Journal* 2, 2, 1975, pp. 83–97.

Jazayery, Laila, 'The migration-development nexus: Afghanistan case study', *International Migration Review* 40, 5—special issue, 2002, pp. 231–52.

Kakar, Hassan, *Government and society in Afghanistan: the reign of Amir 'Abd al-Rahman Khan*, Austin: University of Texas Press, 1979.

Kakar, Hassan, *A political and diplomatic history of Afghanistan, 1863–1901*, Leiden: Brill, 2006.

Kaldor, Mary, 'Introduction', in Kaldor, Mary and Vashee, Basker (eds), *New wars, restructuring the global military sector*, London: Pinter, 1997, pp. 3–33.

Kaye, John, *History of the war in Afghanistan (volume I and II)*, London: Bentley, 1851.

Koser, Khalid, 'Refugees, transnationalism and the state', *Journal of Ethnic and Migration Studies* 33, 2, 2007, pp. 233–54.

Kulakov, Oleg, 'Lessons learned from the Soviet intervention in Afghanistan: implications for Russian defense reform', *Research Paper*, 26, Rome: NATO Defense College, 2006.

Kunz, Egon F., 'The refugee in flight: kinetic models and forms of displacement', *International Migration Review* 7, 2, 1973, pp. 125–46.

Kunz, Egon F., 'Exile and resettlement: refugee theory', *International Migration Review* 15, 1, 1981, pp. 42–51.

Lal, Mohan, *Life of the Amir Dost Mohammed Khan of Kabul*, London: Longman, 1846.

Leithead, Alastair, *Reflection after riots in Kabul*, http://news.bbc.co.uk/1/hi/world/south_asia/5031074.stm (viewed 02/2008), 2006.

Levitt, Peggy, 'Social remittances: migration driven local-level forms of cultural diffusion', *International Migration Review* 32, 4, 1998, pp. 926–48.

Lischer, Sarah Kenyon, *Dangerous sanctuaries: Refugee camps, civil wars and the dilemmas of humanitarian aid*, Ithaca: Cornell University Press, 2005.

Lister, Sarah, 'Caught in confusion: local governance structures in Afghanistan', *Briefing Paper*, Kabul: Afghanistan Research and Evaluation Unit, 2005.

Lister, Sarah, 'Moving forward? Assessing public administration reform in Afghanistan', *Briefing Paper*, Kabul: Afghanistan Research and Evaluation Unit, 2006.

Lister, Sarah; and Wilder, Andrew, 'Strengthening subnational administration in Afghanistan', *Public Administration and Development* 25, 1, 2005, pp. 39–48.

Lowell, B Lindsay; and Gerova, Stefka G, 'Diasporas and economic development: state of knowledge', *Paper prepared for the World Bank*, Washington DC: Institute for the Study of International Migration, 2004.

Loyd, Anthony, 'Yes, for once an Afghan war is winnable', *The Times*, London, 10 March 2007.

Lukes, Steven, *Power: A radical view*, London: MacMillan Press, 1974.

Lyons, Terrence, 'Engaging diasporas to promote conflict resolution: transforming hawks into doves', *Working paper*, Washington DC: Institute for Global Conflict and Cooperation, 2004.

Mabee, Carleton, 'Margaret Mead and behavioural scientists in World War II', *Journal of the History of of the Behavioural Sciences* 23, 11, 1987, pp. 3–13.

Madadi, Abdul Wahab; and Baily, John, 'Dictionary entry', in Sadie, Stanley and Tyrrell, John (eds), *The New Grove Dictionary of Music and Musicians*, London: Macmillan, 2001, pp. 635.

Maimbo, Samuel M., 'The money exchange dealers of Kabul: a study of the hawala system in Afghanistan', *World Bank Working Paper*, 13, Washington DC: World Bank, 2003.

Malkki, Lisa H., *Purity and exile: Violence, memory and national cosmology among the Hutu refugees in Tanzania*, Chicago: University of Chicago Press, 1995.

Manning, Nick; Byrd, William A; Wilder, Andrew; and Evans, Anne, 'Assessing sub-national administration in Afghanistan: early observations and recommendations for action', Kabul: Afghanistan Research and Evaluation Unit/World Bank, 2003.

Marcus, George E., 'Ethnography in/of the world system: the emergence of multi-sited ethnography', *Annual Review of Anthropology* 24, 1995, pp. 95–117.

Marks, Stephen R., 'Durkheim's theory of anomie', *American Journal of Sociology* 80, 2, 1974, pp. 329–63.

Marsden, Peter, 'Repatriation and reconstruction: The case of Afghanistan', in Black, Richard and Koser, Khalid (eds), *The end of the refugee cycle: Refugee repatriation and reconstruction*, New York: Berghahn Books, 1999, pp. 56–68.

Marx, Emmanuel, 'The social world of refugees: a conceptual framework', *Journal of Refugee Studies* 3, 3, 1990, pp. 189–203.

Masson, Charles, *A narrative of various journeys in Baluchistan, Afghanistan and the Punjab including a residence in those countries from 1826 to 1838 (volume I, II and III)*, London: Richard Bentley, 1842.

Médard, Jean-François, 'L'État patrimonialisé', *Politique Africaine* 39, 1990, pp. 25–36.

Medica Mondiale, 'Women, peace and security in Afghanistan: implementation of United Nations Security Council Resolution 1325, five years on: post-Bonn gains and gaps', Cologne: Medica Mondiale, 2007.

Merriam, Alan P., *The Anthropology of music*, Chicago: Northwestern University Press, 1964.

Merton, Robert K., 'Social structure and anomie', *American Sociological Review* 35, 1938, pp. 672–82.

Migration DRC, *Global Migrant Origin Database, version 4*, http://www.migrationdrc.org/research/typesofmigration/global_migrant_origin_database.html (viewed 11/2007), 2007.

Ministry of Foreign Affairs/Sida, 'Country Strategy for Afghanistan, January 01 2002—December 31 2004', Stockholm, Government Offices of Sweden, 2002.

Monsutti, Alessandro, 'Cooperation, remittances, and kinship among the Hazaras', *Iranian Studies* 37, 2, 2004, pp. 219–40.

Monsutti, Alessandro, 'En suivant les réseaux de Kaboul à New York: quelque réflexions méthodologiques sur la recherche ethnographiques parmi les migrants', *Ethnologies* 27, 1, 2005a, pp. 33–53.

Monsutti, Alessandro, *War and migration: social networks and economic strategies of the Hazaras of Afghanistan*, London: Routledge, 2005b.

Monsutti, Alessandro, 'Afghan transnational networks: looking beyond repatriation', *Synthesis Paper Series*, Kabul: Afghanistan Research and Evaluation Unit, 2006.

Monsutti, Alessandro, 'La migration afghane en Australie et en Nouvelle-Zélande', *Afghanistan Info* 61, 2007a, pp. 15–17.

Monsutti, Alessandro, 'Migration as a rite of passage: young Afghans building masculinity and adulthood in Iran', *Iranian Studies* 40, 2, 2007b, pp. 167–85.

Monsutti, Alessandro, 'Afghan migratory strategies and the three solutions to the refugee problem', *Refugee Survey Quarterly* 27, 1, 2008, pp. 58–73.

Mousavi, Sayed Askar, *The Hazaras of Afghanistan: An historical, cultural, economic and political study*, New York: St. Martin's Press, 1997.

Naby, Eden, 'The Afghan diaspora: reflections on the imagined country', in Atabaki, Touraj and Mehendale, Sanjyot (eds), *Central Asia and the Caucasus: transnationalism and diaspora*, London: Routledge, 2005, pp. 169–83.

Nader, Laura, 'The phantom factor: Impact of the Cold War on Anthropology', in Chomsky, Noam (eds), *The Cold War and the university*, New York: New Press, 1997, pp. 107–46.

Nassery, Homira. G., *The reverse brain-drain: Afghan-American diaspora in post-conflict peacebuilding and reconstruction*, http://old.developmentgateway.org/download/195296/The_Role_of_the_Afghan_Diaspora_in_Post.doc (viewed 08/2004), 2003.

Nawanews, *Afghanistan dar markaz e geopolitic nafti jehan*, http://www.nawanews.co.uk/news/energy.html (viewed 09/2006), 2006.

Neuman, Daniel M., *The life of music in North India: The organization of an artistic tradition*, Detroit: Wayne University Press, 1980.

Newland, Kathleen, 'Beyond remittances: the role of diaspora in poverty reduction in their country of origin', *Scoping study for the Department of International Development*, Washington DC: Migration Policy Institute, 2004.

Nixon, Hamish, 'Aiding the state? International assistance and the statebuilding paradox in Afghanistan', *Briefing Paper Series*, Kabul: Afghanistan Research and Evaluation Unit, 2007.

Nixon, Hamish, 'Sub-national statebuilding in Afghanistan 2005–06', Kabul: Afghanistan Research and Evaluation Unit, 2008.

Nixon, Hamish, 'International assistance and governance in Afghanistan', Kabul: Afghanistan Research and Evaluation Unit, n.d.

Noelle, Christine, *State and tribe in nineteenth-century Afghanistan: the reign of Amir Dost Muhammad Khan (1826–1863)*, London: Routledge, 1997.

Olimova, Saodat, *Impact of external migration on development of mountainous regions: Tajikistan, Kyrgyzstan, Afghanistan, and Pakistan*, International workshop on strategies for development and food security in mountainous areas of Central Asia, 6–10 June 2005, Dushambe, Tajikistan, 2005.

Omidian, Patricia A., 'Life out of context: recording Afghan refugees' stories', in Camino, Linda A. and Krulfeld, Ruth M. (eds), *Reconstructing lives, recapturing meaning: refugee identity, gender, and culture change*, Basel: Gordon and Breach, 1994, pp. 151–78.

Omidian, Patricia A., *Ageing and family in an Afghan refugee community: transitions and transformations*, London: Garland Publishing, 1996.

Omidian, Patricia A.; and Lipson, Juliene G., 'Elderly Afghan refugees: traditions and transitions in Northern California', *Selected papers on refugee issues*, 1, Washington DC: American Anthropological Association, 1992.

Pankhurst, Donna, 'The 'sex war' and other wars: towards a feminist peace', in Afshar, Haleh and Eade, Deborah (eds), *Development, women and war: feminist perspectives*, London: Oxfam, 2004, pp. 8–42.

Papa, Massimo, *Afghanistan: tradizione giuridica e ricostruzione dell'ordinamento tra Saria, consuetudini e diritto statale*, Torino: Giappichelli, 2006.

Pennell, T. L., *Among the wild tribes of the Afghan frontier*, London: George Bell and Sons, 1909.

Popitz, Heinrich, *Phänomene der Macht*, Tübingen: JCB Mohr, 1992.

Price, David, 'Cold War anthropology: Collaborators and victims of the national security state', *Identities* 4, 3–4, 1998, pp. 389–430.

Price, David, 'Lessons from Second World War Anthropology', *Anthropology Today* 18, 3, 2002, pp. 14–20.

Qabool, Mohammad, *Afghanistan va gorohbandi haye jadide mantaqayee*, http://www.nawanews.co.uk/news_sco.html (viewed 09/2006), 2006.

Raja Mohan, C., *Back to the Great Game*, http://www.indianexpress.com/story/5766._.html (viewed 02/2008), 2006.

Rasanayagam, Angelo, *Afghanistan: A modern history*, London: IB Tauris, 2003.

Rashid, Ahmed, 'The great trade game', *Far Eastern Economic Review* 166, 4, 2003, pp. 18–19.

Rashid, Ahmed, *Taliban: Islam, oil and the new great game in central Asia*, London: IB Tauris, 2008.

Rasuly-Paleczek, Gabriele, 'Ethnic identity versus nationalism: The Uzbeks of North-Eastern Afghanistan and the Afghan state', in Atabaki, Touraj and O'Kane, John (eds), *Post-Soviet Central Asia*, London: Tauris Academic Studies, 1998, pp. 204–30.

Rasuly-Paleczek, Gabriele, 'Frontiers, hinterlands, centers, peripheries: Adapting to changing fortunes—the Uzbeks of Afghanistan', in Rasuly-Paleczek, Gabriele and Katschnig, Julia (eds), *Central Asia: past, present and future, proceedings of the 7th ESCAS Conference*, Vienna: LIT Verlag, 2004, pp. 81–108.

Ratha, Dilip, 'Leveraging remittances for development', *Policy Brief*, Washington DC: Migration Policy Institute, 2007.

Reyes, Adeleida, *Songs of the caged, songs of the free*, Philadelphia: Temple University Press, 1999.

Riak Akuei, Stephanie, 'Remittances as unforeseen burdens: the livelihoods and social obligations of Sudanese refugees', *Global Migration Perspectives*, 18, Geneva: GCIM, 2005.

Richani, Nazih, *Systems of violence. The political economy of war and peace in Colombia*, Albany: State University of New York Press, 2002.

Rizvi, Gowher, 'The Afghan refugees: Hostages in the struggle for power', *Journal of Refugee Studies* 3, 3, 1990, pp. 144–61.

Roashan, G. Rauf, *Afghan geography and economic prospects*, http://www.afgha.net/?q=node/937 (viewed 02/2008), 2006.

Rogge, John, 'Repatriation of refugees: a not so simple 'optimum' solution', in Allen, T. and Morsink, H. (eds), *When refugees go home*, London: James Currey, 1994, pp. 14–49.

Rouse, Roger, 'Mexican migration and the social space of postmodernism', *Diaspora* 1, 1, 1991, pp. 8–23.

Roy, Olivier, *Islam and resistance in Afghanistan*, Cambridge: Cambridge University Press, 1986.

Roy, Olivier, 'Ethnic identity and political expression in Northern Afghanistan', in Gross, Jo-Ann (eds), *Muslims in Central Asia. Expressions of identity and change*, Durham: Duke University Press, 1992, pp. 73–86.

REFERENCES

Roy, Olivier, 'The new political elite in Afghanistan', in Weiner, Myron and Banuazizi, Ali (eds), *The politics of social transformation in Afghanistan, Iran and Pakistan*, New York: Syracuse University Press, 1994, pp. 72–100.

Roy, Olivier, *Afghanistan: From holy war to civil war*, Princeton: Darwin Press, 1995.

Roy, Olivier, 'Has Islamism a future in Afghanistan?' in Maley, William (eds), *Fundamentalism Reborn? Afghanistan and the Taliban*, New York: New York University Press, 1998, pp. 199–211.

Rubin, Barnett R, *The fragmentation of Afghanistan: state formation and collapse in the International system*, New Haven: Yale University Press, 1995.

Rubin, Barnett R, *Afghanistan's geo-strategic identity*, annual meeting of the American Political Science Association, 31 August—3 September 2006, Philadelphia, 2006.

Rubin, Barnett R., 'Political elites in Afghanistan: Rentier state building, rentier state wrecking', *International Journal of Middle East Studies* 24, 1, 1992, pp. 77–99.

Rubin, Barnett R., 'The political economy of war and peace in Afghanistan', *World Development* 28, 10, 2000, pp. 1789–803.

Rubin, Barnett R., *The fragmentation of Afghanistan, state formation and collapse in the international system (2nd Edition)*, New Haven: Yale University Press, 2002.

Rubin, Barnett R., 'Saving Afghanistan', *Foreign Affairs* 86, 1, 2007, pp. 57–78.

Safran, William, 'Diasporas in modern societies: myths of homeland and return', *Diaspora* 1, 1, 1991, pp. 83–99.

Saikal, Amin, 'The regional politics of the Afghan crisis', in Saikal, Amin and Maley, William (eds), *The Soviet Withdrawal from Afghanistan*, Cambridge and New York: Cambridge University Press, 1989, pp

Saikal, Amin, *Modern Afghanistan: a history of struggle and survival*, London: IB Tauris, 2004.

Saito, Mamiko, 'Second-generation Afghans in neighbouring countries: from mohajer to hamwatan: Afghans return home', *Case Study Series*, Kabul: Afghanistan Research and Evaluation Unit, 2007.

Sale, Florentia; and Edited by Patrick Macrory, *A journal of the first Afghan war*, Oxford: Oxford University Press, 2002.

Sarmast, Ahmad Naser, 'A survey of the history of music in Afghanistan, from ancient times to 2000 A.D. with special reference to art music from c. 1000 A.D.' PhD thesis, Monash University: Department of Musicology and Ethnomusicology, 2004.

Sawyer, R. Keith, *Social emergence, societies as complex systems*, Cambridge: Cambridge University Press, 2005.

Schäfer, Bernd, 'Schmuggel in Afghanistan', *Afghanistan Journal* 1, 2, 1974, pp. 27–31.

Schetter, Conrad, *Ethnizitaet und ethnische Konflikte in Afghanistan*, Berlin: Dietrich Reimer Verlag, 2003.

Schetter, Conrad, 'Kriegsfürstentum und Bürgerkriegsökonomien in Afghanistan', *Arbeitspapiere zur Internationalen Politik und Aussenpolitik (AIPA)*, Cologne, 2004.

Scheyvens, Regina; Novak, Barbara; and Scheyvens, Henry, 'Ethical issues', in Scheyvens, Regina and Storey, Donovan (eds) *Development fieldwork: A practical guide*, London: Sage, 2003, pp. 139–66.

Schiewek, Eckart, 'Administrative boundaries of Afghanistan', Kabul: UNSMA, 2000.

Schlenkhoff, Angela, 'The Conditions for imagining and enacting identity in exile: The discursive production of Afghan identity in London', PhD thesis, University of Kent, Anthropology, 2006.

Shadl, Marcus, 'The man outside: the problem with the external perceptions of Afghanistan in historical sources', *ASIEN The German Journal on Contemporary Asia* 104, 2007, pp. 88–105.

Shahrani, M. Nazif, 'The future of the state and the structure of community governance in Afghanistan', in Maley, William (eds), *Fundamentalism reborn? Afghanistan and the Taliban*, New York: New York University Press, 1998, pp. 212–42.

Shahrani, M. Nazif, 'War, factionalism, and the state in Afghanistan', *American Anthropologist* 104, 3, 2002, pp. 715–22.

Shahrani, M. Nazif, 'Afghanistan's muhajirin (Muslim "refugee-warriors"): Politics of mistrust and distrust of politics', in Daniel, E. Valentine and Knudsen, John C. (eds), *Mistrusting refugees*, Berkeley: University of California Press, 1995, pp. 187–206.

Shain, Yossi; and Barth, Aharon, 'Diasporas and international relations theory', *International Organization* 57, 2003, pp. 449–79.

Shalinsky, Audrey C., 'Gender issues in the Afghanistan diaspora: Nadia's story', *Frontiers: A Journal of Women's Studies* 17, 3, 1996, pp. 102–23.

Shami, Seteney, 'Transnationalism and refugee studies: Rethinking forced migration and identity in the Middle East', *Journal of Refugee Studies* 9, 1, 1996, pp. 3–25.

Sharifzada, Mohammad Jawad, 'Mixed reception for returning professionals', *Afghan Recovery Report*, 152, Institute for War and Peace Reporting, 2004.

Sigrist, Christian, 'Staatsfreie Zonen im Great Game', *Peripherie* 55/56, 1994, pp. 81–93.

Skalnik, Petr, 'Authority versus power: A view from Social Anthropology', in Cheater, Angela (eds), *The Anthropology of power: empowerment and disempowerment in changing structures*, London and New York: Routledge, 1999, pp. 163–74.

Slobin, Dan, 'Music in contemporary Afghan society', in Dupree, Louis and Albert, Linette (eds), *Afghanistan in the 1970s*, New York: Praeger Press, 1974, pp. 239–48.

Smith, Deborah J., 'Community-based dispute resolution processes in Nangahar Province', Kabul: Afghanistan Research and Evaluation Unit, 2009.

Smith, Deborah J.; and Manalan, Shelly, 'Community-based dispute resolution processes in Bamiyan Province', Kabul: Afghanistan Research and Evaluation Unit, 2009.

Sofsky, Wolfgang, *Zeiten des Schreckens, Amok—Terror—Krieg*, Frankfurt: S. Fischer, 2002.

Spanta, Rangin Dadfar, *Speech*, 27th Session of Council of Ministers of SAARC, 1–2 August 2006, Dhaka, 2006.

Stedman, Stephen John; and Tanner, Fred (eds), *Refugee manipulation: War politics and the abuse of human suffering*, Washington: Brookings Institution Press, 2003.

Stigter, Elca; and Monsutti, Alessandro, 'Transnational networks: recognising a regional reality', *Briefing paper*, Kabul: Afghanistan Research and Evaluation Unit, 2005.

Stirling, Paul, *Impartiality and personal morality*, http://www.era.anthropology.ac.uk/Era_Resources/Era/Stirling/Papers/Impartiality/impartiality_1.html (viewed 04/2006), 1968.

Synowitz, Ron, *Afghanistan: amnesty bill could threaten faith in democracy*, http://www.rferl.org/featuresarticle/2007/02/3a334d61-8ab8-4626-a8cc-5-f280c696565.html (viewed 02/2008), 2007.

Tapper, Richard, 'Who are the Kuchi? Nomad self-identities in Afghanistan', *Journal of the Royal Anthropological Institute*, 14, 1, 2008, pp. 97–116.

Tarrius, Alain, 'Territoires circulatoires des entrepreneurs commerciaux maghrébins de Marseille: du commerce communautaire aux réseaux de l'économie souterraine mondiale', *Journal des Anthropologues* 59, 1995, pp. 15–35.

Tarzi, Shah M., 'Afghanistan in 1992, A Hobbesian state of nature', *Asian Survey* 33, 2, 1993, pp. 165–74.

Tellis, Ashley, *Speech*, George C Marshall Center on Security Studies confidence building seminar on Afghanistan and Pakistan, 17 March 2006, Garmisch, Germany, 2006.

Terry, Fiona, *Condemned to repeat: The paradox of humanitarian action*, Ithaca: Cornell University Press, 2002.

The Prime Minister's Office, *Iraq: Its infrastructure of concealment, deception and intimidation*, http://www.pm.gov.uk/output/Page1470.asp (viewed 02/2008), 2003.

Thomas, Gary, 'Afghanistan neighbors influence the political landscape', *Voice of America News Now*, 16 June 2006.

Thompson, Edwina A, 'The nexus of drug trafficking and hawala in Afghanistan', in Buddenburg, Doris and Byrd, William A (eds), *Afghanistan's drug industry: structure, functioning, dynamics and implications for counter-narcotics policy*, Washington DC: World Bank/UNODC, 2006, pp. 155–88.

Tilly, Charles; and Tarrow, Sidney, *Contentious politics*, Boulder: Paradigm, 2007.

Turshen, Meredeth, 'The political economy of rape: an analysis of systematic rape and sexual abuse of women during armed conflict in Africa', in Moser, Caroline O. N. and Clark, Fiona C. (eds), *Victims, perpertrators or actors? gender, armed conflict and political violence*, London: Zed Books, 2001, pp. 55–68.

Turton, David; and Marsden, Peter, 'Taking refugees for a ride? the politics of refugee return to Afghanistan', *Issues paper series*, Kabul: Afghanistan Research and Evaluation Unit, 2002.

Tzemach, Gayle, 'Afghan women break into a 'man's world'', *Financial Times*, London, 10 January 2006.

UN, 'Resolution 1325 (2000): adopted by the Security Council at its 4213th meeting, on 31 October 2000', *S/RES/1325 (2000)*, New York: UN, 2000.

UN, 'Report of the independent expert on the Commission of Human Rights on the situation of human rights in Afghanistan', *A/59/370*, New York: UN: 2004.

UNAMA, 'Afghanistan justice sector overview', Kabul: UNAMA, 2007.

UNDP, 'Afghanistan national human development report 2004. Security with a human face: challenges and responsibilities', Kabul: UNDP, 2004.

UNHCR, *Statistical Yearbook 2001*, http://www.unhcr.org/static/home/statistical_yearbook/2001/toc.htm (viewed 10/2003), 2001.

UNHCR, 'Towards a comprehensive solution for displacement from Afghanistan', *Discussion paper*, Geneva: United Nations High Commissioner for Refugees, 2003.

UNHCR, *Afghanistan: challenges to return*, Geneva: United Nations High Commissioner for Refugees, 2004.

UNHCR, *2006 Global trends: refugees, asylum-seekers, returnees, internally-displaced and stateless persons*, Geneva: United Nations High Commissioner for Refugees, 2007.

UNIFEM, 'Uncounted and discounted: a secondary data research project on violence against women in Afghanistan', Kabul: UNIFEM, 2006.

Vadean, Florin-Petru, 'Skills and remittances: the case of Afghan, Egyptian and Serbian immigrants in Germany', *Working Paper Series 92*, Singapore: Asia Research Institute, 2007.

Valentine, Gill, 'Tell me about...: Using interviews as a research methodology', in Flowerdew, Robin and Martin, David (eds), *Methods in Human Geography: a guide for students doing a research project*, Essex: Longman, 1997, pp. 110–26.

Van Hear, Nicholas, *New diasporas: the mass exodus, dispersal and regrouping of migrant communities*, London: UCL Press, 1998.

Van Hear, Nicholas, 'Sustaining societies under strain: remittances as a form of transnational exchange in Sri Lanka and Ghana', in Al-Ali, Nadje and Koser, Khalid (eds), *New approaches to migration? transnational communities and the transformation of home*, London: Routledge, 2002, pp. 202–23.

Van Hear, Nicholas, 'From durable solutions to transnational relations: home and exile among refugee diasporas', *New Issues in Refugee Research Working Papers*, 83, Geneva: UNHCR, 2003.

Vigne, Godfrey T. A., *A personal narrative of a visit to Ghuzni, Kabul, and Afghanistan, and of a residence at the court of Dost Mohamed*, London: George Routledge, 1840.

Waldinger, Roger, 'Transforming foreigners into Americans', in Waters, Mary C and Ueda, Reed (eds), *The new Americans: a guide to immigration since 1965*, London: Harvard University Press, 2007, pp. 137–48.

Wannell, Bruce, 'Report of a trip to North-West Afghanistan, 1 September 1989–20 January 1990: Enjil and Zendajan districts', Peshawar, unpublished, 1991.

Warwick, Donald P., 'The politics and ethics of field research', in Bulmer, Martin and Warwick, Donald P. (eds), *Social research in developing countries: Surveys and censuses in the Third World*, London: UCL Press, 1983, pp. 315–30.

Watson, Paul, 'In Afghanistan, money tips the scales of justice', *Los Angeles Times*, Los Angeles, 18 December 2006a.

Watson, Paul, 'Justice often carries a price in Afghanistan', *Los Angeles Times*, Los Angeles, 30 December 2006b.

Weber, Max, *Economy and society: An outline of interpretive Sociology (new edition)*, Berkely/Los Angeles: University of California Press, 1978.

Weinbaum, Marvin G, 'Afghanistan and its neighbors: an ever dangerous neighbourhood', *United States Insitute of Peace Special Report*, Washington DC: USIP, 2006.

Weiss Fagen, Patricia; and Bump, Micah N., *Remittances in conflict and crises: how remittances sustain livelihoods in war, crises, and transitions to peace*, Washington: International Peace Academy, 2006.

REFERENCES

Wilder, Andrew, 'Cops or robbers? The struggle to reform the Afghan National Police', *Issues Paper Series*, Kabul: Afghanistan Research and Evaluation Unit, 2007.

Wilson, Ken, 'Thinking about the ethics of fieldwork', in Devereux, Stephen and Hoddinott, John (eds), *Fieldwork in developing countries*, Boulder: Lynne Rienner, 1992, pp. 179–99.

WOMANKIND, 'Taking stock: Afghan women and girls six months on', London: WOMANKIND, 2002.

WOMANKIND, 'Taking stock: Afghan women and girls sixteen months on', London: WOMANKIND, 2003.

WOMANKIND, 'Taking stock: Afghan women and girls five years on', London: WOMANKIND, 2006.

WOMANKIND, 'Tackling violence against women: a worldwide approach', London: WOMANKIND, 2007.

WOMANKIND, 'Taking stock update: Afghan women and girls seven years on', London: WOMANKIND, 2008.

Women Living Under Muslim Laws, *Afghanistan: marriage contract approved by the Supreme Court of Afghanistan*, http://www.wluml.org/english/newsfulltxt. shtml?cmd%5B157%5D=x-157–551952 (viewed 02/2008), 2007.

Woodward, Bob, *Bush at war*, New York: Simon & Schuster, 2002.

Yuval-Davis, Nira, *Gender and nation*, London: Sage, 1997.

Zolberg, Aristide; Suhrke, Astri; and Aguayo, Sergio, *Escape from violence: Conflict and the refugee crisis in the developing world*, New York: Oxford University Press, 1989.

Zolberg, Aristide; Suhrke, Astri; and Aguayo, Sergio, 'International factors in the formation of refugee movements', *International Migration Review* 20, 2, 1986, pp. 151–69.

INDEX

9/11 Attacks, 4, 46, 103, 135–6, 143, 175

Action Plan for Transitional Justice, 53
Afghanistan, 2–3, 16, 35, 59, 65, 70, 96, 114, 173, 184, 187; aid organisation presence in, 19; and CEDAW, 48; Bamiyan Province, 72–3, 75–6, 78–9; Bonn Agreement (2001), 47; borders of, 61, 104, 109, 128; Civil War Period (1992–94), 59; Communist Party, 23, 77, 148; Conflict (2001–Present), 29, 38, 40, 62, 68–9, 78, 99–100, 114, 121; Diaspora of, 17, 21, 141–3, 146–7, 149–50, 155, 162, 183; Durrani, 31–2; ECAS research, 1, 11; economy of, 112, 119; energy resources of, 107–8, 117; Enjil, 130; Federally Administered Tribal Areas, 116; foreign policy toward, 4, 147; Ghazni, 30, 32, 40; geopolitical advantages of, 115, 117–18; government of, 38, 45, 47–8, 56, 66, 109, 111, 152, 154–7, 176; Helmand Province, 35, 39–40, 98; Herat Province, 97; history of conflict, 11; invasion in First Afghan War (1839–42), 31; Jalalabad, 54; Kabul, 36, 38, 42, 54, 61, 67, 90, 97–8, 110–11, 122, 148, 152, 157, 160, 162–3, 167–8, 175, 188; Kandahar, 43; Mazar-i–Sharif, 54, 67, 160, 175; military of, 37; Ministry of Interior, 92–5, 102; Ministry of Finance, 151; Ministry of Women's Affairs, 49, 51; mistreatment of women, 48-9, 51–3, 55–6, 82–3; Nangarhar Province, 72–3, 75–7, 79, 82–3; population of, 5-6, 25, 42, 141, 186; Saur Revolution (1978–79), 91; Soviet Invasion of (1979), 3–4, 41, 57, 59–60, 76, 79, 99, 173, 175; Soviet Withdrawal (1989–92), 59–60, 76; Taliban Period (1994–2001), 59
Afghanistan Research and Evaluation Unit (AREU): research projects of, 71
Amanullah, King: government of, 60
American Anthropological Association (AAA): ethical guidelines of, 12, 24

British Security Service (MI5), 17

Central Intelligence Agency (CIA), 17
China, 104–6, 110; influence of, 108, 117; interest in IPI Pipeline, 108; rivalry with India, 116; rivalry with Pakistan, 104; rivalry with USA, 116; visited by Karzai, Hamid, 104–5
Cold War, 104, 123; end of, 106, 174, 186